Inventing the Universe

Why we can't stop talking about science, faith and God

Alister McGrath

HODDER

First published in Great Britain in 2015 by Hodder & Stoughton
An Hachette UK company

First published in paperback in 2016

1

Copyright © Alister McGrath, 2015

A CIP catalogue record for this title is available from the British Library

ISBN 978 1 444 79848 7
eBook ISBN 978 1 444 79847 0

Typeset in Salon by Hewer Text UK Ltd, Edinburgh

Printed and bound by Clays Ltd, St Ives plc

Hodder & Stoughton policy is to use papers that are natural, renewable and recyclable products and made from wood grown in sustainable forests. The logging and manufacturing processes are expected to conform to the environmental regulations of the country of origin.

Hodder & Stoughton Ltd
Carmelite House
50 Victoria Embankment
London EC4Y 0DZ

www.hodderfaith.com

In memory of
Charles A. Coulson (1910–74)
Rouse Ball Professor of Mathematics, Oxford University, 1952–72
Professor of Theoretical Chemistry, Oxford University, 1972–4
A mentor

Contents

I

From Wonder to Understanding: Beginning a Journey

Most of us know that heart-stopping feeling of awed wonder at the beauty and majesty of nature. I remember well a journey I made across Iran in the late 1970s. I was travelling on a night bus through the vast desert between Shiraz and Kermān, when its ailing engine finally failed. It sputtered to a halt in the middle of nowhere. We all left the coach while its driver tried to fix it. I saw the stars that night as I had never seen them before – brilliant, solemn and still, in the midst of a dark and silent land. I simply cannot express in words the overwhelming feeling of awe I experienced that night – a sense of exaltation, amazement and wonder. I still feel a tingle, a shiver of pleasure, running down my spine when I recall that desert experience, all those years ago.

Rapturous Amazement: A Gateway to Understanding

For some, that sense of wonder – what Albert Einstein called 'rapturous amazement'[1] – is an end in itself. Many of the Romantic poets took this view. Towards the end of his life, the great German novelist and poet Goethe declared that a sense of astonishment or wonder was an end in itself: we should not seek anything beyond or behind this experience of wonder, but simply enjoy it for what it is.[2] But for many it is not a destination, however pleasurable, but is rather a starting point for exploration and discovery.

The great Greek philosopher Aristotle also knew that sense of wonder. For him it was an invitation to explore, to set out on a journey of discovery in which our horizons are expanded, our understanding deepened and our eyes opened.[3] As the great medieval philosopher Thomas Aquinas once put it, this sense of wonder elicits a *desiderium sciendi*, a 'longing to know', whose fulfilment leads to joy as much as to understanding.[4]

This journey of discovery involves both reason and imagination, and leads not to a new place, but rather to a new way of looking at things. There are two main outcomes of this journey of exploration. One of them is *science*, one of humanity's most significant and most deeply satisfying achievements. When I was young, I wanted to study medicine. It made sense. After all, my father was a doctor and my mother a nurse. Knowing my career plans, my great-uncle – who was head of pathology at one of Ireland's leading teaching hospitals – gave me an old microscope. It turned out to be the gateway to a new world. As I happily explored the small plants and cells I found in pond water through its lens, I developed a love of nature which remains with me to this day. It also convinced me that I wanted to know and understand nature. I would be a scientist, not a doctor.

I never regretted that decision. From the age of fifteen, I focused on physics, chemistry and mathematics. I won a major scholarship to Oxford University to study chemistry, where I specialised in quantum theory. I then went on to do doctoral research at Oxford in the laboratories of Professor Sir George Radda, working on developing new techniques for studying complex biological systems. I still have that old brass microscope on my office desk, a reminder of its pivotal role in my life.

Yet though I loved science as a young man, I had a sense that it was not complete. It helped us to understand how things worked. But what did they *mean*? Science gave me a neat answer to the question of how I came to be in this world. Yet it seemed unable to answer a deeper question. *Why* was I here? What was the point of life?

Science is wonderful at raising questions. Some can be answered immediately; some will be answerable in the future through technological advance; and some will lie beyond its capacity to answer – what my scientific hero Sir Peter Medawar (1915–87) referred to as 'questions that science cannot answer and that no conceivable

2

advance of science would empower it to answer'.[5] What Medawar has in mind are what the philosopher Karl Popper called 'ultimate questions', such as the meaning of life. So does acknowledging and engaging such questions mean abandoning science? No. It simply means respecting its limits and not forcing it to become something other than science.

Why We Can't Evade the Big Questions

The Spanish philosopher José Ortega y Gasset (1883–1955) put his finger on the point at issue here. *Scientists are human beings.* If we, as human beings, are to lead fulfilled lives, we need more than the partial account of reality that science offers. We need a 'big picture', an 'integral idea of the universe'. As a young man, I was aware of the need for a 'bigger narrative', a richer vision of reality that would weave together understanding and meaning. I failed to find it. What I found to be elusive I then took to be merely illusory. Yet the idea never entirely died in either my mind or my imagination. While science had a wonderful capacity to explain, it nevertheless failed to satisfy the deeper longings and questions of humanity.

Any philosophy of life, any way of thinking about the questions that really matter, according to Ortega, will thus end up going beyond science – not because there is anything wrong with science, but precisely because its intellectual virtues are won at a price: science works so well because it is so focused and specific in its methods.

> Scientific truth is characterized by its precision and the certainty of its predictions. But science achieves these admirable qualities at the cost of remaining on the level of secondary concerns, leaving ultimate and decisive questions untouched.[6]

For Ortega, the great intellectual virtue of science is that it knows its limits. It only answers questions that it knows it can answer on

3

the basis of the evidence. But human curiosity wants to go further. We feel we need answers to deeper questions that we cannot avoid asking. Who are we, really? What is the point of life? As Ortega rightly observed, human beings – whether scientists or not – cannot live without answering these questions, even in a provisional way. 'We are given no escape from ultimate questions. In one way or another they are in us, whether we like it or not. Scientific truth is exact, but it is incomplete.' We need a richer narrative, linking understanding and meaning. That is what the American philosopher John Dewey (1859–1952) was getting at when he declared that the 'deepest problem of modern life' is that we have failed to integrate our 'thoughts about the world' with our thoughts about 'value and purpose'.[7]

So we come back to that haunting and electrifying sense of wonder at the world. As we have seen, one of its outcomes is science – the attempt to understand the world around us. But there is another outcome. It is one that I initially resisted, believing that it was utterly opposed to science. The shallow materialism of my youth had no space for it. Yet I gradually came to realise that we need a richer and deeper vision of reality if we are to do justice to the complexity of the world, and live out meaningful and fulfilling lives. So just what are we talking about? *The quest for God.*

Like so many young people in the late 1960s, I regarded the idea of God as outdated nonsense. The 1960s were a time of intellectual and cultural change. The old certainties of the past seemed to crumble in the face of a confident expectation of a revolution that would sweep away outdated nonsense, such as belief in God. Without quite realising what I was doing, I adopted a worldview that then seemed to me to be the inevitable result of the consistent application of the scientific method. I would only believe what science could prove.

So I embraced a rather dogmatic atheism, taking delight in its intellectual minimalism and existential bleakness. So what if life had to be seen as meaningless? It was an act of intellectual bravery on my part to accept this harsh scientific truth. Religion was just a pointless relic of a credulous past, offering a spurious delusion of meaning which was easily discarded. I believed that science offered a complete, totalised explanation of the world, ruthlessly exposing its rivals as lies and delusions. Science disproved God, and all honest scientists were atheists. Science was good, and religion was evil.

It was, of course, a hopelessly simplified binary opposition. Everything was black and white, with no sense of the many shades of grey that demanded their proper recognition. But this simplistic outlook suited me just fine then. Without quite understanding what was happening, I had fallen into an 'in-group/out-group' mentality, which consolidates a privileged sense of belonging to a superior 'in-group' by ridiculing, vilifying and demonising its opponents. (It is traditionally understood to be one of the nastier features of religion, but it has now become clear that it is characteristic of any fundamentalism, whether religious or anti-religious.) Religion was intellectually wrong, and morally evil. It was a contaminant, best avoided rather than engaged.

Looking back, I now realise that the world must have seemed very simple to my sixteen-year-old mind. I lacked both the detailed knowledge of the history and philosophy of the sciences that would have shown me that things were rather more complicated than this, and the wisdom to cope with the paradoxes, ambiguity, limits and uncertainty of any serious engagement with reality.[8] Yet for about three years, I was totally convinced of both the intellectual elegance of atheism and the utter stupidity of those who embraced alternative positions.

In December 1970, I learned that I had won a scholarship to study chemistry at Oxford University. Yet I could not begin my studies at Oxford until October 1971. So what was I to do in the meantime? Most of my friends left school in order to travel the world or earn some money. I decided to stay on at school and use the time to learn German and Russian, both of which would be useful for my scientific studies. Having specialised in the physical sciences for two years, I was also aware of the need to deepen my knowledge of biology, and begin to think about biochemistry. I therefore settled down to begin an extended period of reading and reflection.

After a month or so of intensive reading in the school science library in early 1971, having exhausted the works on biology, I came across a section that I had never noticed before: 'The History and Philosophy of Science'. I had little time for this sort of material, tending to regard it as uninformed criticism of the certainties and simplicities of the natural sciences by those who felt threatened by them. Philosophy, in my view, was just pointless speculation about issues that any proper scientist could solve easily through a few well-designed experiments. What was the point? Yet in the end, I decided to read these works. If I was right, what had I to lose by doing so?

By the time I had finished reading the somewhat meagre holdings of the school in this field, I realised that I needed to do some very serious rethinking. Far from being half-witted obscurantism that placed unnecessary obstacles before the relentless pace of scientific advance, the history and philosophy of science asked all the right questions about the reliability and limits of scientific knowledge. And they were questions that I had not faced thus far – such as the under-determination of theory by data, radical theory change in the history of science, the difficulties in devising a 'crucial experiment', and the enormously complex issues associated with devising what was the 'best explanation' of a given set of observations. I was overwhelmed. It was as if a tidal wave was battering against my settled way of thinking, muddying what I had taken to be the clear, still and, above all, *simple* waters of scientific truth.

Things thus turned out to be rather more complicated than I had realised. My eyes had been opened and I knew there was no going back to the simplistic take on the natural sciences I had once known. I had enjoyed the beauty and innocence of a child-like attitude to the sciences, and secretly wished to remain in that secure place. Indeed, I think that part of me deeply wished that I had never picked up those books, never asked those awkward questions, and never questioned the simplicities of my scientific youth. But there could be no going back. I had stepped through a door which up to that point I did not know existed, and could not escape the new world I now began to inhabit.

I found that I could no longer hold on to what I now realise was a somewhat naïve view – that the only authentic knowledge we can possess is scientific knowledge based on empirical evidence. It became clear to me that a whole series of questions that I had dismissed as meaningless or pointless had to be examined again – including the God-question. Having been forced to abandon my rather dogmatic belief that science necessarily entailed atheism, I began to realise that the natural world is conceptually malleable. Nature can be interpreted, without any loss of intellectual integrity, in a number of different ways. So which was the best way of making sense of it?

An Enriched Understanding of Reality

My own rediscovery of the enriched understanding and appreciation of the world made possible through belief in God took place at Oxford University. It was a somewhat cerebral and intellectual conversion, focusing on my growing realisation that belief in God made a lot more sense of things than my atheism did. I had no emotional need for any idea of God, being perfectly prepared to embrace nihilism – if this was right. Yet I mistakenly assumed that its bleakness was an indication of its truth. What if truth were to turn out to be attractive?

Having already discovered the beauty and wonder of nature, I realised that I had – as the poet T.S. Eliot put it – 'had the experience but missed the meaning'. I gradually came to the view so winsomely expressed by C.S. Lewis: 'I believe in Christianity as I believe that the Sun has risen, not only because I see it, but because by it, I see everything else.'[9] It was as if an intellectual sun had

7

risen and illuminated the scientific landscape before my eyes, allowing me to see details and interconnections that I would otherwise have missed altogether. I had once been drawn to atheism on account of the minimalism of its intellectual demands; I now found myself discovering the richness of the intellectual outcomes of Christianity.

It will be clear that my conversion – if that is the right word – was largely intellectual. I had discovered a new way of seeing reality, and was delighted by what I found. Like Dorothy L. Sayers (1893–1957), I was convinced that Christianity seemed to offer an account of reality that was 'intellectually satisfactory'.[10] Yet, also like Sayers, I found my initial delight in the internal logic of the Christian faith to be so compelling that I occasionally wondered if I had merely 'fallen in love with an intellectual pattern'.[11] I did not think of myself as being 'religious' in any way, and my new faith did not result in any habits of 'religiosity'. As far as I was concerned, I had simply discovered a new *theoria* – a way of seeing things which originated in wonder and ended in a deeper understanding and appreciation of reality. To borrow Salman Rushdie's terms, I discovered that 'the idea of God' is both 'a repository for our awestruck wonderment at life and an answer to the great questions of existence'.[12] Like Rushdie, I came to realise the ultimate futility of 'the idea that men and women could ever define themselves in terms that exclude their spiritual needs'.

I tended at this stage to think of my Christian faith as a philosophy of life, not a religion. I had grasped something of its intellectual appeal, but had yet to discover its imaginative, ethical and spiritual depths. I had a sense of standing on the threshold of something beautiful and amazing, which my reason had tantalisingly only grasped in part. Like Einstein, I realised that nature 'shows us only the lion's tail', while hinting at the majesty and grandeur of the magnificent animal to which it was attached – and to which it ultimately led.[13] I was like a traveller who had arrived on an island, and discovered the beauty of the lowlands around its harbour. But beyond lay far mountains and distant landscapes I had yet to explore.

I gradually came to see that I did not need to see my faith as conflicting with science, but as filling in the detail of a 'big picture' of which science was a major part – but only a part. As the theoretical physicist and Nobel Laureate Eugene Wigner pointed out, science is constantly searching for the 'ultimate truth', which he defined as 'a picture which is a consistent fusion into a single unit of the little pictures, formed on the various aspects of nature'.[14] If there was a conflict between faith and science, it was with the view sometimes called 'scientific imperialism' (and now usually abbreviated to 'scientism'), which holds that science, *and science alone*, is able to answer all of life's deepest questions. This distortion of science involves borrowing the language and apparatus of science in order to create the illusion that an essentially *scientific* question is being answered on the basis of what is declared to be 'scientific data', using a universal method that will arrive at a 'scientific' answer. This inflated distortion of science does nobody any favours, least of all scientists themselves.

We all need help in thinking things through. My own thinking on this matter was helped enormously by a conversation with Professor Charles A. Coulson (1910–74), sometime around 1973. Coulson was Oxford's first Professor of Theoretical Chemistry, and was a fellow of Wadham College, Oxford, where I was an undergraduate. As a prominent Methodist lay preacher, it was natural that Coulson should from time to time preach in Wadham Chapel. I heard him preach on the fundamental coherence of nature and faith, and why the idea of a 'god of the gaps' was to be rejected. As a recently converted atheist who was still feeling my way in the mysterious realm of the Christian faith, I talked to him afterwards about some of my questions.

Coulson helped me to see that my new faith did not call upon me to abandon my love of science, but to see it in a new way – indeed, to have a new motivation for loving science and a deepened appreciation for its outcomes. And he persuaded me utterly that the intellectual appeal of Christianity to a scientist did not lie in the location of explanatory gaps that could be arbitrarily and unconvincingly populated with gods. For Coulson, this demanded an indefensible 'dichotomy of existence' and 'intellectual partitioning'.[15]

The solution lay rather in the Christian articulation of a luminous vision of reality that offered insight into the scientific process and its successes, while at the same time setting out a larger narrative that allowed engagement with questions raised by science, yet lying beyond its capacity to answer. Coulson was both gracious and sagacious as we talked, and helped me grasp the idea of the ultimate coherence of science and faith,[16] which remains with me to this day and is set out in this book. Science, like faith, seeks to find and explore a coherent and satisfying understanding of the world in which we live. Might they not do so together, learning from each other's strengths and weaknesses?[17]

Faith and the Appreciation of Nature

But surely, some might reasonably object, faith is more likely to damage than to enrich our understanding of nature? Surely science needs to preserve itself from being contaminated by religion? It is certainly true that some believe any kind of belief in God impoverishes our appreciation of the beauty and wonder of nature. Richard Dawkins, for example, argues – rightly, in my view – that it is perfectly possible to have a sense of 'awe' or reverence for nature without being religious or believing in God. Yet he spoils a perfectly reasonable point by his unevidenced assertion that a religious commitment actually *diminishes* this sense of awe through holding an aesthetically deficient view of the universe.[18] I cannot see the logic of this position, nor is it borne out by empirical research.

In my own experience, a Christian approach to nature deepened my appreciation of the beauty of nature. While I cannot speak for what others might have experienced, it seems to me that there are three ways in which a sense of awed wonder might arise in response to what we observe around us, which help us reflect on the possible influence of religious commitment on our experience of natural beauty.

To begin with, many of us have experienced an immediate sense of wonder evoked by the beauty or vastness of nature, such as I experienced as a young man in the deserts of Iran, or the 'leap of the heart' that the poet William Wordsworth experienced on seeing a rainbow in the sky. Yet this sense of awe occurs *before* any conscious theoretical reflection on what it might imply or entail. To use psychological categories, this is about *perception* rather than *cognition*. It bypasses our conceptual schemes or mental maps, while at the same time motivating us to ask about the origins and goals of this sense of awed wonder. That is why Thomas Aquinas is right when he declares that 'the cause of that at which we wonder is hidden from us',[19] causing us to yearn to make sense of this heart-stopping experience of awe, which we see as a gateway to significance.

This is followed by a derived sense of wonder at the mathematical or theoretical representation of reality that arises from this. Dawkins also knows and approves of this second source of 'awed wonder', but seems to think that religious people 'revel in mystery and feel cheated when it is explained'.[20] But they do not. If anything, a new sense of wonder emerges at the ability of mathematics to represent the natural order in such beautiful ways, and at the spiritual implications of this insight. We will look at this in more detail later in the book (see pages 75–9).

This is linked to a further level of wonder at what the natural world might point to. Unfortunately, Dawkins glosses over the rather important issue of the semiotics of nature – the way in which the natural world functions as a system of signs.[21] From a Christian perspective, the created order bears an elegant and eloquent witness to its Creator: 'The heavens are telling the glory of God!' (Psalm 19:1). It is a theme that resonates throughout Christian history – nature points to God, thus giving a fundamental religious motivation to the study and admiration of the natural world. The great theologian Augustine of Hippo set this out rather nicely in the fifth century:

> Some people read a book in order to discover God. But there is a greater book – the actual appearance of created things. Look above and below you, and note and read. The God that you want to discover did not write in letters of ink, but put in front of your eyes the very things that he made. Can you ask for a louder voice than that?[22]

The natural world is thus appreciated and valued all the more because of its capacity to signify something still greater. The beauty of nature is seen as hinting at the greater beauty of God. That is why so many Christian theologians down the ages have commended the study of the natural sciences, affirming a fundamentally religious motivation for the study of nature.

Yet despite our differences, Dawkins and I agree on something of major importance to this discussion – the ability of a 'grand theory' (such as Marxism, Darwinism [as Dawkins understands it] or the Christian faith), which proposes a larger vision of reality, to evoke awe. Recent work on the psychology of awe has shown how the human sense of awe at the vastness of the universe or the dramatic beauty of a natural landscape or feature (such as a rainbow) could be enhanced by grasping the theoretical foundations or implications of what was being observed.[23]

Theoretical representations of reality are thus beautiful in themselves, while being capable of evoking awe on account of their complexity or their capacity to invoke a 'big picture' view of things. The philosopher Mary Midgley suggests that this may be a reason why Marxism and Darwinism – the 'two great secular faiths of our day' – display 'religious-looking features'.[24] They are based on ideologies, 'large-scale, ambitious systems of thought', which represent 'explicit faiths by which people live and to which they try to convert others'.

Dawkins playfully suggests that a religious approach to the world misses out on something.[25] Having read him in some depth,[26] I still have not quite worked out what this is. A Christian reading of the world denies nothing of what the natural sciences tell us, except the trenchant naturalist dogma that reality is limited to what may be known through the natural sciences. If anything, a Christian engagement with the natural world adds a richness which I have found to be quite absent from Dawkins' account of things, offering me a new motivation for the study of nature. We shall be exploring this theme throughout this book.

The Great Myth: The Perpetual 'Conflict' of Science and Religion

Some will doubtless be surprised at any suggestion that science and religious belief can be held together like this, when the cultural establishment of the West seems to have locked itself into a 'science versus religion' groupthink, a narrow and dogmatic view of reality which holds that any thinking person must choose science over religion. Someone like myself who now sees them, when rightly understood, as having the potential to be mutually enriching is dismissed simply as mad, bad or sad – and possibly all three.

It is a most unfortunate development, which I dislike partly because I think it is inaccurate, but more fundamentally because I detest dogmatism of any kind. It has no place in science, and it ought to have no place in religion. I can see how this misleading perception arises from the explicitly polemical agendas of the New Atheism. After all, Christopher Hitchens remarked that he was not an atheist so much as an 'anti-theist'.[27] Hitchens thus defines his atheism *oppositionally* as a polemical repudiation of theism, not as the simple absence of any theistic belief. This certainly helps us understand how the New Atheism often seems like a mirror of theism. Its leading representatives seem to be defined by an obsession with what it is *against*, like an ex-lover they just cannot stop talking about. Most atheists see a belief in the non-existence of God as functional and unremarkable, and would not think of it as a defining characteristic of their lives. The New Atheism turns it into a fixation.

Yet the problem with the New Atheism goes beyond this puzzling obsession with a God who they believe does not exist. As Greg Epstein, humanist chaplain at Harvard University, writes, adopting anti-theism as a defining characteristic of the movement determines its stridently aggressive approach and dismissive tone.

> Anti-theism means actively seeking out the worst aspects of faith in god and portraying them as representative of all religion. Anti-theism seeks to shame and embarrass people away from religion, browbeating them about the stupidity of belief in a bellicose god.[28]

The unrelenting hostility of the New Atheism towards religion of any kind is part of its rather dogmatic mindset, and leads it to dismiss its opponents with an intellectual arrogance that has no relation to the quality of their arguments. It reminds me of Plato's criticism of the Athenian politics of his day, in which 'rudeness is taken as a mark of sophistication'.[29] It also makes dialogue impossible, in that conversations are framed in terms of defeat or compromise – especially when the New Atheism (unlike more congenial and undogmatic forms of atheism) has invested so heavily in the perennial truth of the conflict of science and faith as a core marker of its identity.

Yet as we shall see, this 'science versus religion' narrative is stale, outdated and largely discredited.[30] It is sustained not by the weight of evidence, but merely by its endless uncritical repetition, which studiously avoids the scholarship of the last generation that has undermined its credibility. When the historical myths are laid to rest, it is clear that there is a plurality of narratives for understanding the relation of science and faith, none of which have the privilege of being self-evidently true or intellectually normative. Furthermore, many of the case studies of the 'warfare' of science and religion often turn out to have many dimensions – and often it is their political, social and institutional dimensions that are the most important.[31] The relationship between science and religion is thus *complicated*, and cannot be reduced to dumbed-down slogans which ultimately serve polemical cultural agendas – such as those evident in Thomas Paine's *Age of Reason* (1794), which sought to minimise the social and cultural influence of Christian churches and leaders by portraying them as irrational. Yes, religion and science *can* be in conflict. But they do not *need* to be at war with each other, and usually have not been so in the past. Both sides of the science and religion 'dialogue' value a quest for understanding and a love of learning, come into conflict with rival approaches, and find themselves involved in 'compromising entanglements with the power of the state'.[32]

The 'conflict narrative' is essentially a social construction, invented to serve the needs and agendas of certain social groups. It is not a timeless truth we have to accept. It is an historical contingency that can be changed. We can choose how we see things. We can rebel against the tyranny of those who tell us what narrative we must adopt, thus forcing us to see history and determine our present possibilities in its light and on its basis. I offer an alternative approach. Like history itself, it is complicated and messy. But it does not try to force our past history or our present options into a narrow preconceived mould. It is about reappropriating an older and wiser approach, which welcomes the confluence of science and faith while respecting their distinct identities and limits. It allows for an enriched narrative of life which weaves together facts, values, meaning and purpose.

Unfortunately, Western culture still tends to look at both history and present experience through this controlling lens of the story of a 'warfare of science and religion', and sees what it wants to see – and does not see what it does not want to see. So how do these narratives become so influential, especially when they are so clearly flawed? In his important work *A Secular Age*, the philosopher and cultural theorist Charles Taylor notes how certain 'metanarratives' – that is, grand stories of explanation and meaning – come to assume social dominance, often for reasons that rest on somewhat flimsy evidential foundations.[33] To challenge or reject these dominant narratives is seen as a sign of irrationality. The 'conflict' narrative is a classic example of a way of thinking that gained traction for cultural, not intellectual reasons, and is sustained by those with vested interests in ensuring its continued dominance. Yet to those who have given careful consideration to the historical evidence, as indicated earlier, this 'science versus religion' narrative seems stale, outdated and largely discredited.

It is surely time to move on, and frame the whole discussion about the relation of science and religion in a new way – or even reappropriate older ways of seeing their relationship, which fell out of favour for reasons that can now be seen as less than persuasive. Sure, it takes a long time for scholarship to filter down to the media. But we need to move on and deal with the way things really are, rather than resting content with a crass simplification of a complex situation. The 'warfare' narrative is falling to pieces of its own accord, breaking apart under the strain of massive scholarly evidence of its shortcomings.

Let's be clear about this. Despite what overenthusiastic New Atheist polemicists may say, science is intrinsically neither for nor against religion, any more than it is for or against politics. It rightly objects when religion (or politics) gets in the way of scientific advance, and rightly applauds when religion (or politics) encourages scientific enquiry and engagement. In the same way, science is neither religiously atheistic or theistic, nor politically liberal or conservative, although it can easily be accommodated within such perspectives. And science is entirely right to challenge religious or political beliefs when these present themselves *as science*.

Some people, for example, improbably argued on *religious* grounds that the Apollo moon landings never took place. A leader of the Hari Krishna movement, Bhaktivedanta Swami Prabhupada, insisted that the Vedic literature taught that 'the Moon is 100,000 *yojanas*, or 800,000 miles, above the rays of the sunshine'. So how could anyone travel to the moon? Not only was the moon too distant; the sun was closer to the earth than the moon. Modern scientific calculations of the moon's distance from earth were unreliable, and the Vedic literature got it right.[34] Prabhupada therefore declared that the so-called moon landings were nothing but an elaborate hoax. Now this is just rambling pseudoscience, and everyone knows it. When religion starts behaving as if it were a science, scientists have every reason to protest against it – and correct it!

It is certainly true that science, if it is to be science and not something else, is committed to a method that is often styled 'methodological naturalism'. That is the way that science works. That is what is characteristic of science, and it both provides it with its rigor and sets its limits. Science has established a set of tested and reliable rules by which it investigates reality, and 'methodological naturalism' is one of them.

But this is about setting rules for exploring reality, not limiting reality to what can be explored in this way.[35] It does not for one moment mean that science is committed to some kind of philosophical materialism. Some materialists argue that the explanatory successes of science imply an underlying ontological materialism. Yet this is simply one of several ways of interpreting this approach, and there are others with widespread support within the scientific community. Eugenie Scott, then director of the National Center for Science Education, made this point neatly back in 1993: 'Science neither denies nor opposes the supernatural, but *ignores* the supernatural for methodological reasons.'[36] Science is a *non-theistic*, not an *anti-theistic*, way of engaging reality. As the philosopher Alvin Plantinga so rightly observes, if there is any conflict between 'science' and 'faith', it is really between a dogmatic metaphysical naturalism and belief in God.[37]

Certainly some – but *only* some – atheist scientists present science as intrinsically atheistic. But maybe that is because they are primarily atheists, not because they are scientists. Virtually all my colleagues who are both scientists and atheists would have no time for the myth that science entails atheism. The great intellectual virtue of science is its radical openness; only frauds and fanatics want to close it down and force it to endorse their own dogmatic worldviews. We all owe it to science to protect it from people like that.

One of the less welcome outcomes of this 'conflict' narrative is the late Stephen Jay Gould's idea of 'non-overlapping magisteria', which treats science and religion as hermetically sealed compartments that never interact with each other.[38] This approach is little more than a retrospective validation of the political realities of modern American academic life, which encourages intellectual isolation and conceptual complacency. We need something better than this bipolar field of discourse, protecting intellectual borders at the price of preventing creative interaction and dialogue.

A solid body of scholarship has gradually built up in recent years, forcing revision of older understandings of the relation of science and faith. It is now clear that the boundaries of 'science' and 'religion' are increasingly recognised to be shaped by historical contingencies. Their respective territories can be mapped in multiple manners and are open to multiple interpretations.[39] Why should we have to put up with an outdated and discredited map of their interactions when this has no privileged claim to truth? We need to call time on this discredited myth. The 'warfare of science and religion' narrative has had its day. We need to draw a line under this and explore better ways of understanding their relationship.

It can be hard to talk to people we disagree with, and to take their ideas seriously. But intellectual integrity demands it. That is how we find out if we need to redirect or recalibrate our own ways of thinking. We need to open our minds, not close them down – and that means talking to people with different perspectives. To its many critics, that is why the New Atheism prefers to ridicule religious people rather than engage seriously with religious ideas. Its rhetoric of dismissal allows it to present its ignorance of religious ideas as an intellectual virtue, when it is simply an arrogant excuse to avoid thinking. And, as we shall see throughout this book, the new scholarship that has emerged over the last twenty years makes it clear that there is a lot of rethinking that needs to be done.

This book is an invitation to journey along another road. I have spent the last forty years exploring this road, and want to tell you about the questions I have faced and what I have found helpful as I travel along it. I am asking you to explore another way of thinking about science and faith – a way that may seem strange to some, but which I believe holds them together in a way that is both rationally satisfying and imaginatively exciting. Science and faith can thus provide us with different yet potentially complementary maps of human identity. I cannot prove it is right, but I can assure you it is deeply satisfying and well worth exploring.

The way of thinking that I shall be describing is not new. It can be tracked back to the Renaissance, before the modern (and very limiting) sense of the words 'science' and 'religion' had emerged. It has simply been forgotten or suppressed, drowned out by the noisy and overheated rhetoric of the New Atheism on the one hand, and a lack of familiarity with the rich pasturelands of our cultural heritage on the other. If anything is new, it is the 'conflict' narrative which swamped the more measured, informed and engaging approaches of the past.

Science and religion are two of the greatest cultural forces in today's world. When rightly framed, a mutual conversation can be enriching and elevating. When rightly constructed, a 'bigger narrative' of reality creates intellectual space for divergence and disagreement, while affirming the intelligibility and coherence of our world.

And that conversation needs to happen. Religion is back in public life and public debate. Despite all the predictions from armchair philosophers and media pundits, God has not gone away; nor has interest in the realm of the 'spiritual'. If anything, it is now the New Atheism that sounds stale and weary. It may have raised some good questions about God and religion; its answers, however, are now seen as glib and superficial. Slick slogans like 'God is a delusion' or 'Faith is a mental illness' made great headlines, but they ultimately failed to satisfy either the minds or the hearts of many looking for deeper answers.

This book offers both a correction of outdated perceptions and a remapping of imaginative possibilities. I want to explore a way of seeing things that is enriched by both science and religion at their best, and that I have found to be both intellectually coherent and imaginatively engaging. Let me emphasise the importance of that word *seeing*. Both scientific theories and theological doctrines can be viewed as invitations to see things in a certain way, to imagine the world in a certain manner – a manner that is believed to be both warranted and truthful, and whose truthfulness is to be measured in part by the degree of intelligibility and coherence it allows us to perceive.

Along the road, we will interact with some of the great issues that arise, many of them fascinating and important in their own right. We will engage with some of the most interesting voices on all sides of the debate – scientists such as Richard Dawkins, Stephen Hawking and Carl Sagan, and philosophers such as Mary Midgley and Roger Scruton. And whether you end up agreeing with me or not, I hope that you will find this journey of exploration of a new way of looking at things interesting and rewarding.

2

Stories, Pictures and Maps: Making Sense of Things

I think I realised why science was so interesting when I was about seven or eight years old. I loved taking things to pieces to find out how they worked. One of my most rewarding experiments in the early 1960s was taking apart my father's watch and figuring out how each of the pieces of the clockwork mechanism functioned. It was fascinating! Unfortunately, putting the watch back together again was not quite so straightforward. Happily, it was quite an old watch and my father was rather less angry than he might have been at having to replace it.

And that is what science does so well – it takes things to pieces to find out how they work. What mechanisms underlie the processes we see around us in the world? How do bees make honey? Why is the sky blue? Why could I never see the far side of the moon? One of the deepest motivations of science is human curiosity. We long to be able to make sense of what we see and experience in the world.

We can think of science as the quest for the best theory. What is the deeper understanding of the structure of the universe that arises from our observations? Because we believe in a rational universe, we also believe in the capacity of human reason to grasp at least something of its structures. As C.S. Lewis pointed out, 'We are not reading rationality into an irrational universe, but responding to a rationality with which the universe has always been saturated.'[1]

The word 'theory' comes from the Greek term *theoria* and means something like 'a way of seeing things'. We need to make a distinction between what we observe and how we understand those observations. A theory is a way of understanding what we observe. It is an intellectual framework that helps us make sense of what we see, or a conceptual net that we throw over what we observe. The historian of science Peter Dear makes this point well:

> The hallmark of natural philosophy is its stress on *intelligibility*: it takes natural phenomena and tries to account for them in ways that not only hold together logically, but also rest on ideas and assumptions that seem right, that make sense.[2]

And that is true of religion as well. As we will see later (page 153), there is growing interest, especially within empirical psychology, in exploring how religion acts as a system of meaning, enabling people to make sense of both the world and their lives, and especially to cope with adversity.[3]

As I prepared to go up to Oxford University to study chemistry in October 1971, I was becoming aware of more profound questions in life that somehow lay beyond the grasp of science. Although I could never quite put my misgivings into words, I was beginning to realise that there was more to life than clarifying natural mechanisms. Science was really good at taking things apart so that we could see how they worked. But was there a way of putting them back together again so that we could see what they meant? If they meant anything, that is.

Meaning and Ultimate Questions

As a young man, I often wondered what life was all about. Did it have any meaning? Was there any purpose to human existence in general, and my own life in particular? I was an atheist at that stage because I believed not merely that there were no valid answers to these questions, but that they simply could not be answered. Intellectual honesty demanded atheism. Yet as I reflected more on these themes, before going up to Oxford, I began to wonder if I had prematurely foreclosed these questions, reaching somewhat hasty answers on the basis of a rather super-ficial reflection on reality.

Science is good – very good – at helping us to understand the processes that brought us into existence in the first place, and keep us alive in the second. Yet there is a major difference between knowing *how* we came into being and knowing *why* we are here. I initially believed science could – or would – give us answers to all our questions about meaning and purpose. Yet my immersion in the philosophy of science in early 1971 led me to the conclusion that science could not provide answers to what the philosopher of science Karl Popper called 'ultimate questions'. Popper argued that science is in no position to 'make assertions about ultimate questions – about the riddles of existence, or about man's task in this world'.[4] Yet this truth, he declared, was open to being misunderstood and misrepresented – for example, in relation to ethics. 'Some great scientists, and many lesser ones, have misunderstood the situation. The fact that science cannot make any pronounce-ment about ethical principles has been misinterpreted as indicating that there are no such principles.'

We shall be considering this issue at several points in this book. Let's turn to reflect on some of its themes.

Science Is Neither Atheist Nor Theist: It Is Just Science

The natural sciences are indeed one of the most reliable forms of intellectual enquiry – perhaps even *the* most reliable – but they achieve and safeguard this enviable reputation for reliability and trustworthiness by acknowledging their limits. We need to guard against overextending ideas beyond the explanatory territory in which they originally took root and within which they work perfectly well.

It is a concern that most scientists recognise. In 1885, Thomas H. Huxley, the great champion of Charles Darwin's ideas in Victorian England, delivered a speech to mark the completion of a statue of Darwin for a London museum. In drawing the speech to a close, Huxley declared that science 'commits suicide when it adopts a creed'.[5] He was right. Science goes terribly wrong when it allies itself with any political, religious or anti-religious world-view. It cannot stop itself being co-opted by ideologues. Yet it can at least protest against this assault on its integrity when it is treated as a weapon by religious or anti-religious activists.

The American evolutionary biologist Stephen Jay Gould (1941–2002) regularly pointed out that science is neither atheist nor theist. It is just science. If it limits itself to the legitimate application of the scientific method – which it should! – it is simply unable to comment on the God-question. The problem lies with some scientists who seem to assume that their authority in their own rather limited field can be transferred to every other area of life.

In response to an anti-evolutionary work which claimed that Darwinism was necessarily atheistic, Gould recalled a less than fond memory of Mrs McInerney, his third-grade teacher, who was in the habit of rapping young knuckles when their owners said or did particularly stupid things:

> To say it for all my colleagues and for the umpteenth millionth time (from college bull sessions to learned treatises): science simply cannot (by its legitimate methods) adjudicate the issue of God's possible superintendence of nature. We neither affirm nor deny it; we simply can't comment on it as scientists. If some of our crowd have made untoward statements claiming that Darwinism disproves God, then I will find Mrs McInerney and have their knuckles rapped for it.[6]

Gould rightly insists that science works only with naturalistic explanations, thus placing discussion of the God-question beyond its reach. It can neither affirm nor deny the existence of God. The bottom line for Gould is that Darwin's theory of evolution actually has no bearing on the existence or nature of God, unless the existence of God is held to entail beliefs that are demonstrably wrong – such as holding that the world is only 6,000 years old. For Gould, it is an observable fact that evolutionary biologists are both atheist and theist. After noting representative examples, including the humanist agnostic G.G. Simpson and the Russian Orthodox Christian Theodosius Dobzhansky, Gould concludes, 'Either half my colleagues are enormously stupid, or else the science of Darwinism is fully compatible with conventional religious beliefs – and equally compatible with atheism.'

Gould was absolutely clear that the natural sciences – including evolutionary theory – were consistent with both atheism and conventional religious belief. Unless half his scientific colleagues were total fools – a presumption that Gould rightly dismissed as nonsense, whichever half it is applied to – there could be no other responsible way of making sense of the varied responses to reality on the part of the intelligent, informed people that he knew.

The veteran British philosopher Mary Midgley is a ferocious critic of the tendency of some scientists to launch into all kinds of 'quasi-scientific speculation' in some of their more popular works – often in their final chapters. Up to that point, the books generally dealt carefully with scientific questions, basing their arguments on reliable evidence. In the final chapter, everything changed! Midgley ridiculed the 'remarkable prophetic and metaphysical passages' that then suddenly appeared, dealing authoritatively (and, it has to be said, often a little pretentiously) with the meaning of life and other great questions.[7]

Midgley is particularly critical of Richard Dawkins, whom she regards as the prime example of a scientist with pretentious and inflated views of the scientific enterprise in general, and of his own prowess as a public intellectual in particular. How, Midgley asked, could *anyone* know the universe is meaningless? How could they show that it has no purpose? These must surely remain open questions.[8]

Science can easily be reconciled with atheism. Of course, it can be just as easily reconciled with Christianity. But science itself entails neither atheism nor any kind of theism, such as Christianity.

It is just science. It is a simple matter of observation that there are scientists who are Christians, there are scientists who are atheists, and there are scientists who hold all kinds of political, social and ethical perspectives on life. That is just the way things are. Science does not entail *any* specific religious, political or social views. It may be argued to be consistent with them; consistency, however, is not the same as entailment.

Seeking Intelligibility and Coherence

As human beings, we try to integrate the many dimensions of life into a coherent and satisfying whole. We want to do more than just make sense of things. We want to position them within a greater whole, of which they are part. Instead of thinking of our mental worlds as a series of disconnected and incoherent thoughts and values, we try to weave them, like threads, into a pattern. We try to develop a 'big picture' of reality which allows us to see science and religion as fitting together within a comprehensive map of the intellectual landscape, allowing an interconnected and enriching view of life. For many of us, the greatest human quest is for a framework of interpretation which can provide overall orientation for our lives.

It is all about stories, pictures and maps. We live in a story-shaped world. But which story makes most sense? Many philosophers now use the word 'myth' to refer to an imaginative pattern that helps us find meaning in life.[9] But which myth is the best? Others prefer to think in terms of 'pictures' that help us visualise and organise our snapshots of life, lending coherence to what might otherwise be disconnected. Or we might talk about 'maps of meaning' that help us make sense of the complex landscape of reality and find our way within it.

Some psychologists use the term 'schema' (plural: 'schemata') to refer to such a mental map of reality, which provides both a framework for representing some aspects of the world and a system of organising information about it.[10] Schemata are often presented and commended through narratives. Good stories, pictures and maps can help us deepen our appreciation of reality – just as inadequate ones can lock us into reduced and impoverished ways of thinking. Get them wrong, and they deprive and demean; get them right, and they illuminate and enrich.

We saw earlier how certain 'grand narratives' captivate the imagination of our culture for a while, before losing their appeal and credibility. Reductionist and materialist ways of seeing the world have now displaced the richer and more holistic approaches of earlier periods in Western culture, especially at the time of the Renaissance. The Renaissance idea of nature as a complex and interconnected living organism has been displaced by a mechanical model of nature. When seen in the light of this dominant 'grand narrative', nature is now interpreted as an impersonal order of matter and force, governed by causal laws.

Yet the cultural dominance of this mechanical narrative does not entail its intellectual precision or existential adequacy. It rose to prominence, and it will one day fade away. There are other stories of meaning, other ways of looking at things, which our culture sidelines and marginalises. And sometimes we need to move on, and recover older ways of thinking which have been silenced and suppressed not because they are wrong, but because they are inconvenient and subversive. The cultural story of science and religion is perhaps the best example of this sort of thing. Let's look at this in more detail.

Stories about Science and Religion

Groups within cultures tell stories to assert and justify their claims to authority and insight on the one hand, and to exclude those who might challenge them on the other. As we noted earlier, the philosopher and cultural theorist Charles Taylor has shown how certain metanarratives – that is, grand stories of explanation and meaning – have come to assume social dominance, despite their often weak grounding in reality.[11] To challenge or reject these dominant narratives is portrayed as a sign of irrationality. Yet those who are wise enough to challenge them are later proclaimed to be prophets, figures of wisdom who saw past the limits of the present to the possibilities of the future.

The prominent postmodern philosopher Michel Foucault (1926–84) made his name with a study of madness in the early modern period.[12] Why was this work so influential? Because it showed how the stigma of 'madness' was widely used by those in power not merely to designate psychological disorders, but also to deal with subversive and inconvenient views that posed a real threat to the political and cultural establishment. The easiest way for the establishment to neutralise dangerous ideas was to declare that they were 'mad'. What was really an act of intellectual suppression was portrayed as an act of public service.

This is exactly what happened with the 'punitive psychiatry' of the Soviet Union, when political and religious dissidents were sent to mental hospitals. There was nothing wrong with them – apart from holding ideas that threatened the dominant ideology of the Soviet Union. It was a neat trick. Sending them to mental hospitals both removed them from contact with society and stigmatised their ideas as 'insane'. Sadly, the same attempt to demonise faith has become a hallmark of the New Atheism. Richard Dawkins' condescending remark that faith is 'a kind of mental illness' may have seemed bold and brilliant to some back in the 1980s; now it just seems prejudiced and grumpy.[13]

Now the stories that dominate our culture do not just *happen*. As cultural analysts since the time of Antonio Gramsci (1891–1937) have shown, they are *made to happen* by those in cultural power and authority. Some intellectuals collude with dominant cultural narratives; others try to challenge them. And often the most powerful challenges to dominant cultural narratives come from scientists. In his essay 'The Scientist as Rebel', the physicist Freeman Dyson declared, 'Science is an alliance of free spirits in all cultures rebelling against the local tyranny that each culture imposes on its children.'[14] Science often finds itself challenging those in positions of cultural authority – such as the religious establishment.

It is a powerful point, and Dyson backs it up with lots of examples. The great Persian mathematician and astronomer Omar Khayyam (1048–1131) regarded science as a rebellion against the intellectual constraints of Islam, just as some of the best Indian physicists of the twentieth century – such as Chandrasekhara Venkata Raman (1888–1970) – saw science as a rebellion against the fatalistic ethic of Hinduism.

Yet at times this rebellion was directed against the political establishment. For example, the first generations of Japanese scientists in the nineteenth century regarded science as a rebellion against their traditional culture of feudalism, just as Raman also saw science as a weapon to diminish the cultural influence of Britain on India during the colonial period.

The culturally dominant story about science and religion being at war with each other is uncritically repeated in the writings of the New Atheism, including Christopher Hitchens' *God Is Not Great* (2007). In this work, Hitchens defends the 'conflict' narrative by a crassly selective appeal to history which amounts to little more than prejudice-driven cherry-picking. Historical details are forced to fit into the author's pet theory, with those obstinately refusing to fit into this predetermined pattern being simply neglected or deliberately marginalised. Hitchens uses carefully selected historical anecdotes as if they were representative of some greater truth to make the somewhat implausible case that those who hold religious beliefs are deluded and hence potentially dangerous to society at large.

Let's look at one of these oracular pronouncements. Hitchens rightly states that the Christian writer Timothy Dwight (1752–1811), a former president of Yale College (which later became Yale University), opposed smallpox vaccination. For Hitchens, Dwight's misjudgement is typical of the backward-looking mind-set of religious people. Dwight's outrageous position, according to Hitchens, just shows how religious obscurantism stood in the way of scientific advance then, as now. Religion poisons all attempts at human progress.

Now this is worryingly light on evidence and heavy on ridicule. Hitchens is right to use smallpox vaccination as a case study in hostility to scientific advance. And he is also right in stating that Dwight opposed smallpox vaccination. But the conclusions he draws are simplistic and superficial, simply revealing his own deep-rooted prejudices and ideological precommitments. The situation is much more complex, and obstinately fails to conform to the 'warfare' narrative that Hitchens so uncritically embraces. Let me give two counter-examples to make this point.

Hitchens clearly thinks that smallpox vaccination is a good thing, so that those who oppose it are to be condemned and those who advocate it are to be commended. Let's go back to the generation before Timothy Dwight. Jonathan Edwards (1703–58), now widely regarded as America's greatest Christian thinker, was the third president of Princeton College (which later became Princeton University). A strong supporter of scientific and medical advance, Edwards was a forceful early advocate of vaccination against smallpox. In order to demonstrate to his students at Princeton that this new medical procedure was safe, Edwards himself received the smallpox vaccine.[15] The vaccination was not successful, and Edwards died shortly afterwards.

Now unbiased readers would not unreasonably expect Hitchens to have given a balanced and accurate account of religious attitudes towards smallpox vaccination, especially as Edwards' advocation of smallpox vaccination cost him his life in the service of scientific advance. Yet Edwards is airbrushed out of the picture. Hitchens is a propagandist, not a scholar. His goal is to defend both the 'warfare' narrative and his own rather dogmatic version of atheism, not to give a fair account of history.

This disturbing bias is confirmed by his astonishing failure to mention that the influential atheist writer George Bernard Shaw (1856–1950) opposed smallpox vaccination in the 1930s, ridiculing it as a 'delusion' and a 'filthy piece of witchcraft'. He dismissed leading scientists whose work so clearly supported it – such as Louis Pasteur and Joseph Lister – as charlatans who knew nothing about the scientific method. Yet Shaw was an *atheist* who made these ludicrous assertions *in the twentieth century*.[16]

Why did Hitchens not mention this famous and shocking example? Of course, Hitchens is free to externalise his own resentments and anxieties about religion in any way he likes. Yet surely he would have been canny enough to realise that his readers might notice this blatant bias?

That is why we need to tell the story fully and properly. And let's be clear that there have unquestionably been times when religion has got in the way of scientific advance. Although Galileo's struggle with the Church over his views on the solar system has been misrepresented, there is no doubt that some senior churchmen did not like what he was saying, for both scientific and religious reasons, and tried to silence him.

But the picture is much more complex than this.[17] At the time, Catholicism was locked in battle with Protestantism, and sought to safeguard its core teachings by refusing to countenance any modification of its traditional interpretations of the Bible. The polemical context created an atmosphere of intense suspicion that was not open to the subtleties of the 'new science'. Galileo's argument that the earth moved was (wrongly) seen as a modification of Catholic teaching which played into the hands of its Protestant opponents.

Contemporary Catholic theology now views Galileo as someone who upheld the consilience of science and faith, and who was misunderstood and misrepresented by his opponents within the Church. Pope John Paul II made this point in 1992, summarising a growing consensus within Catholicism during the twentieth century:

The new science, with its methods and the freedom of research that they implied, obliged theologians to examine their own criteria of scriptural interpretation. Most of them did not know

31

how to do so. Paradoxically, Galileo, a sincere believer, showed himself to be more perceptive in this regard than the theologians who opposed him.[18]

Challenging the 'Warfare' Narrative

There are many ways of challenging the tired and increasingly implausible 'warfare' narrative. One of the most effective is unfortunately also the most tedious – the systematic rebuttal of the leading myths regularly recited as if they were sacred narratives by cultural commentators who really ought to check their sources more carefully. Here is one, taken from the *New York Times* in 2006:

> When 19th-century doctors began using chloroform to alleviate the pain of childbirth, the Scottish Calvinist church declared it a 'Satanic invention' intended to frustrate the Lord's design.[19]

It is amusing, but it is also nonsense. Nineteenth-century opposition to anaesthesia in childbirth was rarely religious in nature; it predominantly came from *medical* sources, arising from concerns about its consequences for mother or child.[20] This is a piece of fiction that has simply been lifted – maybe directly, maybe indirectly, but certainly *uncritically* – from the pages of one of the founding documents of the 'warfare' mythology, long discredited by serious scholarship: Andrew Dickson White's *History of the Warfare of Science with Theology in Christendom* (1896). White was the first President of Cornell University, and wanted to establish it as a bastion of intellectual independence. His severe criticisms of religion were designed to increase Cornell's appeal to students. White's crude 'warfare' narrative is intended to encourage his readers 'to think of polarity where there was confusing plurality, to see monolithic solidarity where there was division and uncertainty, to expect hostility where there was conciliation and concord'.[21]

But there is no point in boring readers with a comprehensive rebuttal of this narrative, correcting distortions accurately but tiresomely. Instead, let's tell a more reliable story, which is probably a lot less interesting than this amusing invented tale of Scottish Calvinists, but which has the unquestionable merit of being more historically trustworthy.

While it is not correct to say that Christianity gave birth to modern science, as if Christianity was the sole causal agent or influence in this important development, it is clear that there is some fundamental synergy between them. For example, Christianity can be seen as providing an intellectual framework conducive to scientific theory and practice.[22] While ridiculous myths still linger within the popular literature – for example, the long-discredited idea that the medieval Church and its theologians taught that the earth was flat and suppressed any idea of its sphericity for religious reasons[23] – scholarship has moved far beyond these outdated fictions and given us a rich, complex and *reliable* account of the interaction of science and faith before and during the Scientific Revolution.

Historians of science in particular generally take the view that religious factors played a significantly positive role in the emergence and persistence of modern science in the West. For a start, many of the key figures in the rise of the natural sciences were individuals with sincere religious commitments; perhaps more importantly, the new approaches to nature that they pioneered were underpinned in various ways by religious assumptions, particularly grounded in a Christian understanding of an ordered creation. Let's note three major themes which historians regard as important to any understanding of the religious origins of the Scientific Revolution in western Europe in the early modern period.

1. A Christian doctrine of creation affirms the notion of a regular universe, whose regularities could be uncovered by empirical study – an idea that was essential to the emergence of science. As the physicist Paul Davies pointed out, 'In Renaissance

Europe, the justification for what we today call the scientific approach to inquiry was the belief in a rational God whose created order could be discerned from a careful study of nature.'[24]

2. Studying nature was widely seen as enhancing and deepening human appreciation for the wisdom and beauty of God.[25] There was thus a fundamental religious motivation for the study of nature, in that the regularities and beauty of nature were seen as reflecting the character of its Creator.

3. Many natural philosophers of the sixteenth and seventeenth centuries became increasingly suspicious of the reliability of unaided human reason as a way of arriving at truths about nature, using the kind of deductive processes familiar from Greek philosophy.[26] This growing anxiety about the limits of the human rational capacity, traditionally expressed by the Christian doctrine of original sin, led natural philosophers to value the empirical method as a means of establishing reliable truths. Experiment, not pure reason, came to be seen as the basis for reliable knowledge of nature.

A Christian conceptual framework, within which science could flourish, is clearly part of the context against which the Scientific Revolution emerged. It is an important fact to set against the myth of a perennial conflict between science and religion. There is a world of difference between saying that 'science and religion are necessarily in conflict' (which is historically indefensible) and saying that 'science and religion are sometimes in conflict, and sometimes work together' (which is historically true, but will seem unexciting to many).

Irrespective of what we might think about the relation of science and faith, it is becoming clear that the boundaries between them are now seen to be more porous and provisional than in the past. As the sociologist Elaine Howard Ecklund recently argued, on the basis of detailed conversations with leading scientists, the notion of an 'insurmountable hostility' between science and religion is 'a caricature, a thought-cliché, perhaps useful as a satire on groupthink, but hardly representative of reality'.[27] This does not necessarily mean that scientists are getting more religious; rather, it points to a growing awareness of failings in the 'warfare' model of the relation of science and faith which used to be built into the worldview of many scientists. In its place we find an increasing openness within the scientific community to the possibility of dialogue and friendly – and possibly *enriching* – co-existence.

Any historian of science knows that the relation between science and religion is ambivalent and cannot be reduced to simplistic dumbed-down slogans. Religious prejudice may certainly have hindered science at points. But what about the occasions when anti-religious prejudice has held up scientific progress? There is no mention of this awkward fact in the highly selective accounts of the interaction of science and religion offered by either Dawkins or Hitchens, but it is an important part of this complex picture – and we need to get this right.

Let's look at an example. In the years following the Second World War it became increasingly clear that the universe had not always existed, as scientists had previously believed. Gradually a scientific consensus began to emerge. The universe came into being in a singular event, which has come to be known as the 'big bang'. This new way of thinking overturned the existing consensus and met some opposition from scientists who disputed the evidence. But it also met opposition in the 1960s from some atheist scientists, such as Fred Hoyle and Steven Weinberg, who were worried that the idea of the universe having an origin 'sounded religious' or resembled the biblical account of creation found in the book of Genesis.

Hoyle's 'steady state' model of the universe was the preferred cosmology of atheists at the time, as it eliminated any possibility of a 'creation'. Speaking at the Massachusetts Institute of Technology in 1967, Weinberg remarked that 'the steady state theory is philosophically the most attractive theory because it *least* resembles the account given in Genesis'. He then ruefully added, 'It is a pity that the steady state theory is contradicted by experiment.'[28]

As this vignette makes clear, the story of science and religion is complex! The myth of the 'warfare' between science and religion resonated well with the social context of England in the later nineteenth century,[29] which pitted 'older, often clerical Gentlemen of Science' against the 'newer career-dependent scientists such as [T.H.] Huxley, who saw entrenched ecclesiastical power as a barrier to their own professional ambitions'.[30] Recent scholarship has suggested that the real conflict of that age was not between science and faith, but between two quite different understandings of science.[31] But a narrative which emerged from the specific social realities of late Victorian England cannot be used as a master template to fix the relation of science and religion in other contexts. It is locked into the agendas of a dead past, and we need to move on.

I propose instead a narrative of enrichment which denies nothing about the empirical sciences save their finality. That is in conflict with the *scientism* that has become so characteristic of the New Atheism, but it is not in conflict with *science*, which has always been willing to recognise its limits.

Scientism is alive and well within the New Atheism, having become the official ideology of the movement. The blogger P.Z. Myers, a loyal defender of the scientism that lies at the heart of the New Atheism, offers this take on the universal validity of the scientific method:

> The New Atheism (I don't like that phrase, either) is about taking a core set of principles that have proven themselves powerful and useful in the scientific world – you've probably noticed that many of these uppity atheists are coming out of a scientific background – and insisting that they also apply to everything else people do.[32]

But *why* should this 'core set of principles' from the scientific world 'apply to everything else people do'? It is a dogmatic assertion that lacks any scientific basis and has the distinct disadvantage of failing miserably when applied to the real world. It is like saying that because microscopes work well in biology, we must use them to sort out the meaning of life, the price of bread and the causes of the First World War. This 'core set of principles' is simply incapable of disclosing the meaning of life, or answering any 'ultimate question'.

The philosopher Mary Midgley brings both wit and philosophical acumen to bear on the excited overstatements which are so characteristic of the less reflective forms of scientism:

> Scientism's mistake does not lie in over-praising one form of [knowledge], but in cutting that form off from the rest of thought, in treating it as a victor who has put all the rest out of business.[33]

In marked contrast to this intellectual sectarianism, real science is wonderful at raising questions that lie beyond its capacity to answer – what Sir Peter Medawar referred to as 'questions that science cannot answer and that no conceivable advance of science would empower it to answer'.[34]

So does engaging such 'ultimate questions' mean abandoning science? No. It simply means acknowledging and respecting the limits of science and not forcing it to become something else. We saw earlier how the philosopher José Ortega y Gasset emphasised that, precisely because we are human beings, we need more than science to satisfy our deep yearnings and intuitions.

The Christian faith is able to enrich this vision of science – not by denying it, nor by proposing itself as a competing science, but by being what it is and doing what it does best, which is raising and answering ultimate questions. Of course, it does much more than this – but it nevertheless does this *distinctively*, and it does it well.

The Christian faith offers an enriched and deepened conceptual framework, a mental map which both accommodates and encourages the scientific enterprise, welcoming its insights and transcending its limitations. It is able to engage the four critical issues identified by the social psychologist Roy Baumeister as central to the human quest for meaning: identity, value, purpose and agency.[35] As Baumeister points out, these are non-empirical ideas which cannot themselves be resolved by scientific enquiry. Yet they matter to us. If our goal is to achieve a rich and integrated understanding of ourselves, we cannot help but ask what Karl Popper termed 'ultimate questions'.

This book is about my own quest for an integrated understanding of reality, leading to a deepened appreciation of our world and our place within it. Because the universe is so complex and profound, we need a rich palette of colours to represent it and enjoy it. We cannot limit ourselves to only one method of exploring reality, or a single level of description or analysis. Reality is so complicated that we need a series of maps to describe it. No single map is good enough for such an integrated engagement with our world, even though it may be adequate for a particular and limited purpose. No single story can do justice to things.

In what follows, we will look at how recognising the need for multiple maps, levels and narratives can help us develop a deeper and fuller grasp of reality.

Multiple Maps of Reality

Theories are about seeing things in a certain way. But, as the philosopher Ludwig Wittgenstein pointed out, theories can easily limit our vision by preventing us seeing things which do not fit their mental maps.[36] We can become trapped within a controlling 'picture of reality' or 'worldview' which prevents us from seeing things that question its adequacy or reliability. This can only lead to an impoverished view of things which denies or filters out anything that does not fit the theory. The best way of avoiding this intellectual tunnel vision is to look at our world through multiple windows.

The philosopher Mary Midgley is a leading defender of the 'multiple maps' approach to grasping the depths and detail of reality. Midgley argues that we need 'many maps, many windows' if we are to represent the complexity of reality, reflecting the fact that 'there are many independent forms and sources of knowledge'. She suggests that it is helpful to think of the world as a 'huge aquarium':

> We cannot see it as a whole from above, so we peer in at it through a number of small windows . . . We can eventually make quite a lot of sense of this habitat if we patiently put together the data from different angles. But if we insist that our own window is the only one worth looking through, we shall not get very far.[37]

No single way of thinking is adequate to explain, on its own, the meaning of our universe. 'For most important questions in human life, a number of different conceptual tool-boxes always have to be used together.'[38] If we limit ourselves to the methods of science in general, or one science (such as physics) in particular, we needlessly lock ourselves into a 'bizarrely restrictive view of meaning'.[39]

Midgley's basic principle of using multiple maps to represent a complex reality raises some challenges and some significant questions – such as the need to develop and deploy an appropriate interpretative framework to settle boundary disputes. Yet it also opens up some important possibilities for integration and enrichment of our vision. We need threads of many colours to represent the complexities of our observations of the world around us and our experience within us.

Yet there is more to how we think about the complexities of our world and experience than 'points of view' or 'perspectives'. We also need to think of different levels of reality, which are engaged in different ways. Let's explore this further.

Multiple Levels of Reality

The philosophy of 'critical realism' is often implicitly presupposed by scientists and occasionally made explicit in their writings.[40] This way of thinking invites us to envisage reality in terms of different 'levels' or 'strata'. Physics, chemistry and biology engage with reality at different levels and have developed subtly different methods of investigation, each adapted to its own domain of competence. Really complex natural systems demand engagement and explanation at multiple levels. Otherwise we only see *part* of the picture and are prone to assume that this is the *whole* picture.

The classic example is any attempt to make sense of humanity.[41] A total account will involve multiple layers of analysis: the physics of vision; the chemistry of phosphates; the biology of cells; the biophysics of the transmission of genetic information; the psychology of learning; the anthropology of culture; the social behaviour of human groups. All of these are studied by dedicated sciences, each of which illuminates one level of human nature. Occasionally, arrogant biologists pretend that they alone see the full picture. But they do not. Science is collaborative, not competitive, patiently building up a rich, multi-layered account of humanity. Biology is one such level – and *only* one such level. And, as we shall see, one level of human nature concerns religiosity. The cognitive science of religion (see pages 125–6) has helped us realise that this is part of who and what we are as human beings.

So how does critical realism help us fit faith into our broader reflections on the universe and life? Critical realism allows us to think of science and religion offering insights about reality and answers to the questions of life *at differing levels*. The best picture of reality is that which weaves together coherently the greatest number of explanatory threads.

The distinguished geologist Frank H.T. Rhodes, who served as President of Cornell University from 1977 to 1995, made this point using the analogy of a boiling kettle. Why, someone might ask, is this kettle boiling? Rhodes notes that two types of explanation might be given. At the scientific level, energy is being supplied which raises the temperature of the water to its boiling point. Yet another answer can be given: 'The kettle is boiling because I put it on to make a cup of tea.' So which of these answers is right?

> Now these are different answers . . . But both are true, both are complementary and not competitive. One answer is appropriate within a particular frame of reference, the other within another frame of reference. There is a sense in which each is incomplete without the other.[42]

Rhodes' basic point is that both answers can be right, because they are concerned with different levels of reality. He affirms a 'complementarity of description' which tries to capture at least something of 'the total picture of reality'.

Multiple Narratives about Reality

We have looked at maps, and thought about levels of reality. Yet there is a third and perhaps a far more important way in which human beings make sense of our world and ourselves within it – by telling stories. As social anthropologists, sociologists, philosophers of history and literary theorists have emphasised, it is natural for us to use stories to explore fundamental questions of meaning.

> [We] are animals who must fundamentally understand what reality is, who we are, and how we ought to live by locating ourselves within the larger narratives and metanarratives that we hear and tell, and that constitute what is for us real and significant.[43]

From an anthropological perspective, narrative is a fundamental means of making sense of experience across human cultures, allowing the narrator to impose order on otherwise disconnected events and to create continuity between past, present and imagined worlds.[44] Sometimes these narratives are local, telling the story of the founding of a city or the identity of a group of people – as, for example, the great narrative of the people of Israel escaping from captivity in Egypt, crystallising their identity in the period of 'wilderness wandering' and finally taking their place in the Promised Land.[45]

Yet the great narratives of humanity have a wider scope, telling stories about the universe and human identity which appeal to the imagination, emphasise our location in the flow of time and convey or generate ideas and values. These 'metanarratives' are grand stories which capture our imaginations and give us a conceptual framework that helps us make sense of things.[46] As literary scholars such as C.S. Lewis and J.R.R. Tolkien have stressed, Christianity primarily takes the form of a narrative, which subsequently and secondarily gives rise to credal and doctrinal formulations, a vision of morality and a sense of meaning.[47] Yet however great its scope might be, this narrative of faith needs amplification in other areas. No single metanarrative is adequate to organise and correlate on its own the complexities of human existence and experience.

As the sociologist Christian Smith points out, this means that we must – and, as a matter of observable fact, we *do* – use multiple narratives to locate ourselves within our world and understand what we experience.[48] Smith notes a number of such narratives encountered in the twenty-first century which provide frameworks of meaning for those who hold them – such as the Christian narrative, the Militant Islamic Resurgence narrative, the Capitalist Prosperity narrative, the Progressive Socialism narrative, the Scientific Enlightenment narrative, the Liberal Progress narrative, and the Chance and Purposeless narrative. Other narratives also emerge from various schools of psychology, anthropology and sociology.

The point is this: even if we are committed to the primacy of one 'master narrative', we find ourselves drawing on others to provide detail, texture and colour. That is just the way we are as human beings. It is natural. And that is what I am doing in this work – weaving together the narratives of science and faith to yield a richer vision and understanding of our world, while respecting and maintaining their distinct identities. I maintain that there are no fundamental intellectual difficulties in doing this;[49] the problem really lies in lingering cultural hostility towards any such synthesis, reflecting the agendas and concerns of a rapidly receding past.

Now in one sense, what I propose is nothing new. These narratives of enrichment were the common currency of earlier ages.[50] These have been displaced by a rival narrative that has already lost its academic credibility and is in the process of losing its remaining cultural appeal. Once the default position of the Western media, its obvious failings and shortcomings have led to it being restricted to the ghetto of militant scientific atheists. We deserve better than this – and we can draw on the wisdom of the past to help us recover better ways of thinking about things which fully engage the human desire for knowledge and meaning.

So where do these reflections on multiple maps of reality, multiple levels of meaning and narratives take us? Science and faith can provide us with different yet potentially complementary accounts of human identity. And we need both if we are to flourish as human beings and lead meaningful and fulfilled lives. Both science and faith are prone to exaggerate their capabilities. Religion cannot tell us the distance to the nearest star, just as science cannot tell us the meaning of life. But each is part of a bigger picture, and we impoverish our vision of life if we exclude either – or both.

In the next chapter we will think more about the place of theories in science, and then compare that with their place in faith.

3

Theory, Evidence and Proof:
How Do We Know What Is True?

We all like things to be simple. As a teenager I exulted in the simplicity of the natural sciences. They proved things! They offered certainties, based on rigorous engagement with the evidence. I read Bertrand Russell's *History of Western Philosophy* when I was about sixteen, particularly enjoying its anti-religious polemic. Yet Russell irritated me at one point. He declared that one of the chief benefits of philosophy was to teach us 'how to live without certainty'.[1] This was ridiculous, in my view. Did he not know anything about science? Did he not realise that it *proved* its theories? Why did we have to live with uncertainty when science gave us certainty?

The Human Yearning for Certainty

At that time I saw science as a wonderfully honest and reliable way of thinking about the world which offered proven answers to the big questions of life. As far as I was concerned, faith – especially religious faith – was just about guesswork and hopeful thinking. I held to what I later realised was a simplistic scientific positivism from which faith was totally excluded by the evidence – a view later expressed so well by Richard Dawkins:

> [Faith] is a state of mind that leads people to believe something – it doesn't matter what – in the total absence of supporting evidence. If there were good supporting evidence, then faith would be superfluous, for the evidence would compel us to believe it anyway.[2]

You only believe what you can prove. That, as far as I was concerned, was why science was so great. When a matter needed to be settled, the scientific community devised experiments that resolved the question. When did anyone ever do an experiment that proved there was a God?

I do not think I ever went as far as Richard Dawkins later did in suggesting that religious people were mentally ill. But I was quite convinced that religion demanded disengagement from reality and taking refuge in an invented universe which bore no relation to what I knew through physics. Religion dealt with a fictional universe in which everything was made up. Science dealt with things that could be proved – that could be shown to be right. It was the most secure and reliable form of knowledge.

Yet every now and then it was as if someone drew aside a curtain, revealing a glimpse of a darker and more complicated world, spoken of only in whispers by those who taught me science at school. It was as if they had sailed 'forbidden seas' – to borrow a nice phrase from Herman Melville's *Moby Dick* – and did not want me to go there just yet. As my fellow students and I studied the nature of light in physics classes in the late 1960s, we were told that people once thought that light travelled through a medium called the 'ether'. Of course, we were assured, nobody believed that sort of nonsense any more! I gained the impression that this was the sort of thing people believed way back in the Middle Ages. Then I realised that my teachers were talking about what scientists believed a mere two generations earlier. So why, I wondered, did science change its mind about so many things? If the evidence compelled us to believe something, surely that was the end of the matter? If something was proved to be true, how could you change your mind about it?

The problem, of course, was that I was being taught a simplified and sanitised version of science, suitable for school kids and nobody else. We were taught that science was about *facts* – an established body of knowledge, proved by experiments. It is an infantile view of science which is still found in low-grade popular works such as Christopher Hitchens' amusing New Atheist manifesto *God Is Not Great*. But it is not the real, hard science I later came to discover. What I and my classmates at school were not told was that the progressive nature of the scientific project meant that what scientists believed today would change over time – sometimes being modified, sometimes being abandoned altogether. The same evidence might be interpreted in new ways – or new evidence might come to light which forced science to abandon existing ways of seeing things. That is why my reading in the field of the history and philosophy of science shook me to my foundations. I suddenly realised that things were much more complicated than I had thought.

Simplistic talk about 'compelling evidence' is seriously misleading for a number of reasons. It suggests that evidence is a purely objective matter, and fails to recognise its complicated subjective aspects. Human beings are creatures who exercise reflective freedom and are perfectly capable of forcing 'evidence' into their preferred and predetermined modes of thinking. The 'Lysenko affair' of the 1940s illustrates this well. The maverick biological ideas of Trofim D. Lysenko (1898–1978) were seen as politically acceptable to the leaders of the Soviet Union, and the scientifically orthodox ideas of his opponents were denounced as 'bourgeois' or 'fascist'. As the sad history of evolutionary biology during the era of the Soviet Union makes clear, a 'groupthink' can emerge which disregards evidence it considers inconvenient, or which accommodates it – often through the application of intellectual violence – within an ideological framework.[3]

Russell was right. We need to cope with uncertainty. And that is challenging, both intellectually and existentially. Looking back on my days as a teenager, I cannot blame myself for longing for certainty. We all do it, in our own ways. We want to know where we stand. Maybe there are deep psychological forces at work within us that incline us to adopt this very naïve model of science, even if we know its limits.[4] This also helps us understand why religious and anti-religious fundamentalisms, which trade in certainties, are so attractive to some people. The real world, outside these bubbles of spurious certainty, is rather more challenging. Yet we have to cope with it and live within it.

Theory in Science: Seeing Things Correctly

The novelist Henry Miller (1891–1980) once spoke of a journey of exploration which led not to a place, but to 'a new way of looking at things'.[5] When confronted with a mass of observations, the scientist's fundamental instinct is to try and figure out what 'big picture' or 'theory' makes the most sense of them. One of the core themes of the natural sciences is that observations are of critical importance. Aristotle spoke of 'saving the phenomena', meaning that observational evidence had to be protected at all costs. A theory was to be judged against the evidence of observation. And if it did not fit the evidence, its validity could be called into question. There can be no question of filtering out observations that inconveniently do not fit with the theory!

The scientific quest aims to find the best way of 'seeing things', the approach that makes most sense of what is actually observed, free from ideological pressures of any kind. What one generation firmly believed to be true may be rejected by a later generation as inadequate – or simply wrong. Science is on a journey and has not yet reached its final destination. That means that things are in flux. It is an unsettling thought, especially for those who like things nice and simple and, above all, *stable*. It is easy to see why some people prefer to think of science in terms of a fixed set of 'scientific' results, rather than as a method whose constant and consistent application leads to changing ideas over time.

A hundred years ago just about everyone believed that the universe had been around for ever; now we believe it had a beginning, opening up some fascinating questions about where it came from in the first place and what its future will be. Neither of these 'beliefs' is arbitrary; they both represent the outcome of reflection on the best evidence available at the time. But the evidence and the theories have changed, and will continue to change. The astronomer Carl Sagan (1934–96) made this point elegantly, and it needs to be heard clearly:

> Science is much more than a body of knowledge. It is a way of thinking. This is central to its success. Science invites us to let the facts in, even when they don't conform to our preconceptions. It counsels us to carry alternative hypotheses in our heads and see which ones best match the facts.[6]

I like that humility. It stands in sharp contrast to those arrogant religious and anti-religious dogmatisms which seem to trade only in certainties. These dogmatic views of reality have no place for the tentativeness, open-mindedness and, above all, the intellectual humility which I now know to be characteristic of both science and religion at their best.

These dogmatic people seem to think that one convulsive act of intellectual assertiveness allows them to escape the complexity that haunts human existence. It does not, and it cannot. I used to think like that, but I do not any more. Even theologians are aware of the need to embrace humility and avoid dogmatism when talking about God. As the nineteenth-century Oxford theologian Charles Gore nicely put it:

> Human language never can express adequately divine realities. A constant tendency to apologize for human speech, a great element of agnosticism, an awful sense of unfathomed depths beyond the little that is made known, is always present to the mind of theologians who know what they are about, in conceiving or expressing God.[7]

Let's follow through on Sagan's wise counsel 'to carry alternative hypotheses in our heads and see which ones best match the facts'. How does that work out in practice? Some examples from the history of science will show us this process in action. Some of the best examples of this process of theoretical change and development come from Sagan's own field of astronomy. In what follows, we will look at some of these and see how they help us make sense of things.

A Case Study: Theories of the Solar System

From the earliest of times, it was known that there were certain 'stars' that seemed to move at different speeds against the background of the fixed stars. The Greeks called these 'planets' (from the Greek word for 'wandering'). So what was special about them? In the second century, the Greek astronomer Ptolemy set out a way of understanding the heavenly bodies which would be accepted by most people for more than a thousand years. Ptolemy argued that the sun, moon and planets all revolved in circular orbits around the earth, but at different distances.[8]

It was a neat model, and it worked reasonably well – partly because, before the invention of the telescope in the sixteenth century, observations of planetary movements were not very accurate. Yet by the dawn of the sixteenth century, it was clear that this geocentric way of looking at things was not good enough. It was therefore modified so that the observations would fit in with the theory. Early medieval astronomers argued that planets moved in more complex ways than people had thought – in effect, in circles within circles (usually referred to as 'epicycles'). By the late Middle Ages, these epicycles had become very complex. What had once seemed a very elegant and simple model was beginning to look forced and unnatural. But what were the alternative ways of seeing things?

In 1543, a new way of seeing things was proposed. The Polish astronomer Nicholas Copernicus published a book arguing that the sun – not the earth – stood at the centre of things.[9] The earth and the planets rotated in circular orbits around the sun. Only the moon revolved around the earth. This heliocentric ('sun-centred') view of the solar system caused some controversy. People were so used to thinking of the sun rotating around the earth that they found this new way of thinking unsettling and disturbing. Surely the Bible taught otherwise? Did Psalm 119:90 not declare that God had 'established the earth, and it stands still'? So how did this fit in with Copernicus's radical new idea that the earth moved? Yet it was soon realised that this was not quite what the text meant. A better translation was easily proposed: God had 'established the earth, and it stands firm'.

Not everyone liked this new way of seeing things. The real opposition to Copernicus came from other scientists, not (as is often suggested) from religious people.[10] There were two major problems with Copernicus's theory. First, it did not account for planetary movements with much greater accuracy than Ptolemy's model. The reason for this was simple. Copernicus wrongly assumed that the planets moved in perfect circles around the sun; we now know that they move in ellipses – somewhat flattened circles, with the sun slightly displaced from their centres. This insight arose decades later, as a result of Johannes Kepler's close study of the movement of the planet Mars in the early seventeenth century.

Second, if Copernicus's theory was right, it meant that the appearance of the fixed stars should change over the period of a year. As the earth moved through space, the relative positions of the fixed stars would be expected to change. This was investigated by the Danish astronomer Tycho Brahe (1546–1601), who found no evidence of this 'parallax effect'. We now know the reason for Brahe's failure to observe this effect. The stars are much further from the sun than anyone realised at the time, and the very small parallax effect – invisible to the naked eye – was only observed as a result of improvements in telescope design in the early nineteenth century. Brahe concluded that the evidence thus pointed to the sun revolving around the earth, rather than the other way round. We need to realise that Brahe's interpretation of the observational evidence was actually *right* on the basis of the evidence available to him at that time.

Now while this brief excursus into early modern astronomy is interesting in its own right, it allows us to appreciate three points of critical importance to any proper understanding of scientific theorising. These three points could be made by looking at other episodes in the history of science; I have chosen these case studies simply because they are very accessible and easy to understand.

1. Science tries to find the theoretical model that provides the 'best fit' for the observations. There is always going to be a debate about which theory is best. For a start, evidence builds up over time. And second, there is always going to be subsidiary debate about what criteria are used to evaluate theories. For example, do we choose the simplest theory? Or the most beautiful? Yet these difficulties do not in any way detract from science's pursuit of the best way of making sense of the universe. Very often, scientists find themselves believing, for good reasons, that a certain theory is right, but are unable to prove it. In fact, they realise that they may *never* be able to prove that it is right. Yet they (rightly) continue to believe it to be true, knowing that a good theory can be trusted until the evidence demands that they abandon it for something that is demonstrably better.

2. This means that scientific theories are provisional. They cannot be proved, as if they were mathematical theorems. At any moment in time, the scientific community will believe that one way of looking at things is (on balance) the best. Yet scientists know perfectly well that their successors in the near or distant future may well look back on them and say, 'Well, that's what they used to think back then. We know better now.' As the scientific journey proceeds, some ways of thinking are left behind. The best theories, however, are never completely lost, but are usually incorporated into better theories. (Think, for example, of the way Einstein's theory of relativity provides a framework for Newton's three laws of motions, accounting for their successes and also explaining their limits.)

3. Most theories have to cope with *anomalies* – that is, observa-tional evidence that does not quite fit the theory. A very naïve scientist might suggest that this is enough to abandon that theory. But science is wiser than that. It knows that things are rarely that simple. The theory may be right, yet needs modifica-tion at minor points. Think of Kepler showing that Copernicus was right about his major belief that the sun was at the centre of our planetary system, but wrong about his minor belief about the circular shape of the planets' orbits around the sun. Or it may be that something we believed to be a major problem for the theory was later shown to be less important than was thought, or rested on a misunderstanding – think of Tycho Brahe's worries about stellar parallax.

Most readers will see that there are important parallels with reli-gious faith at every point. We will be returning to the first two points again and again in this work. But what of the third? What of situations in religious faith where something does not always seem to fit the theory? In the Middle Ages, theologians wrestled with the question of the eternity of the world. The science of their day told them that the universe had always been there; their faith taught them that it had come into being. There was a clear anomaly here, and they found a way of coping with it – in effect by agreeing to live with a divergence which could not be resolved on the basis of the scientific methods available at the time. In the end, science abandoned the notion of the eternity of the universe, adopting an approach which is not identical with a religious idea of creation, but is clearly consistent with it.

Religion has to cope with anomalies as well. In the case of Christianity, I would see the existence of suffering as, at least on the face of it, being such an anomaly. But as Christian writers down the ages have argued, there are ways of understanding suffering that lessen the intellectual burden of this problem and enable us to cope with it in our everyday lives.

While there is more to be said about this, we need to move on and think more about the place of evidence and proof in science, and some of the questions raised by these themes.

Evidence, Proof and Faith in Science

Does science *prove* its theories? The popular stereotype, which I used to believe myself, is that scientists are hyper-rational people who only accept what can be proved on the basis of evidence. As with all stereotypes, there is some truth in this. Science is about the quest for the best explanation of observations. Yet it is often hard to prove that one given theory is the best, partly because nobody is entirely agreed on what criteria to use: simplicity? elegance? comprehensiveness? fruitfulness? But the basic point is clear: science trades in warranted beliefs, on the basis of a public debate about the best interpretation of publicly available evidence.

At this point, a philosopher might raise an objection to our loose way of speaking about science and proof, and point out that in its rigorous sense, 'proof' applies only to logic and mathematics. We can prove that $2 + 2 = 4$, just as we can prove that 'the whole is greater than the part'. It is a fair point. Yet it is still reasonable to say that science provides us with excellent grounds for believing that certain things are true – such as that the chemical formula for water is H_2O, or that the average distance of the moon from the earth is about 384,500 kilometres.

Let's recall Dawkins' views about evidence and faith, noted earlier: 'If there were good supporting evidence, then faith would be superfluous, for the evidence would compel us to believe it anyway.' I have no hesitation in saying that the evidence compels me to believe the chemical formula for water is H_2O, or that the moon is on average about 384,500 kilometres from the earth. But Dawkins fails to make the critically important distinction between the 'total absence of supporting evidence' and the 'absence of totally supporting evidence'. Evidence, as every working scientist knows, can be ambivalent, pointing in several directions, open to several interpretations.

A good example lies in the current debate within cosmology over whether the 'big bang' gave rise to a single universe or a series of universes (the so-called 'multiverse').[11] I have some distinguished scientific colleagues who support the former, and some equally distinguished scientific colleagues who support the latter. Both are real options for thinking and informed scientists, who make their decisions on the basis of their judgements of how best to interpret the evidence, and believe – but cannot prove – that their interpretation is correct.

There is nothing new about this kind of dilemma. It is hardwired into the scientific enterprise. Charles Darwin was faced with a similar problem in developing his theory of 'natural selection'. The evidence just was not good enough to clinch it; in fact, there were several major problems with his theory, including his failure to explain how changes were passed from parents to offspring.[12] Furthermore, everything that was known about the natural world could be accommodated by rival evolutionary theories, such as transformism.[13] We have all read simplistic accounts of how Darwin triumphantly proved his theory. But it is more important to read Darwin himself, who was absolutely clear that he felt he could trust his theory, despite its evidential weaknesses.

Darwin believed that his theory was right, and that it would one day be shown to be right. After all, he pointed out, how could a theory be wrong when it made so much sense of what he observed? Yes, there were loose ends everywhere, and a large number of problems. But his core idea seemed to him to be correct – despite the fact that it could not be proved.

> A crowd of difficulties will have occurred to the reader. Some of them are so grave that to this day I can never reflect on them without being staggered; but, to the best of my judgment, the greater number are only apparent, and those that are real are not, I think, fatal to my theory.[14]

Now there is no way that this recognition of anomalies and difficulties need lead us into some kind of free-floating relativism which allows us to believe whatever we like. It is simply a realistic and principled recognition of the ambiguity of our observations and experience. That is why the standard scientific textbooks rightly emphasise that 'science rests on faith'.[15] We *believe* that certain theories are true, and have good reasons for thinking so – but cannot *prove* that they are true. A failure to recognise that faith is integral to the scientific method ultimately rests on an obstinate refusal to accept the ambiguity of evidence and the inescapable circularity of human experience and interpretation.

Science is on a journey, seeking the best way of explaining and representing reality. Science is primarily about a method, and secondarily about the outcomes of the application of that method. What one generation regards as secure and reliable may be abandoned by the next. Scientific theories are provisional. That does not mean that they are *arbitrary*. It just means that they are not – and never can be – the last word on anything. Richard Dawkins rightly points out that Darwinism is just as provisional as any other scientific theory. 'We must acknowledge the possibility that new facts may come to light which will force our successors of the twenty-first century to abandon Darwinism or modify it beyond recognition.'[16]

I now see that Bertrand Russell was right: we need to learn 'how to live without certainty, and yet without being paralyzed by hesitation'. That is why Michael Polanyi's book *Personal Knowledge* (1958) is so important to reflective scientists. It sparked off a long-overdue discussion about the limits of certainty in science and how scientists ought to respond to this issue. Polanyi (1891–1976) was a Hungarian chemist turned philosopher who found himself to be increasingly troubled by his need to commit himself to what he believed (scientifically) to be true, while knowing that some of this would later be shown to be false.[17] He argued for the need to speak of science as 'personal knowledge' – not absolutely certain, yet still capable of eliciting justified belief.

In many ways, Polanyi's work illuminates the frail condition of humanity as much as the nature of science. Scientific knowledge is not generated infallibly by a mechanical process, but involves our personal – and fallible – judgement that certain beliefs are reliable and to be trusted. Polanyi insisted that we must understand that commitment to beliefs – scientific or otherwise – inevitably transcends the evidence underlying them. And every now and then, evidence emerges that something which scientists *believed* to be true really *is* true. The Higgs boson is a good example.

The Particle of Faith: The Higgs Boson

On 4 July 2012, there was great excitement among the physicists huddled around the Large Hadron Collider in Geneva, Switzerland. The 'Higgs boson' had been seen! Or at least they thought they might have seen it, or something very like it. On 14 March 2013, physicists at CERN (the European Organisation for Nuclear Research) confirmed the discovery. So what was all the fuss about? The Higgs boson is the mysterious particle proposed by physicist Peter Higgs and others back in the 1960s to explain the origin of mass. If its existence could be confirmed, another piece of the jigsaw puzzle of our understanding of the universe would have fallen into place.

The media were fascinated. Not because of the science, though. Most newspapers have discovered that the reading public does not pay all that much attention to science. It does not sell papers! The reason for the huge media interest lies in the nickname given to the Higgs boson back in 1994 by the Nobel Laureate Leon Lederman – the 'God particle'.[18] Journalists loved the nickname. Most scientists hated it, considering it misleading and simplistic. Maybe so. But it certainly got people talking about physics. And maybe it is not such a bad nickname after all. Lederman told people he invented the name the 'God particle' because the Higgs boson was 'so central to the state of physics today, so crucial to our understanding of the structure of matter, yet so elusive'.

Now some people believe that science is about what can be proved. Yet, to say it again, it is just not that simple. Science often proposes the existence of invisible (and often undetectable) things – such as 'dark matter' – to explain what can be seen. (Dark matter is something that is hypothesised by astronomers to account for gravitational effects that appear to be the result of invisible mass.) The reason why the Higgs boson is taken so seriously by particle physicists is that it makes so much sense of scientific observations that its existence seems assured. In other words, its power to explain is seen as an indicator of its truth.

There is an obvious and important parallel with the way religious believers think about God. While some demand proof that God exists, most rightly see this as unrealistic, failing to appreciate either the limits of human reasoning or the nature of God. Believers argue that the existence of God gives the best framework for making sense of the world. God is like a lens which brings things into clearer focus. There is more to God than making sense of things. But for religious believers, it is a great start. The Higgs boson certainly helps us understand how the universe works. Yet it does not answer the rather more interesting question of why there is a universe in which particle physics can be done in the first place.

We have spent quite a lot of time thinking about the role of theories within science. So what about religious theories? What do they do? And are there any parallels with scientific theories?

Theory in Religion: Making Sense of Life

The whole issue of making sense of reality is deeply embedded within both the natural sciences and many forms of religious faith, especially Christianity. In fact, one major factor that led me decisively away from my youthful atheism to Christianity was my growing realisation that the Christian faith made far more sense of what I saw around me and experienced within me than its atheist alternatives.

In what way, then, does religious faith work? What does it do? Scholars give lots of answers to this question, but I am just going to mention the ways in which it works for me. I will put them in the order in which I personally value them, and leave readers to rearrange (or add to) this list as they think appropriate.

1. It helps me make sense of the world by giving me a way of seeing reality which affirms both its intelligibility and coherence.
2. It gives me a framework which allows me to discern meaning and purpose within life.
3. Faith generates a moral vision that is not of my own making and does not serve my own interests.
4. Faith helps me cope with negative situations by allowing me to see them in a new light.
5. Faith brings hope by enabling me to see my life in a wider context of meaning. 'Hope' here does not mean a groundless optimism, but a firm conviction of present significance and future fulfilment.

We will explore these themes later, especially in Chapters 7 and 8. But our concern in this section is to ask what reasons might be given for suggesting that a theory of things is to be trusted in the first place.

We need to make a distinction here between a 'logic of discovery' and a 'logic of justification'. As the American philosopher Charles Peirce (1839–1914) – himself a scientist – pointed out, some of the best scientific theories were developed by great imaginative leaps, rather than by ruthlessly logical analysis.[19] Both imagination and reason play a critical role in theory development. Yet no matter how it was developed, a theory still has to be rigorously checked out against observation and evidence.

A classic example is August Kekulé's theory of the structure of benzene, an organic chemical which did not behave in the way that its simple chemical formula (C_6H_6) suggested. People

came to think that the answer had to lie in its physical structure. Kekulé realised that if benzene was thought of as consisting
of a core ring of six carbon atoms, many of its otherwise
puzzling properties could be explained. He set out his proposal
for the cyclical structure of benzene in a French article of 1865,
and again in a German article of 1866. Slowly the idea found
general acceptance.

But how did Kekulé come up with this idea in the first place?
He did not explain the 'logic of discovery' that led him to this
innovative idea, although he provided an extensive 'logic of justification' for the ring structure of benzene. He was able to show
that its chemical behaviour was accounted for by this new model
of its structure far more successfully than any of the alternative
models then available.

Kekulé finally explained how he thought up the idea of a ring
structure in 1890, at a celebration marking the twenty-fifth
anniversary of his new model – by then widely accepted and
highly acclaimed. Kekulé told his astonished audience that he
had a dream of a snake chasing its own tail and saw how this
might be applied to benzene.[20] (The audience might have been
even more astonished if they had known the deep sexual symbol-
ism that Sigmund Freud later attributed to this image.) But while
the origin of this idea was frankly a little weird, the fact remains
that when it was checked out against the evidence, it seemed to
work. The manner of its derivation might seem strange; the
manner of its verification, however, was perfectly clear – and
ultimately persuasive.

Faith as a Changed Mindset

So what actually happened as I made the transition from atheism to Christianity back in 1971? At one level I began to see
things in a new way. I had viewed what I observed around me
and experienced within me through an atheist lens. Realising
that this did not work as well as I had expected, I tried looking

at it through a theistic lens – and found that it gave me far greater clarity and sharpness of focus than atheism. This certainly did not prove that there was a God, but it made me realise that I needed to rethink things. Maybe belief in God made a lot more sense than I had thought. And that is the line of thought that eventually led me to faith.

Christians talk a lot about repentance, and often gloss this as 'saying sorry to God'. I am sure that is part of the meaning of the idea – but there is a lot more to it than this. The Greek word *metanoia* is much richer, meaning something like 'a radical change of mind', or 'a fundamental intellectual reorientation'. Many Christian Bibles miss the full meaning of this important word when they translate it as 'repent'.

A much better translation of the word *metanoia* would emphasise the idea of a mental transformation – a change of mind and change of heart, which includes turning away from older habits of thought and action and embracing a new way of thinking and living.[21] Paul wrote to the Christian church in Rome explaining that coming to faith is about not being 'conformed to this world', but being 'transformed by the renewing of your minds' (Romans 12:2). That transformation demands alertness to the limits of human reason and openness to the greatness of God. Kathleen Norris put this well: repentance means 'not primarily a sense of regret', but 'a renunciation of narrow and sectarian human views which are not large enough for God's mystery'.[22]

That is what happened to me. I experienced a new way of 'seeing things', as if I had been given a new mental map. Later I read N.R. Hanson's works on the history and philosophy of science, in which he emphasised that observation was shaped by theoretical presuppositions.[23] The process of 'looking at' nature is actually 'theory-laden', in that what we 'see' is often shaped by assumptions drawn from our culture or existing scientific theories. Theories are like a pair of spectacles; they affect what we see.

I was drawn to faith by its ability to explain things – to provide a 'big picture' which wove together the threads of experience to disclose a pattern. I later discovered that both G.K. Chesterton (1874–1936) and C.S. Lewis (1898–1963) returned to faith for a very similar reason. Let's look at what drew them back to faith in more detail.

Returning to Faith: G.K. Chesterton and C.S. Lewis

After a period of agnosticism, Chesterton returned to Christianity because of his discovery that it offered an 'an intelligible picture of the world'. Chesterton realised that testing a theory meant checking it out against observation. How well did theory fit observation? 'The best way to see if a coat fits a man is not to measure both of them, but to try it on.' For Chesterton, what really mattered was the comprehensive ability of faith to disclose a 'big picture', capable of embracing everything.

> Numbers of us have returned to this belief; and we have returned to it, not because of this argument or that argument, but because the theory, when it is adopted, works out everywhere; because the coat, when it is tried on, fits in every crease . . . We put on the theory, like a magic hat, and history becomes translucent like a house of glass.[24]

Now Chesterton overstates things here. Does the coat really fit 'in every crease'? Surely not. No worldview is able to accommodate the totality of human experience of the world. There will always be parts of the mental landscape that are shrouded in mist, even in permanent darkness. As a Christian, I find that the existence of pain and suffering does not fit easily 'in every crease' of the coat of faith. Like most people, I am suspicious of too-neat theories. Yet I believe that Chesterton is right in holding that this coat seems to fit better than other coats – such as atheism.

Chesterton argues that Christianity is to be judged not on the basis of individual arguments or considerations, but on the way of seeing things that is their overall outcome. The plausibility of

Christianity does not depend upon a single argument or affirmation, but is rooted in an interlocking network of ideas and themes. Christianity is like a web of interconnected beliefs and claims, not something that is totally dependent on a single evidential foundation. Some nodes in the web may be of greater importance than others; yet it is the overall coherence of this view of the world that Chesterton sees as being so compelling.

It is a point that was later made by the Harvard philosopher of science W.V.O. Quine (1908–2000). Where some argued for truths that were *analytic* (that is, true by definition, or as a matter of their internal consistency), and others for truths that were *synthetic* (true on account of some contingent fact about the world), Quine argued instead that *all* of our beliefs are linked in an interconnected web which relates to sensory experience at its boundaries. It is not individual nodes of that web, but the web *as a whole*. Quine thus concluded that 'the unit of empirical significance is the whole of science'.[25] The only valid test of a belief, Quine argued, is whether it fits into a web of connected beliefs that accords with our experience *on the whole*.

It is thus the Christian vision of reality as a whole – rather than any of its individual components – that proves so intellectually and imaginatively winsome. Individual observations of nature do not 'prove' Christianity to be true; rather, Christianity validates itself by its ability to make sense of those observations. 'The phenomenon does not prove religion, but religion explains the phenomenon.' For Chesterton, a good theory – whether scientific or religious – is to be judged by the amount of illumination it offers, and its capacity to accommodate what we see in the world around us and experience within us. 'With this idea once inside our heads, a million things become transparent as if a lamp were lit behind them.'

And what about C.S. Lewis, who was an atheist as a young man? Lewis's initial commitment to atheism was grounded in his belief that it was *right*, a 'wholesome severity',[26] even though he conceded that it offered a rather 'grim and meaningless' view of life. He consoled himself by arguing that atheism's intellectual rectitude trumped its emotional and existential inadequacy. Yet Lewis gradually began to become disenchanted with atheism. For a start, it was imaginatively uninteresting. Lewis began to realise that atheism did not – and could not – satisfy the deepest longings of his heart, or his intuition that there was more to life than what was seen on the surface. Lewis put it this way in a famous passage from his autobiography, *Surprised by Joy*, describing the tension he experienced between his reason and imagination.

> On the one side, a many-islanded sea of poetry and myth; on the other, a glib and shallow rationalism. Nearly all that I loved I believed to be imaginary; nearly all that I believed to be real I thought grim and meaningless.[27]

Lewis's 'glib and shallow rationalism' dismissed the deep questions of life, offering only superficial responses. We can prove shallow, superficial and unimportant things. But the things that really matter – the truths by which we live, whether they are political, moral or religious – simply cannot be proved in this way.

Lewis came to rediscover Christianity, mainly because of his realisation that it made imaginative and rational sense, offering a coherent account of the patterns of history, the subjective experience of individuals and the successes of the natural sciences. In an autobiographical memoir of 1930, Lewis remarked that he was an 'empirical theist' who came to faith in God by 'induction'.[28] Induction, of course, lies at the heart of the natural sciences. So what does Lewis mean by this? His fundamental point is that a theory is judged by its ability to fit in with our observations and experiences most elegantly, most simply, most comprehensively and most fruitfully.[29] It gave him a lens that brought them into focus – a source of illumination that allowed him to see more clearly than he otherwise might. That is the point Lewis makes in his engaging and appealing statement of faith, now inscribed on his memorial stone in Poet's Corner, Westminster Abbey: 'I believe in Christianity as I believe that the Sun has risen, not only because I see it, but because by it I see everything else.'[30]

Science and Religion: Can We Prove Theories?

Some readers will protest at this point. 'It's all very well saying that the God-theory makes sense of things. But what is the evidence that the God-theory is right in the first place?' Are religious theories just made up, so that we see a universe that we have invented – a fictitious cosmos that bears no relation to reality? Or are they also attempts to make sense of our world? It is a fair question. Let's look at one of the theories dominant in both physics and cosmology at the moment: M-theory. This theory was put forward by the physicist Edward Witten in 1995 as a means of unifying a number of different 'string theories', which hold that matter is made up of infinitesimally small strings of vibrating energy. It has come to be widely accepted within the scientific community and underlies the recent work of Stephen Hawking and others. What is its appeal? In the end, the answer is this: it is a promissory note which shows signs of being able to unify observations and bring us closer to a grand unified theory.[31]

Yet many scientists remain deeply sceptical of the theory. Yes, they concede, it provides a useful way of looking at things. But what is the actual evidence for this theory, other than its capacity to explain? And how can it be tested empirically? To its critics, M-theory seems to have acquired public respect and credulity in advance of any experimental confirmation. It is, they argue, an unprovable theory that talks of invisible parallel universes and ten-dimensional space. Peter Woit, a professor of mathematics at Columbia University, is one of the more aggressive critics of M-theory, arguing that 'superstring theory has had absolutely zero connection with experiment since it makes absolutely no predictions'.[32] What sort of theory is scientifically untestable? Other physicists disagree with Woit, often strongly, holding that its explanatory potential mitigates its inability to be verified experimentally.

I have no intention of commenting on this debate, other than noting that it is taking place and relevant to our discussion. My point is simple: M-theory is seen by many scientists as a perfectly reasonable way of 'seeing things' which achieves a pleasing – though far from total – degree of holding together what might otherwise be disparate and disconnected aspects of physics. Its virtues are significant; they affirm the intelligibility and coherence of reality by providing a way of seeing things that makes sense of our observations and holds together – or at least opens the way to holding together – quantum theory and gravity. Yet there is no experimental evidence for the truth of the theory: it is trusted precisely because it offers an intelligible and coherent account of reality.

Now there is an obvious parallel with Lewis here. Lewis affirmed the intellectual legitimacy of adopting a theory (God) on account of its capacity to unify and explain, even though the theory itself could not be proved (although Lewis clearly believed that this belief was warranted by the evidence). During the 1920s, Lewis began to realise that he had allowed himself to be trapped inside some kind of rationalist cage, limiting reality to what reason could prove. Yet reason could not prove its own trustworthiness. Why not? Because we would then be using reason to judge reason. Human reason would be both judge and jury in an act of intellectual circularity. 'Unless the measuring rod is independent of the things measured we can do no measuring.'[33]

But what if there was something *beyond* the scope of human reason? And what if the world were full of 'clues' to the meaning of the universe? Gradually, Lewis came to realise that these hints and clues pointed to a world beyond the frontiers of reason. We may hear snatches of its music in the quiet moments of life. Or we may sense its fragrance wafted towards us by a gentle breeze on a cool evening. And if these clues did indeed point to the existence of God, this would provide an intellectual framework that made sense of things.

There is, of course, more to Christianity than making sense of things. It is far more than a cerebral faith, as if it were some form of rationalism with a spiritual veneer. As I grew in my understanding of the Christian faith, I gradually came to appreciate the rich experience of beauty and awe which is so often evoked in Christian worship and which underlies its engagement with the natural world. Yet the intellectual capaciousness of faith cannot be overlooked, especially its discernment of a deeper structure to the world which helps us grasp our own position within it and live out our lives more authentically. As the Harvard psychologist William James suggested many years ago, religious faith is basically 'faith in the existence of an unseen order of some kind in which the riddles of the natural order may be found and explained'.[34]

Not everyone agrees that the virtues of the Christian faith include its ability to make sense of things. The literary critic and cultural commentator Terry Eagleton was severely critical of those who treat religion as a fundamentally explanatory phenomenon. 'Christianity was never meant to be an explanation of anything in the first place,' he wrote. 'It's rather like saying that thanks to the electric toaster we can forget about Chekhov.'[35] Eagleton suggests that believing religion is a 'botched attempt to explain the world' is about as helpful as 'seeing ballet as a botched attempt to run for a bus'.

Now Eagleton is surely right to argue that there is more to Christianity than an attempt to make sense of things. Yet this explanatory theme is – as the novelist Dorothy L. Sayers (1893–1957) came to appreciate – part of its rich heritage. Christians have always held that their faith makes sense in itself, and makes sense of the enigmas and riddles of our experience. The gospel is like an illuminating radiance that lights up the landscape of reality, allowing us to see things as they really are. The French philosopher Simone Weil (1909–43) made this point especially well:

> If I light an electric torch at night out of doors, I don't judge its power by looking at the bulb, but by seeing how many objects it lights up. The brightness of a source of light is appreciated by

the illumination it projects upon non-luminous objects. The value of a religious or, more generally, a spiritual way of life is appreciated by the amount of illumination thrown upon the things of this world.[36]

The ability to illuminate reality is an important measure of the reliability of a theory and an indicator of its truth.

This concern for the illumination of reality naturally leads us to reflect on a statement that the leading British biologist Sir Peter Medawar made towards the end of his life: 'Only humans find their way by a light that illuminates more than the patch of ground they stand on.'[37] It is a striking assertion which invites us to ask: what is the best light to illuminate our patch of ground? My narrative of enrichment suggests that both science and faith, when at their best, help us to make sense of who we are, why we are here and what we ought to do. We need that rich vision to enable us to live our lives to the full.

4

Inventing the Universe: Our Strange World

'If you wish to make an apple pie from scratch, you must first invent the universe' (Carl Sagan). I cannot remember when I first read those words, but they keep coming back to me. Sagan is right. Everything we do – whether making apple pie, writing a book or walking by a river – depends on the existence of the universe. And not just *any* universe, but the specific universe in which we live, which has certain properties that allowed both apples and human beings to come into existence. If you do not have people or apples, you cannot make apple pie.

In this chapter we are going to explore the strange story of our universe and reflect more on its significance. In recent years, a good degree of consensus has emerged about that story – when everything began and how it developed. But there is no agreement on what that story means. For some, such as Richard Dawkins, it means nothing. 'The universe we observe had precisely the properties we should expect if there is, at bottom, no design, no purpose, no evil and no good, nothing but blind pitiless indifference.'[1] I would once have agreed with that. But not now. It is a lot more complicated than that.

The Beginning of Time

So where shall we start? Let's begin our reflections on our universe at the very beginning. Once upon a time, people thought that the universe had always been here. That was what the great philosopher Aristotle taught. Early Christian writers, committed to a notion of the divine creation of the universe, thought that Aristotle was wrong. During the first five centuries they insisted that the universe was not eternal, but had come into being.[2] Nobody seems to have taken much notice of them.

Augustine of Hippo (354–430), probably the greatest and certainly the most influential Christian thinker of that age, taught that, since time was part of the created order, God could not be said to have created the universe *in* time; rather, God created the universe *with* time.[3] God dwelt in a timeless realm, outside the created realm of space and time. Augustine emphasised the importance of not correlating the Christian idea of creation with any dominant philosophical or scientific metanarrative. The doctrine of creation was a theological statement about a universe that came into existence *as God's creation*, not a scientific explanation of how or when that happened.

Augustine argued that God brought everything into existence in a single moment of creation. Yet this created order was not static. God endowed it with the capacity to develop. The creation is meant to change over time, becoming what God intended it to be, rather than having been created in its final definitive form. Now Augustine did not develop these interpretations of Genesis as scientific theories. He was simply unpacking what he saw as the essential *theological* principles of the biblical creation narratives. How ways of reading Genesis mapped onto contemporary scientific narratives was a matter for discussion and debate.

When the great intellectual renaissance of the Middle Ages began, Augustine's approaches to the evolution of the created order and the nature of time did not fit the dominant philosophical narrative of the day, and so were marginalised. Augustine was seen as a major – indeed, *the* major – theological authority of that age. Yet Aristotle was widely regarded as the supreme scientific authority, and his ideas came to dominate the scientific theories of the time. Medieval science was thus committed to the idea of the eternity of the world, because this was such a significant feature of Aristotle's thought. This put Christian theologians in a difficult position. They liked Aristotle, especially his ideas on intellectual method. But they could not go along with his core belief that the universe had always existed.[4] It seemed like an irreconcilable difference between science and religion – between

Aristotle and Augustine. Both sides remained committed to their positions, and no reconciliation was really achieved.

By the end of the nineteenth century, the scientific consensus remained roughly the same on the issue of the eternity of the universe. The great Swedish physicist Svante August Arrhenius (1859–1927), who won the Nobel Prize for chemistry in 1903, wrote a best-selling work entitled *Worlds in the Making* (1906). In this he argued for an infinite, self-perpetuating universe without beginning or end, based partly on the recently discovered principle of the 'indestructibility of energy'. Arrhenius made clear his fundamental 'conviction that the Universe in its essence has always been what it is now. Matter, energy, and life have only varied as to shape and position in space.'[5] Matter and energy might move around the universe; there was, however, no overall change within the system as a whole.

This static view of the universe – which allowed for internal movements of energy and matter, but not for either origination or decay – remained the scientific consensus until the end of the First World War. Religious ideas of creation were regarded as outdated mythological notions, being completely incompatible with cutting-edge scientific knowledge. Then, slowly but surely, evidence began to accumulate suggesting that the universe, far from being eternal, had an origin. It is a fascinating story, and we shall tell some of it in what follows.[6]

During the period between 1900 and 1931 astronomers witnessed three dramatic alterations in their view of the universe. First, the accepted value of the size of the star system increased by a factor of ten; second, the work of Edwin Hubble (1883–1953) led to the realisation that there are other star systems beyond our own galaxy; and third, the behaviour of these external galaxies indicated that the universe was expanding.[7] The expansion of the universe was a difficult idea to accept at the time, as it clearly implied that the universe had evolved from a very dense initial state – in other words, that the universe had a beginning. Some resisted any such suggestion, sometimes fearing the potential religious implications of the idea of the origins of the universe. In 1948, Fred Hoyle and others developed a 'steady state' theory of the universe, which held that the universe, although expanding, could not be said to have had a beginning. Matter was continuously created in order to fill in the voids arising from cosmic expansion.

Opinion began to shift decisively in the 1960s, chiefly on account of the discovery of the cosmic background radiation. In 1965, Arno Penzias and Robert Wilson were working on an experimental microwave antenna at the Bell Laboratories in New Jersey. They were experiencing some difficulties. No matter which direction they pointed their radio antenna, they picked up an unwanted and obtrusive background hissing noise which they simply could not eliminate. Their initial explanation of this phenomenon was that the pigeons roosting on the antenna were interfering with it. Yet even after the enforced depature of the offending birds, the hiss remained.[8]

It was only a matter of time before the full significance of this irritating background hiss was grasped. It could be understood as the 'afterglow' of a 'big bang' – a primal cosmic explosion, the existence of which had been proposed in 1948 by Ralph Alpher and Robert Herman. When seen alongside other pieces of evidence, this background radiation provided significant support for the idea that the universe had a beginning, and caused signifiant difficulties for the rival 'steady state' theory.

Since then, the basic elements of the standard cosmological model have become clarified and have secured widespread support within the scientific community. Although there remain significant areas of debate, this model is widely agreed to offer the best resonance with observational evidence.[9] The universe is now believed to have originated some 14 billion years ago, and to have been expanding and cooling ever since. The two most significant pieces of evidence in support of this theory are the cosmic microwave background radiation and the relative abundance of light nuclei (such as hydrogen, deuterium and helium) synthesised in the immediate aftermath of the 'big bang'.[10] This model entails the recognition that the origins of the universe must be recognised to be a singularity – a unique event, something which can never be repeated, and hence never subjected to the precise experimental analysis that some hold to be characteristic of the scientific method.

It was a dramatic development, which caused a sea-change in thinking about religious language concerning 'creation'. It is often said by atheist apologists that science has eroded the plausibility of faith over the last century. Perhaps that may be true in some respects, yet in others it is demonstrably false. The 'standard cosmological model' resonates strongly with a Christian narrative of creation, much to the annoyance of atheists such as Steven Weinberg (see page 35).

We need to be clear that the Christian narrative of creation and the scientific narrative about the origins of the universe are not *identical*. As we saw earlier, science is, rightly and distinctively, committed to methodological naturalism. Yet any suggestion that the natural world is limited to what can be disclosed by the use of this method is ridiculous. It is a specific lens, an angle of approach, which is characteristic of the natural sciences. Only a crude scientific imperialism claims, arrogantly and wrongly, to be able to know nature in its totality. Science takes one angle of approach; other disciplines diverge, ultimately offering enriched and deepened understandings of our universe.

Although some Christians have read their Bibles as teaching that the world is a mere 6,000 years old, it is clear that this is a figure that has been read into the text on the basis of a series of questionable assumptions which have long been known to be simply wrong. The core themes of the biblical idea of creation are that God created the universe; that this was 'good'; and that it possessed an ordering which in some way reflects the divine rationality.[11] There is plenty of theology – but no chronology.

The scientific narrative of the origins of the cosmos is not the same as the Christian narrative of creation; the two can, however, be intertwined, like a dual helix, to offer a deeply satisfying vision of our universe. The theological notion of creation and the scientific notion of origination are not the same, in that they are framed in terms of different informing conceptual frameworks. Yet there was now a convergence of intellectual focus between these religious and scientific narratives, leading to a synergy of possibilities that had arguably not been possible for a thousand years. 'Creation' and 'origination' are to be seen as two different 'maps of meaning', two different 'levels of explanation' for the universe. They are not identical; they are, however, increasingly being seen as complementary and mutually enriching.

As scientific reflection on this strange universe continued, attention came to focus on two of its most puzzling aspects. Why can we make so much sense of it? And why does it seem to be fine-tuned for life? Let's look at both these questions.

The Strange Rationality of the Cosmos

What exactly do we mean by the universe? It is a word we use all the time, often without thinking about what it means. It comes from the Latin *universum*, meaning 'totality', and is generally taken to mean something like 'everything that exists'. Yet this has become problematic. Let me explain.

There is a major debate within cosmology at the moment about whether there is a single universe, or a multiplicity of universes. Some physicists argue for a 'multiverse' – an aggregate of universes, including our own. We will look at this in more detail later in this chapter. But you can see the problem. If these physicists are right, what we call the 'universe' does not include everything that exists. It is just one universe among many.

So should we stop using the word 'universe'? No. There are two reasons for continuing to use it. First, the multiverse is still only a hypothesis, and remains controversial. We do not yet know if there really are other universes. Second, we can easily retain the word 'universe' to mean 'our universe'. It is like splitting the atom.

The word 'atom' comes from a Greek root meaning 'indivisible', reflecting the idea that the atom was the smallest possible unit of matter. Now we know that this is not right. Atoms are made up of more fundamental components – such as protons, neutrons and electrons. But we still happily use the word 'atom'!

There is another word that we sometimes use instead of 'universe' – and that is 'cosmos' (from the Greek *kosmos*). Traditionally, its origins are traced back to the philosopher Pythagoras, who is said to have been 'the first to call the containing of all things the *kosmos*, because of the order which governs it'.[12] The Greek term *kosmos* thus developed overtones of order and intelligibility. The universe is something that we can *understand*.

That insight is fundamental to the natural sciences. Yet in many ways it is a surprising result. Not only is the universe governed by laws; these laws are comprehensible to us. As the philosopher Roger Scruton remarks, the idea that a universe, left to its own devices, will 'produce conscious beings, able to look for the reason and the meaning of things' is quite remarkable and demands some kind of reasoned explanation.[13] John Polkinghorne, a theoretical physicist noted for his work on quantum theory, is one of many to stress both the curiosity of this observation and its potential implications. Scientists are so familiar with being able to understand the world that most of the time we take it for granted. After all, it is what makes science possible. Yet, Polkinghorne points out, things could have been very different. 'The universe might have been a disorderly chaos rather than an orderly cosmos. Or it might have had a rationality which was inaccessible to us.'[14]

What is particularly puzzling is why the deep structures of the universe can be represented mathematically. How could the great untameable ocean of the universe be represented in the calm, shallow pool of mathematics? This point was made in a classic essay by the theoretical physicist and Nobel Laureate Eugene Wigner, entitled 'The Unreasonable Effectiveness of Mathematics'.[15] One of its closing sentences stands out for me. 'The miracle of the appropriateness of the language of mathematics to the formulation of the laws of physics is a wonderful gift which we neither understand nor deserve.' When scientists try to make sense of the complexities of our world, they use 'mathematics as their torch'. Sometimes abstract mathematical theories that were originally developed without any practical application in mind later turn out to be powerfully predictive physical models.[16] We have got so used to this that we easily forget that this is *strange*. For Wigner, it was a mystery that called out for an explanation.

John Polkinghorne concurs. Why, he wondered, is there such a significant 'congruence between our minds and the universe'? Why does mathematics (the 'rationality experienced within') correspond so closely to the deep structures of the universe (the 'rationality observed without')?[17] He is not alone in being puzzled by it.[18] But what explanations might be offered for this strange observation?

Of course, there are many possible explanations. It might be an extraordinary piece of good luck – even a miracle. Why should mathematics, the outcome of a free exploration of the human mind, bear any relation to the structure of the physical world around us? Now some might suggest that we could leave it there. We do not need to worry about this. Or even think about it. It *works*, and that is all we need to know.

Most, however, will feel that this mystery demands an explanation. As Albert Einstein once remarked, 'The most incomprehensible thing about the universe is that it is comprehensible.'[19] What Einstein was getting at here is that the question of the intelligibility of the world is raised by science, but goes beyond science's unaided ability to answer. It is a good example of the difficulty noted by the philosopher Ludwig Wittgenstein, who correctly pointed out that the *meaning* of a system will not be found *within* the system itself. Science is very good at raising profound questions, the answers to which turn out to lie beyond the scope of the scientific method. So is there what Eugene Wigner himself called 'a picture which is a consistent fusion into a single unit of the little pictures', which can accommodate this observation?

Some would dispute that there is anything to explain. They

would argue that the role of mathematics in basic physical theory is simply organisational, in that we impose meaning and structure on the world. There is thus no particular mathematical order within the universe itself. The human mind likes to organise things, and we are imposing our own ordering on reality by casting a mathematical net over it. The net creates order, but the order is invented, not real.

It is possible, but it is not compelling. As Roger Penrose and others have noted, it fails to explain the extraordinary precision in the agreement between the best physical theories that we have come across and the behaviour of our material universe at its most fundamental levels.[20] Penrose points to Einstein's general theory of relativity, which improves even upon the already amazingly accurate Newtonian theory of gravity. Newton's theory was precise to something like one part in 100 in describing the behaviour of the solar system. Yet Einstein's theory is not merely much more accurate; it also predicts completely new effects, such as black holes and gravitational waves.

Our minds can develop theories which do not simply explain what is already known, but can predict things we have not yet discovered. This is a particularly important point when viewed in the light of the kinds of metaphysical Darwinism which writers such as Daniel Dennett and Richard Dawkins find so puzzlingly persuasive. Dennett, the more philosophically literate of these two atheist evangelists, argues that human thought – including our morality and religion – is shaped by our evolutionary past. Without realising it, we are the prisoners of our genetic history, locked into ways of thinking that were moulded by our need to survive. And that is bad news for lots of traditional ideas – such as God. Dennett sees Darwinism as a 'universal acid', a naturalist philosophy which corrodes religion and ethics, exposing them as relics from a past, with no ongoing place in the present.[21] Dennett's critics, of course, have pointed out that it is bad news for philosophy as well. If human rationality is grounded in our evolutionary past, why rely on it philosophically?

The problems with the kind of approach favoured by Dennett have been understood since the late nineteenth century. In his book *The Foundations of Belief* (1895), Arthur Balfour – a Cambridge academic who went on to become British prime minister – identified a central difficulty within the forms of evolutionary thinking gaining ascendancy at the time. A purely naturalistic philosophy cannot account for the reliable scientific knowledge that we believe we possess. If science turns out to be true, this can only be the result of 'some beneficent accident'. 'We have not merely stumbled on truth in spite of error and illusion, which is odd, but because of error and illusion, which is even odder.'²²

Having shown that naturalism was ultimately self-defeating, Balfour proposed his own solution to the enigma of our rational grasp of the universe: humans can gain access to the truth only because the human mind has been shaped by a divine mind. It is, of course, not necessary to share Balfour's theism to appreciate the point of his argument. As writers as diverse as C.S. Lewis and Alvin Plantinga have shown, a rigorously naturalistic account of the foundations of human knowledge ends up locked into a self-referential argumentative circularity.²³

If Dennett's inflated Darwinian narrative is right, the human mind is to be seen as having evolved in response to the need for survival. So what reason is there for thinking that it can acquire a deep knowledge of reality – such as the fundamental structure of the universe – when all that is needed in order for humans to reproduce their genes is that they avoid making fatal errors too often? There is no convincing evolutionary reason for our ability to develop the rich and complex mathematical theories of our day, speculate about the origins of the universe, or – to focus on our chosen example – to be able to represent the deep structures of reality *mathematically*.

The concerns that Balfour then raised have not gone away. Nor has the continuing realisation that the Christian vision of God makes sense of what is otherwise a puzzling observation – the capacity of mathematics to make sense of the world. This scientific observation of the intelligibility of the world fits easily into a theistic framework. As we saw earlier, G.K. Chesterton noted that 'the phenomenon does not prove religion, but religion explains the phenomenon'. God created the world with an ordered structure, which human beings are able to uncover by virtue of bearing the 'image of God'. That has been a settled conviction of the Christian faith since its earliest days, a thousand years before anyone started to do science seriously and systematically. Yet this intellectual framework fits what we now know – and *did not* know until the 1700s.

The capacity of a theory – a way of seeing things – to 'fit things in', to show that they are an interconnected part of a greater whole, is widely agreed to be an indication of its truth. Now let's be clear that this does not amount to a proof of anything, in the logical or mathematical sense of the term. Science does not work with that form of reasoning. But one of the most fundamental themes of scientific explanation is whether an observation can be satisfactorily accommodated within a way of thinking.[24] This does not prove that a theistic lens is *right*, of course. After all, various forms of Platonism – which hold that there is a mathematical world whose existence is independent of us – also offer a framework for explaining this remarkable, even magical, capacity of mathematics to map the deepest structures of the human mind.[25] Perhaps it is not surprising that Platonism is frequently considered the default metaphysical position for mathematicians. Yet every scientist knows that there are multiple theoretical interpretations of every observation. There are lots of possible explanations; the question is which of these is to be seen as the best.[26] And like it or not, the idea of God remains one of the simplest, most elegant and most satisfying ways of seeing our world.

The Strangeness of Life in the Universe

Why is there life in the universe? In the last few decades, there has been a growing realisation of how the existence of life is dependent on the initial conditions of the universe. Life as we know it depends very sensitively on the form of the laws of physics, and on some seemingly fortuitous accidents in the actual values that nature has chosen for various particle masses, force strengths and so on. If we could play at being God and select values for these natural quantities by twiddling a set of knobs, we would find that virtually all of their settings would make the universe uninhabitable. Some knobs would have to be tuned with enormous precision if life were to flourish in the universe. This has led many to speak of the universe being 'fine-tuned' for life.

Many recent scientific studies have emphasised the significance of certain fundamental cosmological constants which, if varied slightly, would have significant implications for the emergence of human existence.[27] For more technical readers, examples of the 'fine-tuning' of fundamental cosmological constants include the following:

1. If the strong coupling constant were slightly smaller, hydrogen would be the only element in the universe. Since the evolution of life as we know it is fundamentally dependent on the chemical properties of carbon, that life could not have come into being without some hydrogen being converted to carbon by fusion. On the other hand, if the strong coupling constant were slightly larger (even by as much as 2 per cent), the hydrogen would have been converted to helium, with the result that no long-lived stars would have been formed. In that such stars are regarded as essential to the emergence of life, such a conversion would have led to life as we know it failing to emerge.

2. If the weak fine constant were slightly smaller, no hydrogen would have formed during the early history of the universe. Consequently, no stars would have been formed – and the biologically significant chemical elements of carbon, nitrogen and oxygen were formed in the cores of stars, not in the original big bang. On the other hand, if it were slightly larger,

supernovae would have been unable to eject the heavier elements necessary for life. In either case, life as we know it could not have emerged.

3. If the electromagnetic fine structure constant were slightly larger, the stars would not be hot enough to warm planets to a temperature sufficient to maintain life in the form in which we know it. If smaller, the stars would have burned out too quickly to allow life to evolve on these planets.

4. If the gravitational fine structure constant were slightly smaller, stars and planets would not have been able to form, on account of the gravitational constraints necessary for coalescence of their constituent material. If stronger, the stars thus formed would have burned out too quickly to allow the evolution of life.

In short: if the values of certain fundamental constants of the universe had been slightly different, life would not have been possible. Without carbon, oxygen and nitrogen, there would be no life in the universe – no apples, and no human beings.

We live in a universe which has apples, and which has human beings who can use them to make pies. Modern cosmology helps us realise that the seemingly commonplace existence of apples and humans is actually nothing less than astonishing. The simple act of making an apple pie is far more wonderful than many have grasped!

Now 'fine-tuning' has become an accepted notion in modern cosmology. But what does it mean? It might, after all, mean absolutely nothing. There might be zillions of universes, and all the rest are barren and sterile. We just happen to be in the one that supports life. Our number came up, and we are here as a result. That is just the way things are. Yet the odds against a life-friendly universe are massive – unimaginably massive. The extreme improbability of life makes us wonder if we can really be satisfied with this explanation. As Freeman Dyson once remarked, 'The more I examine the universe and study the details of its architecture, the more evidence I find that the universe in some sense must have known that we were coming.'[28]

And Dyson is not on his own here. The British astronomer Fred Hoyle was notoriously hostile towards the idea of the origins of the universe, fearing that it would sound 'religious'. Yet he was clear that there was something strange about the way the universe was set up.[29]

A common sense interpretation of the facts suggests that a superintellect has monkeyed with physics, as well as with chemistry and biology, and that there are no blind forces worth speaking about in nature. The numbers one calculates from the facts seem to me so overwhelming as to put this conclusion almost beyond question.

So how does a theist, like myself, respond to these observations and comments? First, let's be clear that these observations *prove* nothing. Yet as philosophers of science, such as Charles Peirce, have emphasised, one of the goals of scientific explanation is to set surprising observations in a context which makes them seem unsurprising, perhaps even predictable. As I have stressed throughout this book, Christianity gives us a 'big picture', a lens which brings things into focus. And if Christianity is right in its understanding of God, isn't something like this just what we should expect?

Critics of Creation: Stephen Hawking and Laurence Krauss

So what might critics of the idea of divine creation say in response? In this section, we are going to look at two recent high-profile works from leading scientists who have argued that modern scientific thinking allows us to dispense with God altogether. I have chosen these two books on account of their cultural impact, as judged by sales figures and associated stories in print and other forms of media.

Stephen Hawking is one of the world's greatest theoretical physicists, with a rare gift for popular communication. His most famous book, *A Brief History of Time* (1988), stayed on the British *Sunday Times* best-sellers list for a record-breaking 237 weeks. In 2010, Hawking teamed up with the American physicist Leonard Mlodinow to write *The Grand Design*,[30] an interesting account of unified field theories and superstring theories, along with a highly speculative ramble through philosophical and theological byways. The work attracted media attention mainly because of its bold statements of the explanatory redundancy of God (it is not clear whether these are to be tracked back to Hawking himself, or to Mlodinow). We do not need, they declared, 'to invoke God to light the blue touchpaper and set the universe going'. It was a vivid turn of phrase, and got people talking. But what did they mean? Is there a 'blue touchpaper' which needs to be lit to 'set the universe going'? And if God did not light it, who or what did?

The Grand Design turns out to be a rather self-congratulatory manifesto of a somewhat crude scientific imperialism, which brashly – and prematurely, as it turns out – declares that 'philosophy is dead', leaving the field clear for scientists to become 'the bearers of the torch of discovery in our quest for knowledge'.[31] This is nonsense, and the remainder of the book at least serves as a powerful demonstration of the continuing need for serious philosophy, if only to challenge and counter the inflated and muddled claims of some scientists. What Hawking and Mlodinow provide is not pure physics, but a poorly argued metaphysics whose failings are all too evident.

The basic idea of *The Grand Design* is that the laws of physics are adequate in themselves to account for the origins of the universe. We therefore have to choose between God and the laws of physics, as if they could not both be true, or were somehow in mutual conflict. Since 'there is a law such as gravity, the universe can and will create itself from nothing'.[32] Yet it is difficult to see how physical laws can ever provide a complete explanation of the universe. After all, laws themselves do not create anything, in that they are merely a description of what happens under certain conditions.[33] The 'laws of nature' cause nothing to happen; they are a framework of thinking which helps clarify regularities of action that happen within nature. Laws themselves cause nothing; they help us to make sense of the causalities that we observe within the universe.

I work in Oxford, and happened to be walking through the University Parks late one summer morning on my way to a meeting. I encountered two American visitors, who were watching a game of cricket. It soon became clear that they were baffled by what they were seeing. 'Can you tell us what's going on here?' they asked me. It was an unwise question, as I have never been a great fan of cricket. However, I tried to explain the rules. My feeble attempt seemed to work quite well. The batsman hit the ball and it soared into the air. 'That's six runs, right?' my new friends asked me. And sure enough, the scoreboard changed a moment later. They had grasped something of the rules of cricket!

That lunchtime experience came back to me when I read *The Grand Design*. Its authors seemed to think that laws amount to agency. Laws are a description of what happens in certain situations, or an enumeration of observations. They do not cause anything; they do not create anything; they are a summary or account of what happens within the universe. The laws of cricket did not cause the batsman to hit a six. The batsman simply hit the ball in a certain way, and the laws of cricket decreed that this was worth six runs. The batsman did all the work; the laws simply provided an interpretative or evaluative framework.

Hawking seems to think that having laws makes things happen. It does not. Agency is one thing; explanation is another. And where did these laws come from in the first place? What explains the explainers? Surely there is a regress here, in which explanation is merely deflected, rather than effected? It is a fair point to make, given that Hawking and Mlodinow hold that such a 'deflection' can be used as an argument against God. 'It is reasonable to ask who or what created the universe, but if the answer is God, then the question has merely been deflected to that of who created God.'[34] It is a rather obvious point, but consistency is important in any rational argument. If Hawking and Mlodinow believe that the answer to the question of who or what created the universe is 'the laws of gravity', then the question has merely been deflected to that of who or what created the laws of gravity. Maybe we still need philosophy after all.

A second recent critique of the idea of creation is found in Lawrence Krauss's *Universe from Nothing* (2012).[35] Krauss, a professor of physics at Arizona State University, describes himself as an 'anti-theist' and sees his understanding of physics as demolishing theism. Interestingly, Krauss had hoped to have Christopher Hitchens (1949–2011), a leading representative of the New Atheism, write the preface to his book. Hitchens seems to know nothing about science, to judge by his pontifications on the matter, but he certainly shares Krauss's hostility towards religion. Having read Krauss's book closely, I think it is best seen as another of the New Atheist critiques of religion, rather than a serious attempt to think through the implications of science. In this work, Krauss argues that science is well on the way to explaining how the universe emerges from 'nothing' without any need to reference a creator God.

I first read this book with eager anticipation, since Richard Dawkins had declared it to be the best thing on the question of creation since Darwin's *Origin of Species*. Although I disagree with Dawkins on many points, when someone I regard as a leading atheist says this is the best atheist critique of religion, I have to take it seriously. Let me just say that, if this is the best atheist critique of religion since Darwin, atheism is in a very bad place. Darwin's book – which I have read many times – is a brilliant, articulate work of science, based on rigorous argument and cautious understatement. And Darwin – in contrast to Dawkins – did not see *Origin of Species* as anti-theistic. Nor did his leading interpreter, Thomas H. Huxley.[36] Krauss's work is a sloppily written, poorly argued atheist tract trading on the cultural reputation of science which left me intellectually dissatisfied. The uncritical effusive praise meted out for this disappointing work by leading New Atheist commentators does nothing to conceal its obvious argumentative and evidential failings.

The first major section of *Universe from Nothing* focuses mainly on such overdiscussed (and not particularly controversial) ideas as 'dark matter'. It is only in the last forty pages or so that Krauss gets round to discussing the issue of how 'something' emerges from 'nothing'. So what does Krauss mean by 'nothing'? Here is what he says. 'By *nothing* I do not mean nothing, but rather *nothing* – in this case, the nothingness we normally call empty space.' Krauss seems to think that italicising 'nothing' solves a metaphysical problem, when all it does is indicate that Krauss's 'nothing' is not 'nothing' at all.

Krauss surely knows perfectly well that 'empty space' is not really empty: there is *something* there, in the form of electromagnetic fields and virtual particles in the 'Dirac sea' of particle-antiparticle pairs. 'Empty space' is thus not 'void', but contains transient electromagnetic waves and particles that pop into and out of existence. 'Nothing', as I understand the word, would mean 'an *absence* of fields, virtual particles and anything else'. Krauss is not a clear writer, and there are points at which it is difficult to follow his argument – especially towards the end of the work. But it seems clear that all he has succeeded in doing is showing *how something can emerge from something else*. But that is just how the universe works.

Maybe that is why Krauss used that important qualification: 'the nothingness we *normally* call empty space' (my emphasis). Is this meant to imply that there is a 'popular' understanding of 'empty space', which is to be contrasted with a more rigorously scientific account of 'empty space' – which would begin by emphasising that it is not 'empty' at all?

The last century has seen huge advances in quantum theory and has forced us to rethink many 'common-sense' notions, such as the idea of the 'emptiness' of space. Well, space may be physically (nearly) empty; but it is populated by fields and forces, all of which have the potential to cause things to happen. David Albert, a professor of philosophy at Columbia University with a PhD in physics, put his finger on the central flaw of Krauss's book:

> If what we formerly took for nothing turns out, on closer examination, to have the makings of protons and neutrons and tables and chairs and planets and solar systems and galaxies and universes in it, then it wasn't nothing, and it couldn't have been nothing in the first place.[37]

But there is another issue. The laws of quantum mechanics do not actually help us to answer what we might call 'ultimate questions'. They do not tell us why the universe should be made up of a particular kind of fields (or why it should have any kinds of fields in the first place), or why there should be a universe at all. They do not tell us where those fields came from. They give us an important, revisable, intellectual framework to make sense of the workings of the universe. We can track its history and infer the principles that seem to govern its development and its present state of functioning. But we cannot say *why* the universe is there; just that it *is there*. The scientific narrative does not possess a methodology which allows it to answer that 'why' question, which would require access to whatever existed before the 'big bang'. And at the moment, that is simply inconceivable.

The fact that the relation of the scientific narrative of origination and the Christian narrative of creation is being discussed with such enthusiasm makes it clear that this is no 'dead' question. And it is clear, even on the basis of this very brief consideration of these works, that they do not have anything like the significance or impact on theism that some – perhaps including their authors – might think. It is more complicated than they seem to realise.

What is eternity?

Finally, let's consider a question that emerges from recent scientific theories about the origins of the universe and concerns the nature of time. We naturally think of the origins of the universe as happening *in* time. In other words, we imagine a graph with a timeline, and at a certain point along that line the universe comes into existence. Except it is not like that. We have to speak of the 'birth of space-time'. In other words, both space and time came into existence – not *in* time or space, but *as* time and space.

Most of us find it impossible to visualise this. We are so conditioned by living in a world of time and space that we cannot escape thinking in terms of time and space. Where were time and space before they came into being? It seems a hopelessly counter-intuitive question, just as ridiculous as 'what is the universe expanding into?' But we have to learn to adapt our thinking to the deeper structures of rationality. That is one of the core themes of the scientific method – not to be trapped into 'common-sense' or 'rational' ways of thinking, but to let the universe tell us what it is really like. So what is the relevance of this for our thinking about eternity? Most of us work with a common-sense notion of eternity as 'an infinitely extended period of time'. But that is not what the word means. It means 'timelessness'.

Now there are two important points to make here. First, Christianity understands – as it has always understood – God to be *outside* time. God creates the universe *with time*, not *in time*. It is virtually impossible for us to visualise this, as we are locked into habits of thought and mental image-making that are shaped by the world around us. Christianity thinks of God creating space and time, not standing in space-time and rearranging things that were already there. God therefore is not an object in the world, but someone who stands beyond our world. While the idea of heaven is notoriously difficult to visualise, we could think of this as a realm beyond the world of space and time that we presently know and inhabit.

This poses imaginative challenges for us. C.S. Lewis suggests that we experience problems visualising complex realities because we are 'Flatlanders' – two-dimensional people trying to visualise three-dimensional objects. Lewis invites us to imagine what it would be like to live in a two-dimensional universe, and trying to visualise or describe a three-dimensional reality. 'Flatlanders attempting to imagine a cube, would either imagine the six squares coinciding, and thus destroy their distinctness, or else imagine them set out side by side, and thus destroy the unity.'[38] Lewis suggests that our mental difficulties – whether scientific or religious – arise from seeing things from a limited and limiting perspective. We cannot break free from the world that we know; yet we are invited to imagine a 'strange world' (Einstein) that seems to operate by different rules! We think of time; we are invited to think instead of timelessness.

In this chapter, we have reflected on some themes relating to cosmology. We now need to move on and reflect on what many see as a 'game-changer' in the relation of science and religion – the controversies about evolution associated with Charles Darwin.

5

Darwin and Evolution:
New Questions for Science and Faith

Darwin's theory of evolution is often cited as the supreme demonstration of the irreconcilability of science and religion. The leading New Atheist Richard Dawkins presents Darwin as an atheist apologist who demolished the credibility of theism. The subtitle of Dawkins' influential work *The Blind Watchmaker* (1986) emphasises one of its core themes: 'Why the evidence of evolution reveals a universe without design.' For Dawkins, Darwin marks a turning point in the history of atheism. A milestone had been passed, and there was no turning back.

It is certainly true that Darwin has been seized upon by a coalition of vested interest groups in pursuit of their own agendas. Materialists, atheists and radical secularists saw his ideas as a way of finally getting rid of God from the public square,[1] while aggressively anti-scientific religious fundamentalists saw them as an excuse for getting rid of science in schools. If there is one situation in which the ailing 'warfare' narrative of the relation between science and religion has any plausibility, it is right here in this battle of fundamentalisms. But what of those caught in the middle of this nasty firefight? What of those who do not share these extremist ideologies?

In this chapter, we will explore the question of the significance of Darwin's theory of evolution, looking at its historical development, its contemporary statements and how it might impact on religious belief. Let's begin by setting the context for Darwin's ideas.

The Context of Darwin's Theory of Evolution

The nineteenth century was a period of scientific advance in many Western nations, especially Great Britain. Many of these new insights called into question long-standing assumptions about the nature of the world which had shaped cultural attitudes. Science works with the available evidence. Some histories of science create the impression that earlier generations were backward-looking because they thought the sun went around the earth in 1300, or failed to realise the earth was at least millions of years old in 1700. This is clearly unfair. Science rests upon the interpretation of *evidence* – and the evidence for these beliefs that most now take for granted was not available at those times.

In the late eighteenth century, a growing consensus developed within scientific circles that the earth was much older than had previously been assumed. Geologists were beginning to uncover evidence that life forms that were now extinct had once inhabited the earth.[2] Gradually, these ideas began to percolate downwards into popular culture. Although there was suspicion about the notion of an ancient earth, especially during the 1830s,[3] the idea gradually gained popular support, not least on account of the public's fascination with dinosaurs.

The term 'dinosaur' was invented in 1842 by the palaeontologist Sir Richard Owen (1804–92) to refer to large reptile-like primitive animals that were now extinct, whose skeletons had been unearthed in the previous thirty years.[4] Owen commissioned a set of full-sized sculptures of dinosaurs for the Great Exhibition in London's Crystal Palace in 1854. This collection of models of various extinct Mesozoic reptiles included a reconstruction of their original environment complete with an artificial lake with islands. They caused a sensation and were widely seen as the most memorable feature of the exhibition.[5]

This growing awareness of the antiquity of the earth was accompanied by speculation about how biological life forms developed. In the first half of the nineteenth century, terms such as 'progressionism' and 'transmutation' began to be used to refer to the view that life forms had changed over geological time. Many German biologists conceived of life evolving according to some set of predetermined laws, analogous to the way in which an embryo develops in the womb.

As early as 1794, Erasmus Darwin – Charles Darwin's grandfather – outlined a theory of the succession of life forms through successive adaptations. The fossil record suggested (although its interpretation was disputed) a progressive emergence of higher forms of life. Some interpreted this in terms of a series of special divine creations; following the publication of *Vestiges of the Natural History of Creation* (1844), this began to be formulated in terms of a purposeful and progressive transformation within nature, guided by some basic developmental principles ultimately grounded in divine providence.[6]

The phenomenon of what we would now call 'evolution' was increasingly accepted by about 1850, with a number of theories emerging to account for its specific features – most notably the 'transformist' model developed decades earlier by the French biologist Jean Baptiste Lamarck (1744–1829). These approaches met with some resistance on both religious and scientific grounds.[7] Yet the most significant opposition in England to Lamarck's theory of evolution seems to have been political. Lamarck's theory was initially seen as associated with dangerous continental radicalism, both political and religious.[8] The memory of the violence of the French Revolution was still fresh in England at that time! Gradually, this unhelpful perception weakened as the idea of biological evolution came to be reframed in terms of reform and progress – two core values of the Victorian age.

Religious hostility towards any notion of biological transformism emanated from a number of sources. One of the most interesting was William Paley's *Natural Theology* (1802), which declared that the complexity of biological structures – such as the human eye – was evidence of divine 'contrivance'; that is, design and construction.[9] Paley used the image of a watch to make his point: its intricate mechanism showed clear evidence of design and construction. Natural complexity, Paley argued, could not have arisen through chance; it was a witness to divine design. Yet by 1850, Paley's influence had dwindled as scientific evidence of biological development began to make its mark.

It is interesting to note that Dawkins' *Blind Watchmaker* is specifically aimed against Paley's approach, which Dawkins seems to think is representative of Christianity as a whole. It is not. Dawkins' strongly negative assessment of the religious implications of Darwinism actually depends on depicting a local historical contingency as if it were a universal theological necessity. Paley's approach – including the controlling image of the watch – is firmly located in the scientific and cultural world of the early eighteenth century. By the middle of the nineteenth century, English Christianity had moved on, developing more sophisticated approaches to the manner in which the natural world displayed signs of a creator. Dawkins makes a superb case for abandoning Paley. Sadly, he seems to think this also entails abandoning God.

By 1850, most British intellectuals were receptive to the notion of biological evolution. But what mechanism lay behind it? What theory could be advanced to explain how the evolution of species took place? Lamarck's transformist account of evolution seemed increasingly acceptable to many in Victorian England, despite its lingering associations with French political radicalism. It was easily assimilated to an ethos of self-improvement, in which the characteristics of animals developed in response to environmental challenges.

Charles Darwin is therefore to be remembered not for demonstrating the *phenomenon* of biological evolution (although he unquestionably amplified its scope), but for offering a *theory* of the way in which this process took place. In what follows, we shall look at some aspects of this theory.

Darwin's Theory of Evolution: The Core Themes

A full treatment of Darwin's theory of evolution would consider the slow development of his ideas and show how they gradually fell into place.[10] For our limited purposes in this chapter, we shall focus on the three leading themes of this new understanding of the phenomenon of biological evolution, set out in *The Origin of Species* (1859):

1. The Principle of Variation. Variation arises among individuals within any given population – for example, in relation to their physical structures.
2. The Principle of Heredity. Offspring resemble their parents more than they resemble unrelated individuals.
3. The Principle of Selection. Some forms of life are more successful at surviving and reproducing than other forms in any given environment.

Darwin thus thinks of evolution as a sorting process within nature which filters out certain forms of life through differential reproduction. Darwin named this process 'natural selection'. Let's look at his approach in more detail.

A scientific theory aims to explain what is observed. So what did Darwin believe needed to be explained? *The Origin of Species* identifies a number of observations that Darwin believed were not satisfactorily accounted for by existing theories of evolution, such as Lamarck's 'transformism', or Paley's theory of special divine creation. A good example is the observation that many creatures have what are known as 'vestigial structures' or 'rudimentary structures' which have no obvious function – such as the nipples of male mammals, or wings on many flightless birds. So how could these be explained on the basis of Paley's theory, which stressed the importance of the individual design of species? Why should God design redundancies?

The core of Darwin's theory is the notion of 'natural selection'.

Darwin invented the term 'natural selection' to refer to a hypo-
thetical process within nature which was analogous to the process
of 'artificial selection' used by breeders of cattle or pigeons.
Darwin began to study pigeons in March 1855, trying to understand how breeders were able to develop new characteristics – such
as 'neck ruffles'. Darwin came to see that these breeds of pigeons
had all developed from a common ancestor – the so-called 'rock
pigeon' (*Columba livia*). If humans were able to bring about such
change in pigeons over hundreds of years, might there be some
analogous process operating within nature, acting over much
longer times, which might bring about comparable changes?

Very similar ideas were developed around the same time by
Alfred Wallace (1823–1913), who helped Darwin develop aspects
of his theory in the late 1850s. Darwin and Wallace presented their
evolutionary ideas together at a meeting of the Linnaean Society in
July 1858, although their presentations do not seem to have led to
any significant interest developing in the question. While Darwin
and Wallace developed very similar ideas of natural selection in the
late 1850s, there are some significant divergences between them.[11]
These are often differences of emphasis. For example, Darwin
emphasised the importance of competition between individuals of
the same species to survive and reproduce, whereas Wallace placed
an emphasis on local environmental pressures on varieties and
species which led to divergent populations in different locations.
Yet these divergences are minor when compared with their clearly
convergent positions on natural selection.

Darwin later set out the evidence for natural selection fully in
his *Variation of Animals and Plants under Domestication* (1868).
Yet his realisation that Wallace had come to more or less the same
conclusions independently in 1858 spurred him to publish his
ideas on evolution earlier than he had intended. He had already
written about 250,000 words of a large projected book on natural selection,[12] and realised that he would have to produce
something shorter and more focused if he was to gain a wider
readership. In 1859, Darwin published *On the Origin of Species*

by Means of Natural Selection, or the Preservation of Favoured Races in the Struggle for Life. It is now universally known by the shorter title *The Origin of Species*. In what follows, I will set out the core elements of its argument.[13]

Darwin begins by setting out three *facts*, confirmed by extensive observation:

1. Every species is fertile enough that if all offspring survived to reproduce, the population would become larger.
2. Despite periodic fluctuations, populations remain roughly the same size.
3. Resources such as food are limited and are relatively stable over time.

From these facts, the following *inference* is then drawn: that a struggle for survival ensues, in that there are not enough resources to sustain all living forms. Both Darwin and Wallace had read Thomas Malthus's *Essay on the Principle of Population* (1797), which had emphasised that the population size was limited by resources. Darwin and Wallace both argued that living species were competing for limited resources, leading to a struggle for survival.

Two further sets of observations are now woven into the argument. For these Darwin drew on his knowledge of pigeon-breeding.

4. Individuals in a population vary significantly from one another.
5. Much of this variation can be passed down from one generation to another – even though the mechanism for this was unclear.

This led Darwin to draw two further inferences.

6. Individuals which are less suited (or 'adapted') to their environment are less likely to survive, and hence less likely to

reproduce. In contrast, individuals that are more suited to the environment are more likely to survive, and hence are more likely to reproduce and leave their heritable traits to future generations. This is the 'filtering process' that Darwin termed 'natural selection'.

7. This process, which proceeds over extended periods of time, results in populations changing to adapt to their environments, and these variations eventually accumulate over time to form new species.

Darwin's *The Origin of Species* went through six editions and Darwin worked constantly to improve his text, adding new material, amending existing material and, above all, responding to criticisms. Some 60 per cent of these modifications took place in the last two editions, which introduced some 'improvements' that now seem unwise – for example, his incorporation of Herbert Spencer's potentially misleading phrase 'the survival of the fittest'.[14]

The contents of these successive editions of *The Origin of Species* make it clear that Darwin's new theory faced considerable opposition on many fronts. As we shall see, some Christian thinkers saw it as a threat to the way in which they had interpreted their faith. Yet other Christians saw Darwin's theory as offering new ways of understanding and parsing traditional Christian ideas. More importantly, Darwin's theory provoked scientific controversy, with many scientists of his day raising concerns about the scientific foundations of 'natural selection'. If the successive editions of *The Origin of Species* are anything to go by, Darwin's theory appears to have met more sustained opposition from the scientific community than from its religious counterpart, especially on account of its failure to offer a convincing account of how innovations were transmitted to future generations.

A good example of such scientific criticism is found in the concerns raised by Henry Charles Fleeming Jenkin (1833–85) about 'blending inheritance'.[15] Jenkin, sometime Regius Professor of Engineering at the University of Edinburgh, identified what

Darwin clearly believed to be a potentially fatal enquiry flaw in his theory. He pointed out that, on the basis of existing understandings of hereditary transmission, any novelties would be diluted in subsequent generations. Yet Darwin's theory depended on the transmission, not dilution, of such characteristics. In other words, Darwin's theory lacked a viable understanding of genetics.

The answer, of course, lay in the writings of the Austrian monk Gregor Mendel, later incorporated into what is sometimes known as the 'neo-Darwinian synthesis'. Mendel's theory of genetics made it clear that individual characteristics could be passed down from parents to offspring. Yet that theoretical advance was unknown to Darwin or his critics at the time. Nevertheless, the fact that such characteristics were passed down from parents to offspring was well known at this time, even though its mechanism was not understood. Darwin's appeal to the methods and outcomes of 'artificial selection' among pigeon-breeders connected well with his readership.

So much for the science. But what of its religious significance?

The Religious Significance of Darwin's Ideas

Some popular writers, especially those sympathetic to the New Atheism, suggest that Darwin's *Origin of Species* launched a new phase in the relation of science and religion (which, of course, they frame using the obsolete 'warfare' narrative), with Darwin taking the role of a bold atheist defender of truth against obstinate clerical creationists. The reality, as might be expected, is much more complex and interesting.

First of all, let's look at Darwin's own religious views. These have been carefully studied by scholars and they are reasonably well understood, especially when seen in the light of his Victorian context.[16] Darwin's religious views changed over time, from the Christian orthodoxy of his period at Cambridge University, through a form of deism around the time of publication of *The Origin of Species*, to an essentially agnostic position in later life.

It is certainly true that Darwin's religious beliefs veered away from what we might loosely call 'Christian orthodoxy'. Yet Darwin declined to be considered as an atheist. Furthermore, we do not find anything in Darwin remotely resembling the aggressive and ridiculing form of atheism characteristic of some of those who have presented themselves as his champions in more recent times. In his later life, Darwin remained respectful towards those who retained religious beliefs, while expressing hostility towards any form of dogmatism, whether religious or atheist.

What we do find in Darwin's works, particularly his letters, is a specific critique of some aspects of Christianity, which he clearly distinguishes from a more generic belief in a God who governs the world through the laws of nature.[17] Yet Darwin's misgivings about Christianity seem to have little to do with his new idea of 'natural selection', or his theory of evolution in general. For Darwin, the problem was belief in divine providence. Some of his biographers have suggested that a crisis in Darwin's religious convictions came about as a result of the death of his daughter Annie in 1851 at the age of ten.[18] Darwin was also concerned about the amount of suffering he saw in the natural world. While in South America, he witnessed at first hand the terrible struggle for existence faced by the natives of the Tierra del Fuego. And as a biologist, he found himself uneasy about the violence and suffering entailed in the vicious natural food chain.

Yet, despite his own waning personal religious beliefs, Darwin was emphatic that he did not see his evolutionary ideas as liable to cause legitimate difficulties for religious believers. Others may now interpret those ideas as causing religious discomfort, or as entailing atheism; but Darwin himself did not see things this way. Darwin seems to have been willing not merely to go on record concerning, but to *emphasise*, the consilience of religious faith and the theory of natural selection. In a letter of 1879 Darwin declared, 'It seems to me absurd to doubt that a man may be an ardent Theist & an evolutionist.' He further added that, even in his 'most extreme fluctuations', he had 'never been an atheist in the sense of denying the existence of a God'.[19] In that same letter he remarked that the 'most correct description of my state of mind', especially as he grew older, would be 'agnostic'.

One of the major themes in *The Origin of Species* is the notion of 'laws impressed on matter by the Creator', which is actually given a higher profile in the second edition of the work than in the first.[20] Darwin seems to have conceived of evolutionary law in the realm of biology as being analogous to gravitational law in the realm of astronomy. This is certainly suggested by the three highly significant quotations that Darwin placed before the main text of *The Origin of Species*. Two of these were present in the first edition; the third was added in the second edition. These three citations are designed to frame Darwin's exposition of natural selection within a framework of natural laws.

The first of these sentences is taken from the writings of William Whewell, a Cambridge philosopher of science: 'Events are brought about not by insulated interpositions of Divine power, exerted in each particular case, but by the establishment of general laws.' Whewell's words echo the widely accepted theological framework – found in theologians such as Thomas Aquinas and scientists such as Isaac Newton – which held that God does not normally intervene in the natural order, but acts indirectly through the created laws of nature. This idea is clearly implicit in the 'big book' on natural selection on which Darwin worked from about 1856 to 1858: 'By nature, I mean the laws ordained by God to govern the Universe.'[21]

The second quotation, present from the second edition onwards, is taken from Joseph Butler's *Analogy of Religion,* a classic eighteenth-century work of Anglican theology, affirming that God's actions can be considered as operating through the regular processes of nature, rather than as being superimposed upon it: 'What is natural as much requires and presupposes an intelligent agent to render it so, i.e. to effect it continually or at stated times, as what is supernatural or miraculous does to effect it for once.'

The final quotation, taken from Roger Bacon's *Advancement of Learning*, appeals to the classic Renaissance image of the consilience of science and religion – the metaphor of the 'two books', the book of God's word (the Bible) and the book of God's works (nature). Nobody, Bacon declared, should think 'that a man can search too far or be too well studied in the book of God's word, or in the book of God's works; divinity or philosophy; but rather let men endeavour an endless progress or proficience in both'.

One of the major achievements of Darwin's *The Origin of Species* was to show how an explanation could be given for what he described as the 'mystery of mysteries' – the successive appearance of new life forms that could be seen in the fossil record. If new species could emerge from pre-existing species by a process of natural selection, it was no longer necessary to suppose the occurrence of what Darwin called 'independent acts of creation'. Darwin developed his theory in terms of 'laws impressed upon matter by the Creator' rather than individual divine actions of creation.

The dominant form of Christianity in England in Darwin's time was the established Church of England, which was a powerful presence within the academic and cultural world of the day. It soon became clear that many of its senior figures were supportive of Darwin's ideas, seeing evolution as God's preferred method for bringing biological diversity into being.

One such figure was the novelist and Christian social reformer Charles Kingsley (1819–75), to whom Darwin refers as 'a celebrated author and divine'. Knowing of his interest in the topic, Darwin sent Kingsley an advance copy of *The Origin of Species*. A week before its publication, Kingsley wrote back to Darwin to express his delight at the work, making a theological judgement that would resonate with many within the Church. It was, he declared, 'just as noble a conception of Deity, to believe that He created primal forms capable of self-development' as it was 'to believe that He required a fresh act of intervention to supply the lacunas which He Himself had made'.[22] Kingsley declared that he, like Darwin and many others, had 'learnt to disbelieve the dogma of the permanence of species', which he considered to be contradicted by the intelligent observation of nature, particularly the development of new forms of plants and animals through selective breeding for agricultural purposes.

In an 1871 lecture, Kingsley – by then a canon of Westminster Abbey, a citadel of the religious establishment – argued that the word 'creation' implies a process as much as an event. Darwin's theory had clarified the mechanism of creation. 'We knew of old that God was so wise that he could make all things; but, behold, he is so much wiser than even that, that he can make all things make themselves.'[23] Where Paley thought of a static creation, Kingsley argued that Darwin made it possible to see creation as a dynamic process, directed by divine providence. Instead of a 'chilling dream of a dead universe ungoverned by an absent God', Kingsley declared that Darwinism, when rightly interpreted, offered a vision of a living universe constantly improving under the wise direction of its benevolent Creator. 'Of old it was said by Him without whom nothing is made: "My Father worketh hitherto, and I work." Shall we quarrel with Science if she should show how those words are true?'

This approach was later widely adopted by senior churchmen. This warm ecclesiastical endorsement of Darwin continued to his death. Although Darwin wanted to be buried near his home, it was eventually arranged that he would be buried in Westminster Abbey.

Many readers, however, will find such a warm reception for Darwin's ideas from senior clergy of the Church of England puzzling. After all, was one of the church's bishops, Samuel Wilberforce, not a vicious and ignorant opponent of Darwin? This naturally brings us to consider one of the great legends of the 'warfare' narrative of science and religion – the debate between Samuel Wilberforce and Thomas H. Huxley at Oxford in 1860.

The Legend of the 1860 British Association
Meeting in Oxford

The myth that science and religion are permanently at war with each other is often justified through an appeal to the meeting of the British Association at Oxford on 30 June 1860, which pitted Samuel Wilberforce, Bishop of Oxford, against Thomas H. Huxley on the topic of Darwin's theory of evolution. A generation later, this debate was propelled to iconic status as a classic example of the 'warfare of science and religion'. However, in the last generation, historians have offered a much more informed and balanced account of the meeting, which is now seen in a very different light.[24]

The popular image of Huxley's triumphant defeat of a reactionary religious opponent of evolution is now generally seen as a myth created by the opponents of organised religion in the 1890s. This revisionist account of the meeting does not deny its historical factuality. This new research calls into question overblown and inaccurate accounts of its significance and offers an informed reconstruction of the debate which accounts better for the historical evidence at our disposal.

The British Association for the Advancement of Science was scheduled to meet in Oxford in 1860. As Charles Darwin's *The Origin of Species* had been published the previous year, it was natural that it should be a subject of discussion at the 1860 meeting. Darwin himself was in poor health and was unable to attend the meeting in person. Huxley – then a young man – was invited in his place. Samuel Wilberforce, Bishop of Oxford, was also invited to speak. He had been vice-president of the British Association in the past and was known to be familiar with Darwin's ideas and writing. Although he was Bishop of Oxford at that time, he was not present as a representative of the Church of England at this meeting.

In his address, Wilberforce set out the main themes of Darwin's work, emphasising that the British Association discussion was about science, not religion. In his extended review of Darwin's *Origin of Species*, published in *The Quarterly Review* in the same month as the British Association meeting, Wilberforce made it clear that he had 'no sympathy with those who object to any facts or alleged facts in nature, or to any inference logically deduced from them, because they believe them to contradict what it appears to them is taught by Revelation'.[25]

According to a popular legend that is regularly and uncritically reproduced in many older biographies of Darwin, Wilberforce attempted to pour scorn on the theory of evolution by suggesting that it implied that humans were recently descended from monkeys. Would Huxley, he asked, prefer to think of himself being descended from an ape on his grandfather's or grandmother's side? He was then duly rebuked by Huxley, who turned the tables on him, showing him up to be an ignorant and arrogant cleric. Even the BBC perpetuated this nonsense in the 1970s, representing a 'young, handsome, heroic Huxley' triumphing over a sulky and villainous Wilberforce.[26]

The classic formulation of this legendary demonisation of Wilberforce dates from 1898 and takes the form of an autobiographical memory from Mrs Isabella Sidgewick, published in *Macmillan's Magazine*. This idiosyncratic account is inconsistent with most accounts published or in circulation closer to the time of the meeting itself, nearly forty years earlier, raising some awkward questions about the reliability of Mrs Sidgewick's memory. A review published shortly after the event in the *Athenaeum* expressed the consensus of 1860. Wilberforce and Huxley, it declared, 'have each found foemen worthy of their steel, and made their charges and countercharges very much to their own satisfaction and the delight of their respective friends'.

It is quite clear from Wilberforce's careful and insightful published review of Darwin's *The Origin of Species* that religious issues did not feature prominently in his mind; the issue was the scientific case for evolution, not its religious implications or complications. The fact that Wilberforce was Bishop of Oxford has clearly led many to conclude that religion was at the forefront of the debate and that Wilberforce opposed Darwin on religious grounds. The evidence does not support this interpretation of events. The debate was primarily about the scientific merits of Darwin's theory and Wilberforce – who, it must be noted, was actually present in his capacity as a former vice-president of the Association, not as a bishop of the Church of England – was clearly well informed about the matter. Darwin himself remarked, after reading Wilberforce's review of his work, that it was 'uncommonly clever; it picks out with skill all the most conjectural parts, and brings forward well all the difficulties'.[27] Furthermore, recent scholarship has suggested that the real debate at that time was not between science and religion, but between two quite distinct visions of science, one defined by 'naturalist' assumptions and the other more open to theistic beliefs.[28]

Yet there is another point about this Oxford meeting of 1860 which has generally been overlooked. On Sunday 1 July, the day after the confrontation between Wilberforce and Huxley, the conference delegates heard a sermon preached on the theme of 'The Present Relations of Science to Religion'. The preacher was Frederick Temple (1821–1902), who had strong local connections and good scientific credibility. He had been a fellow of Balliol College, Oxford, and had gone on to be headmaster of Rugby School, where he had established scholarships in natural science and was in the process of planning a school science laboratory.

Temple did not comment on the debate of the previous day, but instead praised scientists for trying discover as much as possible about the structures and laws of the universe, within which the 'the finger of God' might be discerned. The harmony between science and the Christian faith, he declared, was not concerned with the superficial 'petty details of facts' but was seen at a more profound level.[29] This harmony was at the level of a 'deep identity of tone, character, and spirit' between Scripture and nature – a relationship traditionally expressed using the 'two books' metaphor.

Temple was a rising star in the ecclesiastical firmament and went on to become Archbishop of Canterbury. Temple confirmed what was now emerging as the preferred ecclesial framing of Darwin's ideas.[30] As he declared in some Oxford lectures of 1884, God 'did not make the things, we may say; no, but He made them make themselves'.[31]

This is not to say that there were no religious concerns about Darwin's ideas, in that many, including Charles Kingsley, had difficulties with the notion of the continuity that Darwin's theory seemed to imply between humans and their animal ancestors – something that was hinted at in *The Origin of Species*, but was not stated more explicitly until *The Descent of Man* (1871). Yet this does not amount to an uncritical rejection of the theory. It was simply a recognition that there were further questions that needed to be explored – some scientific, some religious, some ethical.

Social Darwinism: The Problem of Eugenics

Darwin's theory of evolution was adopted by those with progressive political agendas, particularly the improvement of the human race. It is not difficult to understand Darwin's appeal to social progressives of the age. If Darwin allows us to understand the mechanism of evolution, might we be able to use that understanding to improve the quality of humanity? Or at least to prevent certain defective human beings from being born? These are contentious issues which will raise concerns for many readers. Yet we must consider how Darwin's insights were applied by his successors, whether rightly or wrongly.

The first major attempt to apply Darwinian insights to safeguarding the human future was the 'eugenics' movement which emerged in the first half of the twentieth century. The scientific basis of this movement seemed to be unassailable. Sir Francis Galton (1822–1911), a cousin of Charles Darwin, had noted the implications of Darwin's theory of natural selection and influenced a significant passage in *The Descent of Man* which laid the foundation for eugenics.[32] Darwin noted that 'with savages, the weak in body or mind are soon eliminated; and those that survive commonly exhibit a vigorous state of health'. Civilised societies, however, inhibit this 'process of elimination' through medical and social care, thus enabling 'the weak members of civilised societies' to 'propagate their kind'. Darwin saw this as 'injurious' to the future of the human race:

> No one who has attended to the breeding of domestic animals will doubt that this must be highly injurious to the race of man. It is surprising how soon a want of care, or care wrongly directed, leads to the degeneration of a domestic race; but excepting in the case of man himself, hardly any one is so ignorant as to allow his worst animals to breed.

Darwin's implicit support for the notion of selective breeding for humans, paralleling the best practices of stockbreeders, was one of many factors which led to eugenics becoming increasingly influential within Victorian culture. Since the process of genetic transmission in evolution was now understood, why should it not be applied to ensure the future of the British Empire? Galton argued that breeding should be limited to those possessing 'eugenic value' – qualities which seem remarkably close to the virtues and values of Victorian England.[33] Galton's proposals included the suggestion that extra credit should be given for 'family merit' in competitive examinations for the civil services or other professional posts if the candidate had superior breeding potential, as judged by the success of family members in their chosen professions. He also recommended that the requirement for celibacy for Fellows at Oxford and Cambridge Universities should be abolished, since these intelligent males could be expected to have superior offspring and thus ought to be encouraged to breed.

It soon became clear that there was a darker side to eugenics. Galton's science quickly became the victim of politics and prejudice. Normative judgements about 'eugenic value' soon extended to race and social class. Some argued for a form of scientific racism, holding that 'the negro' was less biologically advanced than 'the Mongolian or the European'.[34] For such reasons, some argued that certain 'undesirable' social groups should be prohibited from reproducing. Although this problem was especially pronounced in the case of Adolf Hitler's racial policies of the 1930s, many progressive and liberal thinkers of that period – both in Great Britain and the United States – argued for the forcible sterilisation of individuals or social groups deemed to have limited eugenic value. While such acts could arguably be given some scientific justification, the chief difficulty was that eugenic value was all too often defined in terms of class, race or creed. In effect, self-appointed social 'in-groups' sought to prevent 'out-groups' from reproducing.

In England, Marie Stopes (1880–1958) founded the Society for Constructive Birth Control and Racial Progress to 'promote eugenic birth control' in 1921. Stopes' book *Radiant Motherhood* (1920) reflected the consensus then emerging within British progressive circles. Its final chapter, entitled 'A New and Irradiated Race', advocated sterilisation as a means of preventing the 'rotten and racially diseased' from endangering the 'higher and more beautiful forms of the human race'.[35] Stopes framed her vision of the enforced sterilisation of those lacking eugenic value in terms of ensuring the beauty of the race. 'The evolution of humanity will take a leap forward when we have around us only fine and beautiful young people.'[36] This final chapter of *Radiant Motherhood* needs to be read carefully, not least because it provides important insights into the racial and class prejudices of the British cultural elite of the 1920s, who felt themselves threatened by a growing working class. 'If the good in our race is not to be swamped and destroyed as the fruit tree by the parasite, this prolific depravity must be curbed.'[37]

Although seen as progressive during the 1920s, eugenics is now widely regarded as a failed amalgam of Darwinian ideas with transient social and political agendas. This is not a criticism of science, nor of Darwin's ideas (although many will feel uneasy with Darwin's implied criticism of public health care). It is a reminder of the way in which science can be abused by those in power and redirected towards political goals. Above all, it undermines any suggestion that science is *necessarily* associated with liberal values. History tells us otherwise and we cannot ignore it.

So what questions might Darwin's theory of evolution raise for religion, particularly for Christianity? Let's consider these in the next section.

Tensions between Darwinism and Faith

The publication of Darwin's *Origin of Species* (1859) and *Descent of Man* (1871) gave rise to significant cultural debates, with attention often focusing on the place and status of human beings in a Darwinian world. There were unquestionably religious elements to those debates, but it would be a serious misjudgement to think that they solely or mainly concerned religion. Darwin's views on the evolutionary origins of humanity had enormous social, political, ethical and religious implications which left many wondering how to make sense of this strange new world, in which human beings seemed to have been relocated conceptually.

Some of the most perceptive explorations of these concerns are found in the novels and poetry of the late Victorian age rather than more technical writings.[38] In his 'Lucretius' (1868), Alfred Lord Tennyson (1809–92) offers a somewhat grim view of the implications of Darwinism, portraying the Roman philosopher's materialism and his increasing awareness of his own animalistic desires as ultimately driving him to suicide. George Meredith (1828–1909) offered a radically different take on the matter in his 'Ode to the Spirit of Earth in Autumn' (1862), embracing the prospect of a new paganism in which human beings could accept their place as an ephemeral part of nature while living out their biological natures to the full.

There are three major themes that emerge from Darwin's ideas which create tensions for some traditional religious beliefs, including those of Christianity. In what follows, we shall note these briefly. Our concern here is not so much with the historical debates of the Victorian age, but with their counterparts in the twenty-first century.

1. Darwinism offers a materialist understanding of human nature

One of the most distinctive and central themes of Darwin's *Descent of Man* is that 'man is descended from some lowly-organised form'.[39] Human beings are to be understood as participants within, rather than merely observers of, the evolutionary process. Perhaps influenced by the ideology of progress that was so characteristic of his age, Darwin saw this as eliciting hope for the future:

> Man may be excused for feeling some pride at having risen, though not through his own exertions, to the very summit of the organic scale; and the fact of his having thus risen, instead of having been aboriginally placed there, may give him hopes for a still higher destiny in the distant future . . . Man still bears in his bodily frame the indelible stamp of his lowly origin.[40]

Such a recognition of the evolutionary links between humanity and the animal kingdom causes the human to appear more animal and the animal to appear more human. Within Darwin's theoretical framework – though not within Lamarck's – human beings cannot in any sense be said to be either the 'goal' or the 'apex' of evolution. From a religious point of view this raised a number of concerns, perhaps most notably the traditional belief that human beings alone possess immortal souls. We shall consider this question in more detail in the following chapter.

Yet this belief goes way beyond religion. Most Darwinists would insist that it is a corollary of an evolutionary worldview that we must recognise that we are animals, part of the evolutionary process. Darwinism thus critiques the absolutist assumptions concerning the place of humanity within nature that lies behind 'speciesism' – a somewhat cumbersome term introduced by Richard Ryder and given wider currency by Peter Singer, currently of Princeton University. This has raised awkward questions far beyond the realm of traditional religion, in that many political and ethical theories are predicated on the assumption of the privileged status of humanity within nature, whether this is justified on religious or secular grounds.

We shall explore some of these themes in the next chapter, which reflects further on the relation of scientific and religious accounts of human nature. But here let's look at a specifically religious issue which arises from Darwin's theories.

2. God is eliminated from the world

A common religious concern is that Darwin's evolutionary theory led to the elimination of God from any role within the world. It does not require divine action in order for it to take place, and the random nature of variation is inconsistent with the idea of divine creation and providence, which is linked with the ideas of design, purpose and intentionality. Richard Dawkins thus argues that Darwin's theory renders belief in God superfluous. Many conservative Protestant writers agree, arguing that the role attributed to random events is inconsistent with the biblical material. Creationist writers often consider this one of the most important elements of their critique of Darwinism.

However, the force of this point is open to question. B.B. Warfield (1851–1921), perhaps one of the most influential conservative Protestant theologians of the late nineteenth century, pointed out that evolution could easily be understood as a seemingly random process which was nevertheless divinely superintended. God's providence, he argued, could be seen as directing the evolutionary process towards its intended goals.

Warfield – seen by some as the founder of an 'inerrantist' view of the Bible – also pointed out that if a way of interpreting the Bible was in conflict with science, it might be because that way of understanding the text was wrong and needed review.[41] While some would see this as a weak 'accommodationist' argument, Warfield wanted to acknowledge that biblical interpretation needed to take science into account.

Some Anglican writers of the late Victorian age took a very different approach, holding that Darwin liberated Christianity from a cold and arid deist idea of God as a 'watchmaker', popularised by William Paley and others. The nineteenth-century Anglican theologian Aubrey Moore (1848–90) famously argued that, under the guise of a foe, Darwin had done Christianity the work of a friend. How? By liberating it from this defective vision of God.

Yet the most widely proposed mechanism which Christian writers have put forward to account for God's involvement in the evolutionary process is the classic notion of secondary causality, particularly as this was developed by Thomas Aquinas in the thirteenth century.[42] For Aquinas, God's causality operates in a number of ways. While God must be considered capable of doing certain things directly, God delegates causal efficacy to the created order. Aquinas understands this notion of secondary causality to be an extension of, not an alternative to, the primary causality of God. Events within the created order can exist in complex causal relationships without in any way denying their ultimate dependency upon God as final cause. The created order thus demonstrates causal relationships which can be investigated by the natural sciences. Those causal relationships can be investigated and correlated – for example, in the form of the 'laws of nature' – without in any way implying, still less necessitating, an atheist worldview. God creates a world with its own ordering and processes. Aquinas in effect offers a more rigorous framework for exploring the insight of Charles Kingsley: God 'can make all things make themselves'.

3. A challenge to traditional interpretations of the book of Genesis?

Darwin's evolutionary theories impacted on a religious question which was particularly significant for Christians and Jews – the interpretation of the early chapters of the book of Genesis, which speak of the creation of the world and humanity.[43] Some popular Christian writers of the seventeenth century interpreted this text as implying that God created the world and human beings about six thousand years ago – one famous suggestion being 4004 BC.[44] In fact, the biblical narratives give no chronology for the act of creation; this figure depends on some very speculative mathematics and creative interpretations of the biblical texts.[45] By the middle of the eighteenth century, geological data had made it clear that the earth was much older than a few thousand years.

In some ways, the problem was that some Christians of the Victorian age were reading the Bible naïvely, as if it were a science textbook, failing to realise the complexity of its language, the theological intentions of its authors or the literary conventions of its context.[46] Early Christian writers of the fourth and fifth centuries were much more sensitive to this complexity, reading Genesis as a literary text with a theological message to convey. Core elements of that theological message included the idea that there is one Creator God who made all things that exist; that the material creation is 'good', not evil; and that human beings have a special place in this creation, including a responsibility to care for the created order.

Despite the fact that sermons were one of the most important means of exploring the interface of science and religion during the Victorian age, few preachers engaged Darwin or his ideas seriously.[47] Indeed, many popular English preachers of the early nineteenth century treated Genesis in a crudely literal manner, seeing it as using straightforward descriptive prose to convey a factual scientific message about the chronology of the world.

This tendency developed further within American Protestant

fundamentalism, which holds to a literal reading of the Genesis text. Fundamentalists argue that the best weapon against what they regard as 'bad science' is 'good science' – that is, science based on a literal and factual reading of Genesis. This view, which involves reading the Bible as a scientific textbook rather than as a religious text, has now come to be known as 'creationism'.

The rise of various forms of creationism in the United States and elsewhere is a relatively recent development, dating from more than a century after Darwin's *The Origin of Species*.[48] It is normally tracked back to a single book, *The Genesis Flood* (1961). This work, written by two American fundamentalists, John C. White and Henry M. Morris, laid the foundations for what was improbably called 'scientific creationism'. Unlike traditional Christian understandings of creation, this movement develops its thinking within a polemical framework, failing to make any distinction between the languages and approaches of theology and science.

For reflective Christians, it is important to appreciate that there are alternative models to thinking about these issues within the long tradition of reflection on the Bible, which can easily be reappropriated today. A good example is the approach to the interpretation of the Genesis creation narratives developed by Augustine of Hippo a thousand years before the 'Scientific Revolution' of our modern period and fifteen hundred years before Darwin's *The Origin of Species*.[49] There is no way in which Augustine can be considered to have 'accommodated' his biblical interpretation in order to fit in new theories about the 'big bang' or natural selection. Augustine's classic work *On the Literal Meaning of Genesis*, written between 401 and 415, was intended to be a 'literal' commentary on the text ('literal' here means something along the lines of 'in the sense intended by the author'). This 'traditional' – i.e., ancient – way of reading Genesis predates by more than a millennium the literal readings of this text which became characteristic of English-speaking Protestantism in the eighteenth and nineteenth centuries.

For Augustine, the natural meaning of the Genesis creation

accounts is that God brought everything into existence in a single moment of creation. Yet the created order is not static, in that God endowed it with the capacity to develop. Augustine uses the image of a dormant seed to help his readers grasp this point. God creates seeds, which will grow and develop at the right time. Using more technical language, Augustine asks his readers to think of created order as containing divinely embedded causalities which emerge or evolve at a later stage. Yet Augustine has no time for any notion of random or arbitrary changes within creation. The development of God's creation is always subject to God's sovereign providence. The God who planted the seeds at the moment of creation also governs and directs the time and place of their growth and development.

Now this is not a theory of biological evolution as we would now understand the term. Neither Augustine nor any of his contemporaries had access to the geological or biological information that would have opened up this issue for them. They were not anti-evolution; the idea just never occurred to them, because there was no evidence available to them to open up this line of thought. Yet Augustine's approach can be developed, easily and naturally, to respond to this new insight. And many would argue that, if British theologians of the nineteenth century had had a better knowledge of their intellectual heritage, their response to the challenge of Darwinism would have been more interesting, constructive and productive.

In this chapter, I have looked at some of the issues that arise from evolutionary thought. There is much more that needs to be said about these issues, much of which has already been said by others and merits attention.[50] Yet one matter clearly demands further discussion now: human nature. How do the narratives of science and faith help us understand who we are and why we matter? We shall consider these issues in the next chapter.

6

Souls: On Being Human

People do some weird things. In 1907, Dr Duncan MacDougall carried out a bizarre series of experiments in Haverhill, Massachusetts.[1] MacDougall weighed patients who were dying of tuberculosis and reported a strange and sudden weight loss at the moment of death in four cases. Having observed that 'from one-half to a full ounce departed from the body at the moment of expiration', MacDougall seems to have concluded that the 'departure of the soul from the body' could be 'recorded by physical means'.

The experiment is now regarded as hopelessly flawed, and the idea of the soul weighing about an ounce is widely ridiculed. But that is not the point. MacDougall's experiment is a telling indicator of the continuing influence of the idea of an immortal soul, trapped within the human body and only able to escape at death. It is not a specifically religious idea, let alone a Christian idea. It actually originated within classical Greek philosophy, at least five hundred years before Christianity appeared on the scene. Yet it is still deeply influential in Western culture.

So how do we think about humanity? What is distinct about human beings? Do we *have* souls? *Are* we souls? Anyway, what exactly is a soul? In this chapter, we will consider some of the deepest questions we ask about ourselves. Let's begin by thinking about the widespread belief that we are nothing but a collection of chemicals.

Physical Reductionism: Are We Just Atoms and Molecules?

Human beings can be described or defined at multiple levels. Each level helps us understand the complexity of human nature. The physicist will tell us that we are made of atoms and molecules.

She is right. But she is wrong if she adds that ridiculous word 'just'. The chemist will tell us that life is the result of complex chemical reactions, leading to food being converted to energy. The physiologist will tell us about the various organs that make up the human body and what each of them does. These are all true. Yet we transcend all of these levels of description. If humanity is defined by anything, it is not by what we find at the bottom of the ladder, but by what we find at the top. That is what makes us different. That is what makes us human.

One of the reasons why science is so successful concerns its use of 'reductive explanation', by which complex systems are reduced to more manageable, simpler mechanisms. Although there is a growing realisation that this form of explanation experiences difficulties in coping with many aspects of the biological sciences,[2] its usefulness in the field of physics is beyond doubt. So what are we to make of strongly reductive accounts of human nature, such as this oracular pronouncement from the biologist Francis Crick?

> 'You', your joys and your sorrows, your memories and your ambi-
> tions, your sense of personal identity and free will, are in fact no
> more than the behaviour of a vast assembly of nerve cells and their
> associated molecules . . . You're nothing but a pack of neurons.[3]

Crick's highly reductive approach to our human identity assumes that a complex system is no more than the sum of its parts. It may be a little more sophisticated than the routine declaration that 'we're nothing but atoms and molecules', but its basic assumption remains the same. Human identity is framed in terms of the basic components of the human body; there is no recognition of the emergence within human beings of any properties that transcend those of our individual components.[4] Emergence is a natural process by which high-level properties arise within systems through interactions at lower levels that do not themselves exhibit such properties. Higher levels of systems thus cannot be reduced to the lower levels.

One of the key lessons from the concept of emergence is that if we fully understand things on one level of reality, that does not mean we can explain – or predict – what happens at the next level. Physics cannot predict biology.

Another reductionist approach to human nature is based on our biological history rather than our chemical or biological components. We are just 'naked apes' – to quote the title of a book by the English zoologist Desmond Morris, which became a bestseller when it appeared in 1967.[5] It gets headlines, but it is just wrong. We are actually *ex*-apes.[6] We have evolved beyond that. To imagine that human nature can be defined in terms of our ancestry is to deny both *biological* evolution and, more importantly, *cultural* evolution. Anthropology supplements a purely biological account of human evolution by stressing the importance of cultural factors in enabling human beings to evolve beyond their biological limits.

Yet perhaps the best-known form of biological reductionism in recent years is the view that genes are the basic elements of biological reality. In what follows, we will look at this interesting approach.

Genetic Reductionism: Dancing to the Music of DNA?

Richard Dawkins is one of the most high-profile defenders of the 'gene's eye' view of evolution, which was very popular back in the 1980s, although it has since fallen out of favour.[7] This approach sees biological organisms – such as human beings – as complicated machines controlled by our genes. For Dawkins, everything is determined by our DNA – the complex biological molecule which transmits genetic information. 'DNA neither cares nor knows. DNA just is. And we dance to its music.' We are simply there to allow our genes to transfer themselves to future generations. Viewed through the lens of Dawkins' scientific reductionism, human beings are just gene-perpetuating machines.

> [Genes] swarm in huge colonies, safe inside gigantic lumbering robots, sealed off from the outside world, communicating with it by tortuous indirect routes, manipulating it by remote control.

They are in you and me; they created us, body and mind; and their preservation is the ultimate rationale for our existence.[8]

So that's settled, then. That is what science tells us about human nature and identity.

But it does not. This is metaphysical pontification, not scientific analysis. Dawkins is offering his own idiosyncratic interpretation of the science, not the neat science itself. What is there in Dawkins' words, cited above, that can be *proved* experimentally? It is mostly speculation, passed off as if it were a solid scientific consensus. The best criticism of Dawkins' genetic reductionism comes from Denis Noble, the distinguished Oxford biologist credited by many with the invention of 'systems biology' – an approach to biology which recognises the complexity of biological systems, noting particularly the failure of reductionist approaches to biology to explain how the properties of such systems emerge.[9] Noble argues that the observed complexity of biological systems demands scepticism about reductionist interpretations. We are forced to recognise that properties emerge within these systems which transcend those of their individual components.

So what does Noble make of Dawkins' genetic reductionism? Not much. For Noble, the only factually correct element in Dawkins' bold statement, quoted above, is that genes 'are in you and me'. The rest is non-empirical metaphysical speculation which smuggles in all kinds of unverified ideological precommitments. To make this point absolutely clear, Noble playfully rewrote Dawkins' statement, turning his metaphysical assumptions on their head while retaining the single empirically verifiable statement in Dawkins' original piece.

[Genes] are trapped in huge colonies, locked inside highly intelligent beings, moulded by the outside world, communicating with it by complex processes, through which, blindly, as if by magic, function emerges. They are in you and me; we are the system that allows their code to be read; and their preservation is totally dependent on the joy that we experience in reproducing ourselves. We are the ultimate rationale for their existence.[10]

Here, humans are represented as being in control. We are active; our genes are passive.

So what in Noble's passage is observable, and what is speculative? As before, the only thing that can be evidentially confirmed is that genes are 'in you and me'. The remainder is speculative and lies beyond empirical investigation. Dawkins and Noble see things in completely different ways. They cannot both be right. Both smuggle in a series of quite different values and beliefs. Yet their statements are 'empirically equivalent'. In other words, they both have equally good grounding in observation and experimental evidence. So how could we decide which is to be preferred on scientific grounds? As Noble observes, 'no one seems to be able to think of an experiment that would detect an empirical difference between them'.[11]

Now science helps us understand how we *function*; but there is a lot more to human identity than this. C.S. Lewis regularly protested against reductionist accounts of reality. In *The Voyage of the Dawn Treader*, one of the children shows off his scientific knowledge of astronomy to Ramandu, an old man who lives on a Narnian island. 'In our world,' says Eustace, 'a star is a huge ball of flaming gas.' The old man is not impressed. 'Even in your world, my son, that is not what a star is, but only what it is made of.'[12] Lewis's point was that we too easily fall into the trap of believing that describing the components of a star is equivalent to establishing its identity.

Science uses reductionist approaches as one of several tools to study a system. It makes sense. If you break the system down into its individual parts, you will end up understanding the behaviour of the whole system better. But that is not the full picture. When the components of a system come together, new properties emerge at the level of the system as a whole which were not present in any of its components beforehand.[13] A complex system – such as the human body – has properties that we often cannot anticipate or predict from our knowledge of the properties of the individual parts. Reductionism has severe limits – especially in biology.

Is There a Soul?

There is a line in one of Plato's dialogues that always makes me sit up. 'Some say that the body [*sōma*] is a tomb [*sēma*] of the soul [*psychē*] since the soul is buried for the time being.'[14] The slogan 'the body is a tomb' – which rhymes in Greek – has had a deep impact on Western thought. Plato suggested that the soul could be liberated from its imprisonment by philosophy. The Greek mystery religions held that the immortal soul, imprisoned or entombed in a material body, was only liberated at death. More recently, the philosopher René Descartes (1596–1650) developed a similar position which defined human nature in terms of a physical body and immortal soul.[15]

This popular view of human nature, reflected in some Christian theologians, drew a distinction between a physical human 'body' and an immaterial human 'soul' (Latin: *anima*). Humans, it was argued, were distinguished from all other animals and inanimate objects by the possession of this immaterial immortal soul, which was liberated from the body at the moment of death. This approach was held to be justified on biblical grounds, in that the New Testament generally speaks of 'body and soul', and occasionally of 'body, soul and spirit'. References to the 'body' were understood by some older Christian writers to refer to the physical and material parts of humanity, whereas the 'soul' was understood as an immaterial and eternal spiritual entity which merely resided within the human body.

Yet it is widely agreed that this is not how the writers of the Bible understood these ideas. The notion of an immaterial soul was a secular Greek concept, not a biblical notion. The Old Testament conceives of humanity 'as an animated body and not as an incarnate soul'.[16] The biblical vision of humanity was that of a single entity, an inseparable psychosomatic unit with many facets or aspects. 'Soul' is an Anglo-Saxon term used to translate a variety of biblical terms, often having the general sense of 'life'. Thus the Hebrew word *nephesh*, translated as 'soul' in some older English Bibles, really means a 'living being'.

We find the same pattern in the New Testament. In his letters, Paul does not use terms such as 'flesh' and 'spirit' to refer to parts of the human body; rather they are to be seen as different modes of human existence. As the New Testament scholar James Dunn points out, Paul adopts an 'aspective', not a 'partitive', understanding of terms such as 'soul', 'flesh' and 'body'. 'Paul's conception of the human person is of a being who functions within several dimensions.'[17] To 'live according to the flesh' does not mean being directed by some specific part of the body, but simply to live at a purely human level.

Modern neuroscience has no place for the idea of a 'soul', understood as some immaterial part of the body. Neither does the Christian Bible. The 'soul-body' dualism lives on in popular culture, both secular and Christian. Yet the best view – found in both contemporary neuroscience and Christian theology – is to think of humanity as a physical unity: a single body, not a 'body and soul'.[18]

So how does this affect Christian thinking about personal identity and the hope of heaven – areas in which the idea of an immortal 'soul' might seem to be useful? Most Christian theologians frame their understanding of both identity and hope in relational terms. It is a way of thinking that is rooted in the Bible and sees a believer's identity as rooted in and sustained by their relationship with God. Each of us exists within a network of relationships: parents, children, relatives and friends. Our social identity is framed in terms of these relationships. That is one of the reasons why the theme of being 'remembered' by God is so important. We do not need the idea of a 'soul' to make sense of this idea; the concept of a relationship works perfectly well, and has been reappropriated since the First World War within both philosophy and theology to help articulate our understanding of our personal identity as human beings.[19]

Why We Cannot Stop Talking about God

Whether you think Christianity is right or wrong, there is no getting away from one of its core ideas – that we are in some way hardwired to think about, even long for, God. It is an idea that is set out in the opening paragraph of what is now increasingly regarded as the most important theological text in Western Christianity: Augustine of Hippo's *Confessions*, written between 397 and 400. Here is the prayer in which Augustine sets out this idea: 'You have made us for yourself, and our hearts are restless until they find their rest in you.'[20]

This idea of a 'natural desire for God'[21] has been developed in all sorts of ways within the Christian tradition – such as Pascal's idea of a God-shaped 'abyss' within human nature which is too deep to be satisfied by anything less than God, or C.S. Lewis's idea of a deep sense of yearning for significance which both originates from and leads back to God.[22] But the basic idea is simple: belief in God, like the phenomenon of religion itself, is natural. The Christian narrative tells us about a natural desire for God; a scientific narrative tells us about a desire for God that is natural. It is not difficult to see how these narratives can be interwoven at this point.

The rise of the 'Age of Reason' saw this view challenged in a number of ways. Many argued that religion was imposed upon people. Far from being something natural, it was something that was demanded of us by our culture, or which arose from pressures of social conformity. Yet there are now strong indications that religion is something natural. That does not make it right or wrong. Where rationalism held that religion arose through the 'sleep of reason' – in other words, through the suspension of normal human critical and rational faculties – there is now a growing consensus that religion is best understood as a natural phenomenon, a cognitively natural human activity which arises through – not in spite of – natural human ways of thinking.[23]

There are many fascinating questions that need to be explored arising from this recognition of natural religious tendencies. First, suppose we grant that religious beliefs arise naturally in human cognitive development. Is this good news or bad news for theism or atheism? The jury is out on this one, although I personally think that it works more in theism's favour. Second, does a natural inclination towards religion imply that theism is natural? After all, 'religion' takes many forms (it is not an empirical notion),[24] and theism is one of them. And third, how do people move from this 'natural religion' to a specific religious tradition – for example, Christianity? Older discussions of these issues may still retain some of their importance,[25] but it is clear that the whole field has now moved on significantly.

The empirical discipline which has explored this topic is a relatively new arrival on the scene. The term 'cognitive science of religion', introduced by the Oxford scholar Justin Barrett (born 1971), has come to designate approaches to the study of religion that are derived from the cognitive sciences. One of the basic empirical findings of this school of thought is that religion arises through normal processes of thought, not in opposition to them.[26] It is a natural aspect of being human, whether it is right or wrong. Religion is natural, in that it arises from human cognitive processes that are automatic, unconscious and not dependent on culture.

The core narrative of Christianity and Judaism speaks of humanity being created 'in the image of God', with some kind of homing instinct for its Creator. The emerging scientific narrative speaks of religion as cognitively natural human activity. These narratives are not the same. But they are clearly related. Might the notion of humanity bearing God's image map onto cognitive accounts of natural religious instincts? There are clearly important possibilities for dialogue here.

These findings have led to some surprising conclusions. Thus Robert McCauley, Director of the Center for Mind, Brain and Culture at Emory University, has argued that, while religion is a natural outcome of human cognitive processes, the natural sciences are not.[27] McCauley's point is that both science and theology involve abstract formulations that are seriously counterintuitive and require cultural support. This leads McCauley to conclude that science depends more fundamentally than religion on institutional and cultural support. If civilisation were to collapse, religion would persist, whereas science would have to be rebuilt.

McCauley also draws the important and potentially controversial conclusion that this approach to religion suggests that people with certain cognitive impairments – such as autism or any autistic spectrum conditions – will find religion to be 'largely inscrutable' and 'cognitively challenging'.[28] In other words, they just will not get what religion is all about. A recent empirical study appears to confirm this conclusion, finding that 'mentalizing deficits' associated with the autistic spectrum, which are more commonly found in men than in women, may undermine this intuitive cognitive support for religion.[29] It remains to be seen whether this is confirmed by more detailed studies and what the implications of this might be for contemporary discussions about religion and atheism.

This cognitive approach to religion unquestionably helps us understand why religion is ubiquitous in human culture: religion is so common within and across cultures because of its 'cognitive naturalness'. C.S. Lewis may have overstated things when he suggested that the human search for meaning was as natural as sexual desire or physical hunger and thirst. But you can see what he was getting at, and why the new cognitive approaches to the origins of religion reinforce his point.[30] The origins of religious belief do not lie so much in cultural or social conditions, as in the intuitions that arise from normally developing and functioning human cognitive systems.[31]

This strongly suggests that the secular humanist and New Atheist visions for a totally secular human world are simply unrealistic, in that religion will naturally re-emerge, even where it is suppressed.[32] It also suggests that non-religious people possess natural capacities and tendencies which might otherwise lead to religion, but which have either not yet been activated by any triggers in their environment or experience, or been suppressed by social or cultural pressures.

So why are we hardwired in this way? Nobody really knows,

and it is tempting to present somewhat speculative 'just so' stories as if they were genuine explanations.

But before we can offer a Darwinian explanation of the origins of religion, we need to determine whether religion is biologically adaptive or not. Does religion help us to survive? Some scholars argue that there is no obvious adaptive function to religion,[33] while others hold that religion can clearly be understood in adaptationist terms.[34] There is simply no scholarly consensus on this matter at present.[35]

Unfortunately, that has not stopped some New Atheist writers from presenting their own somewhat trenchant views on the nature and value of religion as if they were the solid findings of reputable science. In *The God Delusion*, Richard Dawkins declares that religion is non-adaptive and damages people. If religious beliefs are adaptive in any sense, he insists, it is only in that they act successfully as cultural parasites within their human hosts. Yet his analysis is conspicuously lacking in empirical engagement of any kind. As the leading evolutionary theorist David Sloan Wilson argued, *The God Delusion* suggests that Dawkins 'is just another angry atheist, trading on his reputation as an evolutionist and spokesperson for science to vent his personal opinions about religion'.[36]

Yet there is a point that needs further comment here. If religion is natural, what does this have to say about the movement that calls itself 'humanism'?

Why 'Humanism' Needs to Find a New Name for Itself

From about 1983 to 1988, I spent a lot of my professional life studying the emergence and intellectual characteristics of Renaissance humanism, especially in the great cities of Switzerland in the first decades of the sixteenth century.[37] It was a wonderful experience, in which I came to admire – and even to share – some of the key beliefs and aspirations of the great humanists of that age, such as Erasmus of Rotterdam (1466–1536). I shared their belief in the importance of *studia humanitatis* ('humane studies' – what we would now call the 'humanities'), especially grammar, rhetoric, poetry, moral philosophy and history. In the Renaissance, a humanist was someone who valued the humanities and recognised their transformative potential, both for individuals and for culture as a whole. It was easy to see why they believed that European culture could be renewed by a return to the wisdom of the past, as found in the writings and architectural styles of classical Rome and Athens.[38]

There was no particular hostility towards religion within Renaissance humanism, although Erasmus and other humanists of his age delighted in lampooning the more ridiculous aspects of the institutional Church. Anyone who bothers to read Erasmus's commentaries on the New Testament or his landmark *Enchiridion Militis Christiani* ('Handbook of the Christian Soldier') will discern his love of God and his belief that religion, when properly implemented, was of enormous cultural importance.[39]

So why do we now think of humanism as anti-religious? Why do people now use the word 'humanism' to refer to a worldview that rejects God? After all, the Renaissance invented the word 'humanist' and it meant nothing like this. The answer is that one specific form of humanism – an explicitly *secular* humanism – gained the cultural ascendancy in the West during the twentieth century, leading people to equate 'humanism' and 'secular humanism'. This transformation in the cultural understanding of humanism was primarily due to Paul Kurtz (1925–2012), one of America's most prominent secular humanists.[40] Kurtz was instrumental in reshaping American humanism in a specifically secular direction during the late 1970s and early 1980s, largely by suppressing its historic religious origins and continuing religious associations and commitments.

Kurtz disliked the original American 'Humanist Manifesto' (1933), which made specific approving reference to religious humanism and was drafted by a range of individuals, including many religious figures.[41] Kurtz vigorously advocated a more secular form of humanism and established the 'Council for Secular Humanism' to lobby for a radical change in direction of the American Humanist Association. He was clearly successful: most people now tend to think of 'humanism' as *secular* humanism', having lost sight of the rich range of possibilities – many of which are religious – that were once associated with the term. Kurtz was one of the two primary authors of 'Humanist Manifesto II' (1973), setting out a vision for a form of humanism that was systematically evacuated of religious possibilities and affirmations.

I have no problem with anyone using the phrase 'secular humanism' to refer to this movement. But this must never be confused with the generous and noble vision of humanism we find in Erasmus and the leading figures of the Renaissance. Erasmus would be appalled at the dogmatism and anti-religious tone of this more recent variant of the movement he once so proudly represented. Given Renaissance humanism's love of the humanities, it is shocking to realise how far the movement has lost its intellectual and cultural bearings when so many of its representatives are scientific imperialists who dismiss the humanities as irrelevant.

Mary Midgley, who clearly considers herself to be a non-theistic humanist, makes an important point about how an aggressively anti-theistic humanism can pull the rug out from under itself. In an important essay entitled 'The Paradox of Humanism', Midgley points out the vulnerability of reductive forms of humanism which eliminate the transcendent in the mistaken belief that this safeguards the human.[42] Humanism, she argues, exists to 'celebrate and increase the glory of human life', without having to express any devotion towards any entities outside it – such as God. But as soon as anyone starts to eliminate those entities, 'valuable elements in human life' begin to unravel. 'The center begins to bleed.' Why? Because the 'patterns essential to human life turn out to be ones that cannot be altogether contained within it'. As Midgley puts it, 'to be fully human seems to involve being interested in other things as well as human ones, and sometimes more than human ones'.

But the new cognitive science of religion raises a much deeper question. The cognitive science of religion tells us that humans are naturally religious. So if it is natural to be religious, how can any form of humanism be *opposed* to religion? It is time to suggest that 'secular humanism' needs to name itself for what it really is and abandon any pretentions to stand in the noble tradition of Erasmus and the Renaissance. Any form of humanism rests on an understanding of what human nature really is – and what longings, desires and aspirations are naturally human. A Christian humanist declares that humanity finds its true goal in finding God. A secular humanist declares that humanity finds its true goal in rejecting God. But to pretend that 'humanism' is *necessarily* 'secular humanism' is indefensible. It is surely time to move on. Christian humanism is alive and well, even if secular humanism pretends it does not – and cannot – exist.

The Dark Side of Human Nature

There are some things that are not true, but I wish that they were true. Probably because I am an academic, I often want to cling to the charming but rather naïve view that human beings are essentially good. I would like to think that if there is anything wrong with people, it can be sorted out by educating them properly. After all, education is about more than providing people with skills to earn a living; it is about making them into better human beings. It is a noble vision for education, and one that I admire. Yet, deep down, I know that it is not that simple. In fact, it is probably just wrong.

We all know about the darker side of human nature, even if we prefer not to talk about it, perhaps fearing where such thoughts might lead us. Any worldview which fails to do justice to this fundamental ambiguity within human nature ends up causing massive cognitive dissonance, as the harsh realities of observation and experience obstinately refuse to fit the neat little theoretical box.

When I was younger, I happily accepted the Enlightenment's

worldview of the constant improvement of the human condition through science and technology. I do not any more – not because I have lapsed into some kind of irrationality, but simply because the evidence so strongly suggests it is wrong. I share the views of the cultural theorist Terry Eagleton, who describes the 'dream of untrammelled human progress' as a 'bright-eyed superstition', a fairy tale which lacks any rigorous or defensible evidential base. 'If ever there was a pious myth and a piece of credulous superstition, it is the liberal-rationalist belief that, a few hiccups apart, we are all steadily en route to a finer world.'[43]

What sort of things does Eagleton have in mind? Rather a lot, to judge from his analysis, most of which relates to the twentieth century. If humanity were on an upward trend, surely we would have been seen at our best by that stage? If we are constantly improving, things ought to be really great by now. Yet the reality does not fit this narrative at all. Humanity has failed to progress. We may know more than we used to, but we seem to end up using this knowledge badly.

The Second World War provides us with ample (if unsettling and sobering) food for thought. The significance of the Nazi extermination camps for any account of human nature can hardly be overlooked. They prompted George Steiner's famous observation that someone could read great poetry or play great music in the evening, and then take part in mass murder on an industrial scale the next day. 'We know that a man can read Goethe or Rilke in the evening, that he can play Bach and Schubert, and go to his day's work at Auschwitz in the morning.'[44]

While I personally doubt if many of those running the death camps read Rilke or Goethe, or were even capable of playing Bach or Schubert, Steiner's point remains important. German poetry and music – emblematic of one of Europe's most sophisticated and humane cultures – ultimately failed to humanise. Or we might think of the infamous Wannsee Conference of January 1942, which did so much to prepare the way for the extermination of the Jews at camps like Auschwitz.[45] The majority of those present at that meeting of Nazi technocrats were highly educated, with doctorates or medical qualifications from German universities. Once more, education had failed to humanise.

Now these observations prove nothing. But they do point to a pattern – not a consistent pattern of pure evil, and certainly not of pure goodness, but of *human complexity* and *ambiguity*. My own view, adopted with regret in the light of the evidence, is that simplistic narratives of fundamental human goodness and inevitable progress have to be rejected as myths, representing a blind faith in a utopian human nature which bears little obvious relation to what we see in history and culture, especially in the darker moments of the history of Europe in the twentieth century. We need a better narrative if we are to do justice to reality and face up to its implications.

We need to draw on a richer, if more disturbing, view of reality to help us here in our conversation about human selfishness and evil – such as Carl Jung's notion of the 'shadow',[46] or Richard Dawkins' notion of the 'selfish gene', or the Christian notion of 'original sin' – which boldly faces up to this disquieting aspect of human nature that the 'Age of Reason' understandably but wrongly preferred to gloss over.[47]

In his influential work *The Selfish Gene*, Dawkins notes that what he terms 'gene selfishness' will normally 'give rise to selfishness in individual behaviour'. Humans struggle to resist the 'tyranny of the selfish replicators',[48] which predisposes them to behave in selfish ways. While Dawkins believes that human beings are able to resist such 'gene selfishness', his point about our innate predisposition towards selfish behaviour is an important corrective to naïve views about human goodness. For Dawkins, we might be able to make ourselves good – but this happens by fighting against our genic inheritance.

One of the aspects of the Christian vision of reality that I have increasingly come to appreciate over the years is the notion of 'original sin'. This is often misunderstood and misrepresented;[49] when rightly understood, however, it offers a realistic account of human nature as morally ambiguous, capable of good, yet with a

tendency – even a propensity – to seek the lesser good or experience the lure of evil and fall into unhelpful patterns of habituation
and dependency. Original sin is not about personal fault or guilt,
but affirms the uncomfortable insight that human nature is
wounded and damaged and thus prone to think and act wrongly.
Perhaps it is no wonder that many Enlightenment writers were so
hostile towards this idea, which called into question its assumptions about the goodness and rationality of human nature. If
'man is the measure of all things' (Alexander Pope), what happens
if we are flawed?

That was the point that the Soviet dissident and novelist Aleksandr
Solzhenitsyn (1918–2008) made in his famous commencement
address at Harvard University in 1978. After his experiences of the
brutal political and intellectual repression of the Soviet Union,
Solzhenitsyn had no doubt about the limitations of human nature.
The dreadful events of the twentieth century made it clear to any
thinking person that the Enlightenment vision of humanity was a
delusion, a fiction with no counterpart in reality.

> It has made man the measure of all things on earth – imperfect
> man, who is never free of pride, self-interest, envy, vanity, and
> dozens of other defects. We are now paying for the mistakes which
> were not properly appraised at the beginning of the journey.[50]

The paradox is that we need human beings to expose the limitations of human nature, adopting a self-critical attitude which
challenges some core assumptions of our self-understanding.

The Christian faith gives us a critical lens through which to view
the complex motivations and mixed agendas of human beings. We
bear God's image, yet we are sinful. We are capable of good, just
as we are capable of evil. We often find ourselves trapped by our
own natures, ending up doing wrong rather than right and wondering what can be done to liberate ourselves from this dilemma.[51]
This way of thinking allows us to frame the complex picture we
see of human culture and history, characterised by aspirations to

greatness and goodness on the one hand, and oppression and violence on the other.

Earlier in this work, I suggested that science and religion were two of the greatest – if not *the* greatest – outcomes of human civilisation. But in the light of the above discussion, we need to ask a difficult and uncomfortable question. What happens when they go wrong? We are all human beings, with the strengths and weaknesses that this brings. It is great when science and religion work well. But since both are undertaken by human beings, both can go badly wrong. And let's be honest about this: *both do go wrong*.

When Science Goes Wrong

Is science a religion? Richard Dawkins is often asked this question, and has a standard answer: no. The sciences, he argues, have all the good points of religious belief and none of their bad points. They evoke a sense of wonder at reality and offer humanity uplift and inspiration. And they are immune from the problems of faith. It is a neat answer, and it makes sense if science at its best is compared with religion at its worst. But it is just not that simple. Scientists are human beings. And human beings naturally mess things up – including both science and religion. So let's try to tell a more reliable story.

Every scientist I know is aware of the problems that science faces in universities – relentless pressure to generate more research income and perform well in institutional league tables. Alongside these institutional pressures, some scientists – as human beings – long for fame and fortune. So should we be surprised that some scientists cheat and produce 'research papers' that turn out to be based on forged results? It is becoming a serious problem and many journals are tightening up their review processes as a result, following growing evidence of manipulation of the process by assumed and fabricated identities. I have no intention of discussing any of these cases in detail.[52] My point is simple and irrefutable.

Some scientists do bad things. But that does not make science bad. Like anything that human beings do, it can go wrong.

And science can go wrong in other ways – again, reflecting human evil, naïvety or downright stupidity. One of the greatest threats we face today is from weapons of mass destruction, such as nuclear weapons. Who invented these? *Scientists*. Now if someone were to use the flawed logic of Christopher Hitchens (a few members of group X do bad things, therefore group X is bad), you could write off science as morally disastrous and wicked. Since it spawned such evil, it must itself be evil. But everyone knows this is nonsense. Things are more complicated than this.

Let me give a case study which illustrates the problems, and then comment on it. When I was studying chemistry at Oxford back in the early 1970s, I frequently had to read the works of one of America's greatest scientists, Louis Frederick Fieser (1899–1977), as preparation for tutorials. Fieser, who became Professor of Chemistry at Harvard University in 1930, was famous for developing the artificial synthesis of a series of important naturally occurring compounds, including Vitamin K, necessary for blood coagulation.[53] His work also prepared the ground for the synthesis of steroids, such as cortisone, with important medical applications. He was clearly well regarded within the world of organic chemistry in those days and was referenced regularly and appreciatively in organic chemistry lectures I attended at Oxford.

Later, I discovered that Fieser invented something else that was not mentioned in those Oxford lectures. The United States had entered the Second World War following the bombing of Pearl Harbor on 7 December 1941. The Department of Defense soon realised that operational requirements in both the European and Pacific war theatres required the development of new chemical weapons. Fieser created what the Department of Defense was looking for on Valentine's Day 1942 at a secret Harvard war research laboratory. He invented napalm – a chemical gel which, once ignited, stuck to human bodies and could not be removed. It burned at high temperatures and could not be extinguished.[54] On the night of 9–10 March 1945, the US Air Force dropped 1,700 tons of napalm bombs on the city of Tokyo, causing massive loss of civilian life. It is thought that over 87,500 people died that night – an immediate loss of life greater than that caused by either of the atom bombs dropped a few months later on the cities of Hiroshima and Nagasaki.

So what are we to make of this? An aggressive ideological critic might argue that this demonstrates the fundamental immorality of science. I do not see it that way. It is just one of many signs of human failure and weakness, by which good things are abused and put to bad uses. That is what human beings are like. We need to be honest about the problem and face up to the fact that science *can be*, and as a matter of fact *is being*, abused. But that does not make science bad. If there is a problem, it lies deeper – in human nature itself.

And that is true of religion as well.

When Religion Goes Wrong

Religion can go wrong, and does go wrong. In 1932, William Temple (1881–1944) – then Archbishop of York, and later Archbishop of Canterbury – declared that what he called 'bad religion' was not only the most serious problem facing humanity in the modern world, but its chief enemy.

> Religion itself, when developed to real maturity, knows quite well that the first object of its condemnation is bad Religion, which is a totally different thing from irreligion, and can be a very much worse thing.[55]

Temple is right. Religion can turn bad. It can go wrong, and when it does, it must be challenged and changed. That is why Temple singled out the prophets of Israel and Jesus of Nazareth as reformers who called into question the religious conventions of their day.

Yet while Temple sees religion as something that *can go wrong*,

New Atheists such as Christopher Hitchens see it as something that *is intrinsically wrong.* Hitchens is clearly using an ideological, rather than an empirical, perceptual framework which conflates religiosity with irrationality, and irrationality with evil acts. Yes, religion can go wrong, invoking God's name to incite evil. But sadly, most human ideals get abused like this.

We need to inject a note of realism here. Just about anything that human beings do can go wrong. Science is no exception; neither is religion. Michael Shermer, a noted critic of religion, rightly points out that religion has been implicated in some tragedies and outrages such as holy wars. Yet it is more complicated than this. As Shermer insists, we need to tell the *full* story.

> However, for every one of these grand tragedies there are ten thousand acts of personal kindness and social good that go unreported . . . Religion, like all social institutions of such historical depth and cultural impact, cannot be reduced to an unambiguous good or evil.[56]

Science has been grossly abused – witness the forms of 'social Darwinism' which emerged in Nazi Germany, now widely condemned as an abomination yet seen as progressive by many social liberals at the time. I am perfectly prepared to accept that this is bad science, and not to judge science by its bastardisations. Both science and religion can spawn monsters. But they need not do so, nor should either be judged by its pathological forms. But there is a really interesting question here which secular humanists have overlooked. *What does bad religion tell us about humanity?*

Bernard Williams (1929–2003) has long been one of my favourite philosophers. From conversations around Oxford, I know I am not on my own here. His writings on ethics are always stimulating, especially his critique of the modern tendency to evaluate the moral standards of the past in terms of what we believe today.[57] Williams is hostile towards religion and dubious of its intellectual and moral virtues. However, his philosophical acuity leads him to pose an awkward question about human nature which has never been given its due weight by the secular humanist establishment. Since secular humanism believes that religious morality is based on a fiction, what does this tell us about human nature itself?

> For granted that religion's transcendental claim is false, human beings must have dreamed it, and we need an understanding of why this was the content of their dream. (Humanism – in the contemporary sense of a secularist and anti-religious movement – seems seldom to have faced fully a very immediate consequence of its own views; that this terrible thing, religion, is a *human* creation.)[58]

It is a point that will probably have occurred to the more reflective readers of the anti-religious tracts of the New Atheism, which portray human beings as morally good and rational people who are oppressed by religion. Yet there is an obvious problem here. Christopher Hitchens assures us that 'God did not create man in his own image. Evidently, it was quite the other way about.'[59] The point he hoped to make was that God is a human invention. Yet he unintentionally made a far more damaging admission: God looks like his human creators. And if God turns out to be a genocidal tyrant (as Hitchens colourfully, but somewhat improbably, suggests), then that is what we are like as well.

In scapegoating God or religion for the rational and moral failings of human beings, the New Atheism has exposed a serious incoherence in its own worldview. Everything that is wrong with the world, we are told, can be blamed on God or religion. But if God and religion are human inventions, then it is human beings – not some non-existent god – who are to blame for any evil and violence they cause. If God is evil and pernicious – as New Atheist writers assure us is indeed the case – then this God was invented by evil and pernicious human beings. If religion perverts us, we have merely perverted ourselves.

Now let me make it clear that I see no reason to share this puzzling notion that God is evil. But suppose – purely for the sake of argument – that the New Atheism is justified in asserting that this invented God is evil. If we create God in our own image, and this God is evil, what does that say about *us*? If there is no God, we cannot blame this non-existent God for human evil. The fault is ours alone. Our beliefs about God are a mirror which shows up what we are really like.

The only way out of this dilemma is to appeal to the moral dualism that underlies so many failed philosophies and religions of the past. This version of this flawed worldview holds that there are bad people who invent religion, and there are good people who oppose it. That is the philosophy that lies behind the 'Bright' – a frankly rather patronising self-designation for an atheist, unwisely endorsed by Richard Dawkins and Daniel Dennett, which rather unsubtly implied that everyone else was dim. Christopher Hitchens wisely repudiated this piece of arrogant nonsense and lambasted Dawkins and Dennett for their 'cringe-making proposal that atheists should conceitedly nominate themselves to be called "Brights"'.[60] But however unsatisfactory the idea of the 'Bright' may have been, it seemed the only way out of this lethal contradiction of the New Atheism's own making.

So where does this leave us? The philosopher John Gray insists that we need to be critical of human nature and recognise its limitations and aberrations. Yes, he declares, religion can go badly wrong.

> But the fault is not with religion, any more than science is to blame for the proliferation of weapons of mass destruction or medicine and psychology for the refinement of techniques of torture. The fault is in the intractable human animal.[61]

Perhaps we should not be surprised that some human animals are now actively seeking to overcome those limitations – not by retreating into an implausible world in which humanity is declared to be good, but by redirecting the evolutionary process.

Transcending Our Limits? Changing Our Natures?

Human beings have always dreamed of creating better worlds and better people. Mary Shelley's novel *Frankenstein* (1818) has become the archetypal statement of the dream of creating new life through technology, and the nightmare of what happens when this new life form turns against its creator.[62] H.G. Wells' novel *The Island of Doctor Moreau* (1896) explored more explicitly Darwinian themes – such as whether evolutionary processes can be short-circuited, allowing an immediate transition from animals to humans.

These dreams have now been given new energy by scientific and technological advances. Darwin, many argue, showed us how we evolved. Why can we not now take charge of the process and direct our own future evolution? Why should we not take charge of the gene pool and make sure that defects are excluded, thus ensuring the future of humanity? Since we understand so much about the human body, why should we not enhance its capacities, going far beyond our present capabilities and significantly extending our life expectancies?

Such questions have evoked deep cultural concerns about scientists playing at being God.[63] It is a criticism that is easily dismissed, but which cannot be ignored. If human beings were as rational and moral as we would like them to be, there might not be a serious problem. But human beings are very good at getting things wrong. And technology lets them mess things up in a way that might turn out to be irreversible. In this section, we will look at the emergence of the movement now known as 'transhumanism', and ask where this is taking us.

So what is transhumanism? Transhumanism can be described in a number of ways. The movement affirms both the possibility and desirability of fundamentally improving the human condition through applied reason, especially by developing and making widely available technologies to eliminate ageing and thus to enhance human intellectual, physical and psychological capacities.

This goal is to be achieved by the use of technology, which means studying the promises and potential dangers of technologies that will enable us to overcome our present fundamental human limitations. The transhumanist agenda thus goes beyond using technology for therapeutic purposes alone. Transhumanism argues for the *acceleration* of human evolution through technological enhancement.[64]

So is this Darwinian? Not really. Human evolution cannot be described in purely Darwinian terms, on account of the role of culture in enabling humanity to transcend its biological limitations. Darwinism certainly accounts for the biological evolution of humanity; the cultural evolution of humanity is probably better described using a Lamarckian model – in other words, in terms of intentional development.[65] Transhumanism sees no reason to wait for humanity to evolve further; it wants to take charge of the evolutionary process and construct a new humanity, including a new rationality, liberated from its original biological limitations.[66] Some transhumanists are optimistic that the human life span can be extended indefinitely through technology, in effect reviving classic ideas about a 'fountain of youth'.

Transhumanism is still an emerging movement, showing significant differences in emphasis and outlook within its ranks. It is still too early to evaluate it properly. However, it seems appropriate to note a question which is being widely discussed within the transhumanist movement itself. This is the question of 'existential risks', defined as risks that threaten the entire future of humanity.[67] Natural risks – such as asteroid impacts, supervolcanic eruptions, earthquakes or gamma-ray bursts – have always been present and will remain so. The new concern is that as humanity's powers expand, so will the scale of their potential consequences. An increasingly powerful humanity may make mistakes which threaten its own existence. After all, humanity has already developed the means for destroying itself, and can be expected to develop further such tools in the coming century.

Yet these 'anthropogenic existential risks' – that is, those caused by human activity – might not necessarily arise from war or terrorism. Some of the biggest existential risks will arise through potential future technological breakthroughs that may radically expand our ability to manipulate the external world or our own biology. The development of advanced forms of biotechnology and machine intelligence may have outcomes that we cannot predict and may not be able to control.

So will technological advance lead to wiser and better decisions than humanity has made in the recent past? Let's hope so. But our history is not reassuring at this point. We are not very good at learning from our mistakes. So does the enhancement of human technological possibilities mean that we need moral enhancement to be able to cope with the new challenges we face? Do we need to be rebooted morally? Ingmar Persson (University of Gothenburg) and Julian Savulescu (Oxford University) have raised concerns which need to be addressed. Modern technology provides us with the means to cause our downfall, yet our natural moral psychology does not provide us with the means to prevent this. Therefore, they argue, the moral enhancement of humankind is necessary if we are to find a way out of this predicament.[68]

This worries many of us. Who will carry out this enhancement? Who will reprogramme us? There is a clear and uncomfortable dilemma here, in that these 'moral enhancements' will need to be developed and chosen by morally questionable human beings who could easily adapt them to advance their own vested interests and concerns.

Perhaps we do need a new morality. Then again, maybe we need to revisit older options and adapt them to the new situations we may face. We face difficult questions as human beings, and science is not going to answer them on its own. We will come back to that question in a later chapter, when we reflect on the basis of ethics.

7

The Quest for Meaning and the Limits of Science

Scientists are human beings. Because they are scientists, they have highly developed ideas about how the universe works. Because they are human beings, they also have views on deeper questions such as, amongst many other things, the meaning of their own individual existence and how to live a good life. But what happens if science cannot answer these deeper questions? In the end, most scientists end up believing rather a lot of things that lie beyond the scope of the scientific method. These are things that really matter to us – not the shallow truths of reason, but the deep existential truths about who we are and why we are here.

Does Science Have Limits?

Over the years, I have come to share the widely held view that there are limits to what science can tell us. These are not arbitrary and self-serving limits imposed upon science by politicians, religious leaders or cultural commentators who feel threatened by the natural sciences. They are intrinsic to the scientific method itself. If science is science – and not something else – then there are certain domains of knowledge and opinion that lie beyond its scope. Science maintains both its integrity and its distinct identity by focusing on what it can investigate empirically, fully recognising that this means some larger questions of life will remain beyond its scope. Albert Einstein rightly declared that 'science can only ascertain what *is*, not what *should be*, and outside of its domain value judgements of all kinds remain necessary'.[1]

Now not everyone agrees with this. Some, such as the philosopher Bertrand Russell, argue that there are, as a matter of fact, no limits to the scope of the natural sciences. 'Whatever knowledge is attainable, must be attained by scientific methods; and what science cannot discover, mankind cannot know.'[2] This neat little overstatement has never persuaded me. For a start, the logic is deeply flawed. 'What science cannot discover, mankind cannot know' is not actually a *scientific* statement at all. So if it is true, it is false (if you see what I mean). It is like the irritating enigma of the slogan on the college noticeboard: 'Every statement on this board is false.' More worryingly, what about the great truths of logic and mathematics – fields that Russell knew very well – which offer proofs of an intellectual rigour that exceed anything that the natural sciences can offer? Surely we can know those?

In this chapter, we shall reflect on whether there are limits to science and what the implications of this might be. To begin with, we shall consider 'ultimate questions' and reflect on how we can answer them – if, of course, we can answer them at all.

Ultimate Questions: Why We Need Answers

Let's go back to the great Spanish philosopher José Ortega y Gasset (1883–1955), with whom we engaged earlier in this work. As we noted earlier, Ortega makes an important observation concerning the place of natural sciences in human culture:

> Scientific truth is characterized by its precision and the certainty of its predictions. But science achieves these admirable qualities at the cost of remaining on the level of secondary concerns, leaving ultimate and decisive questions untouched.[3]

Ortega points out that, because scientists are human beings, they want – they *need* – to go further than science can legitimately take us. Science nourishes part – but only a small part – of the human quest for wisdom, knowledge and understanding. If science, using its proper methods, comes to a halt at a certain point, we as human beings long to go further and explore what lies beyond the scientific horizon.

> How can anyone live if we silence these ultimate dramatic questions? Where does the world come from, and where is it going? What is the supreme power of the cosmos? What is the essential meaning of life? We cannot breathe if we are confined to a realm of secondary and intermediate themes. We need a comprehensive perspective [*una perspectiva íntegra*], with primary and ultimate levels, not a fractured landscape, or a truncated horizon which lacks the awe evoked by infinite distances.[4]

Because we are human beings, we cannot avoid asking 'ultimate questions'. It is an insight reinforced by the cognitive science of religion. And we have three main options here. We can choose to ignore these questions; we can try to answer them using science itself, pushing it to its limits; or we can use multiple maps or narratives to flesh out a purely scientific description. Let's consider each of these three possibilities.

1. Ignoring ultimate questions

First, we can either dismiss or ignore these ultimate questions about meaning and purpose. We might agree that they might be interesting. In fact, they might even be important. But if they cannot be answered, why worry about them? The moment we step outside the safe world of science, we find ourselves in the wastelands of philosophy or theology. Who wants to go there? Let's limit ourselves to the world of what has been proved and ignore what lies beyond it.

It is attractive to some. It is seen as a safe option, following the stern intellectual precept of the mathematician W.K. Clifford (1845–79): 'It is wrong always, everywhere, and for anyone, to believe anything upon insufficient evidence.'[5] It is a noble statement, with which I agree entirely in principle. But it is hard to make it work in the real world. It is now seen as little more than a platitude. Why?

For a start, there is a major problem with that elusive word 'insufficient'. Who decides what counts as sufficient evidence and what does not? A judgement, itself lying beyond the reach of evidence, is required in order to determine how much evidence is required to legitimise a belief. Clifford was a mathematician, used to working within a world of theorems in which conclusive proof was a realistic possibility. But outside the world of mathematics and logic, things are a lot more ambiguous and fuzzy.

In fact, this approach turns out to have limited relevance even within the natural sciences, despite its initial promise. What about rival theories that are empirically equivalent – that is to say, deemed to be equally supported by the available evidence? We have already seen that two distinguished Oxford biologists – Richard Dawkins and Denis Noble – set out diametrically opposed approaches to the causality of genes, which cannot be resolved experimentally (see pages 119–20). But other examples are easily given. For instance, why did the Copenhagen interpretation of quantum theory win out over hidden variable theories or the De Broglie–Bohm theory, when these three are empirically equivalent? Why did the Copenhagen theory gain most support, when it was no more successful at explaining the evidence than its rivals? The answer lies in the contingencies of history, not the scientific evidence itself.[6]

Furthermore, as the modern debates about cosmology indicate, many theories that were once believed to be well evidenced eventually turn out to be inadequate or completely wrong. We may think, for excellent reasons, that something is right *today*; in the future, it may be seen to be wrong. And, for the same reasons, we may think that something is wrong *today*; in the future, it may be seen to be right. The recognition of the difficulties with the seemingly simple idea of a 'crucial experiment' and of the general under-determination of theory by evidence dates from after Clifford's time.[7] Clifford's intention in formulating this principle was excellent; its application has turned out to be rather more complicated and ambivalent.

In practice, human beings tend to work with more pragmatic criteria of justification than those allowed by Clifford. It is not because people are fools. Quite the reverse; it is because they can see the obvious problems with his approach. The Harvard psychologist William James emphasised that we have to search for truth in a world in which the evidence is profoundly ambivalent and open to multiple interpretations. If the true goal of intellectual enquiry is to identify true beliefs rather than simply avoid error, then we will sometimes have to take the risk of believing something to be true without compelling evidence that this is the case.[8] It may be noted here that Darwin's approach in *The Origin of Species* (1859) is much more supportive of James's viewpoint than Clifford's, especially in regard to coping with the counter-evidence that Darwin knew posed a significant threat to his theory.[9]

And, perhaps most importantly, what about great questions of meaning and ethics which are integral to human existence? These clearly lie beyond the scope of Clifford's austere and severely limited account of the legitimate outcomes of human rationality. We can, of course, close these discussions down and declare them to be improper. We can be like Richard Dawkins and declare that taking non-scientific answers to 'ultimate questions' seriously is merely 'resorting to superstition'.[10] Yet pronouncing this kind of rationalist incantation does not solve anything. As William James pointed out, we still end up having to make big decisions – usually moral – and need to base these on *something*. We cannot opt out of life and the value-based decisions that we need to make.

2. Hoping science can answer ultimate questions

The second approach concedes the importance of such ultimate questions, but argues that science will *eventually* be capable of answering all of life's fundamental questions – provided that they really do have answers. If reality is like a landscape, there may be parts of it which are beyond the reach of science *at the moment*. But eventually, science will be able to answer all of life's questions. It is just a matter of time. And if science cannot answer a question, then there is no answer to be given.

Richard Dawkins holds that science can answer all of life's great questions – and if it cannot answer them today, it will be able to answer them in the future. Since science discloses no meaning to the universe, the only reasonable conclusion is that there is no meaning to find. His comment is worth repeating: 'The universe we observe has precisely the properties we should expect if there is, at bottom, no design, no purpose, no evil and no good, nothing but blind pitiless indifference.'[11]

Dawkins tries to resolve this problem of meaning by developing the idea of a 'Universal Darwinism' which inflates Darwin's provisional scientific account of the origin of species into a grand metanarrative, able to answer ultimate questions about meaning and morality.[12] Dawkins himself uses this informing Darwinian metanarrative to generate his own moral values, some of which have generated considerable controversy. In 2014, he declared categorically that it would be 'immoral' for a mother to allow a pregnancy to continue if it was known that the foetus had Down's syndrome. Dawkins issued this piece of moral guidance in response to a woman who admitted she would face 'a real ethical dilemma' if she became pregnant and learned that the baby would be born with the disorder. Dawkins tweeted what many thought to be an insensitive and callous response: 'Abort it and try again. It would be immoral to bring it into the world if you have the choice.'[13] Yet Dawkins' moral judgement – although perhaps delivered with what might seem to some to be indecent haste, and widely ridiculed – was perfectly consistent with the Darwinian metanarrative that informed it.

So how reliable is that metanarrative? To its critics, this represents a metaphysically bloated 'Darwinism', recontexualised within twenty-first-century debates.[14] Darwin has been transfigured into an iconographic figurehead of viewpoints which he did not advocate and for which he probably would have had little sympathy. This 'Darwinian ideology' represents what George Steiner provocatively termed a 'substitute theology' – a system of belief whose structures and aspirations are religious 'in strategy and in effect' (though not, of course, in name).[15]

The major difficulty that Dawkins faces here concerns the transition from Darwin's provisional and corrigible theory of natural selection to a universally valid narrative of meaning. After all, Dawkins himself rightly emphasised the provisionality of Darwin's approach, which it shares with all other scientific theories. 'New facts may come to light which will force our successors of the twenty-first century to abandon Darwinism or modify it beyond recognition.'[16] To give him due credit, Dawkins rightly realised that, if science was to have deeper cultural traction, it needed to develop a deeper and broader narrative about reality, from which moral values could be developed.

One of the most thoughtful critics of the view that science can provide robust and reliable answers to questions of value and meaning is the Nobel Laureate Sir Peter Medawar (1915–87), a 'paragon of rationalism'[17] whom Richard Dawkins once described as the 'chief spokesman for the scientist in the modern world'.[18] Medawar achieved respect far beyond the scientific community on account of his willingness to engage creatively and constructively with the humanities, recognising the respective strengths and weaknesses of every intellectual discipline – including his own. Medawar had no hesitation in denouncing mystical nonsense wherever and whenever he found it – as in his celebrated dismissal of the French palaeontologist Pierre Teilhard de Chardin's mystical views of evolution, which he regarded as being credible only to those incapable of rational thought.[19]

Yet Medawar was aware of the danger of exaggerating the reach of either science or reason. 'Young scientists', he once wrote, must never mistake 'the necessity of reason for the sufficiency of reason'. Rationalism, he declared, 'falls short of answering the many simple and childlike questions' that people ask about their origins and purposes. 'It is not to rationalism that we look for answers to these simple questions because rationalism chides the endeavour to look at all.'[20]

Medawar's position on the limits of science diverges radically from Dawkins'. Medawar drew a distinction between 'transcendent' questions, which he thought were best left to religion and metaphysics, and questions about the organisation and structure of the material universe, which were dealt with authoritatively by the natural sciences. Medawar insisted that it is 'very likely' that there are limits to science, given 'the existence of questions that science cannot answer, and that no conceivable advance of science would empower it to answer'.[21]

Some – such as those whom Medawar dismisses as 'doctrinaire positivists' – would ridicule these questions, dismissing them as 'nonquestions or pseudoquestions such as only simpletons ask and only charlatans of one kind or another profess to be able to answer'.[22] Such a glib response, Medawar suggests, leaves people 'empty and dissatisfied'. These questions are both real and important to those who ask them.

3. Using multiple maps of meaning to answer ultimate questions

The third approach, advocated in this work, is to recognise the importance and legitimacy of these 'ultimate questions' and use multiple maps of meaning to offer an enriched – but not an *inflated* – vision of reality, engaging both cognitive and existential questions. It is part of our human nature to seek a richer and deeper vision of reality which enables us to do justice to the complexity of the world and live out meaningful and fulfilling lives. Even Sigmund Freud, who may well have been the least religious person of the twentieth century, knew that there was some deep instinct in human nature that causes us to seek meaning and transcendence. We look for reassurance that, however fragmented our world of experience may seem at times, there is a richer narrative which holds things together in a coherent web of meaning. That is what the philosopher Ludwig Wittgenstein was getting at when he declared that 'to believe in God means to see that life has a meaning'.[23]

As I have made clear throughout this work, I have found that the Christian faith offers a persuasive and deeply satisfying enrichment of a scientific engagement with reality. While I give some of the reasons underlying my judgement in this work, I do not expect all of my readers to agree with me. After all, my position can be criticised on perfectly reasonable grounds. The most important of these, in my view, is the perception that Christianity rests on a less secure evidential foundation than the natural sciences.

I concede this point, although I must point out that it needs qualification in two important respects. For a start, we need to remind ourselves of the provisionality of *all* scientific judgements. What is accepted today may be rejected tomorrow, as further evidence becomes available. Furthermore, *any* worldview – including Dawkins' metaphysically inflated 'Darwinism' – lies beyond empirical verification. As the writings of Thomas Aquinas, G.K. Chesterton and C.S. Lewis make clear, Christianity may certainly be *justified*, in that good reasons may be given for accepting its ideas; it cannot, however, be *proved* to be right. But then neither can atheism. Or Buddhism. Or anything that goes beyond the domain of the empirical – including any quest for meaning in life or for a viable morality. The human condition is such that only shallow truths can be proved; the deepest truths lie beyond absolute proof – but may nevertheless be trusted.

In the end, we have to recognise that all three of the approaches just outlined will cause – or certainly *ought* to cause – those who hold them a certain degree of intellectual discomfort. None of them are self-evidently right, despite the bullying rhetoric and condescending tone of some cultural commentators with vested interests in the matter. All of them face intellectual challenges which are easily ignored, dismissed or misrepresented by earnest ideologues, yet which are rightly troubling to genuine seekers after truth. Yet we have to make a choice between them and will have to make that choice *believing* that it is justified. That is not necessarily a bad thing. As the literary critic Terry Eagleton noted, 'We hold many beliefs that have no unimpeachably rational justification, but are nonetheless reasonable to entertain.'[24]

In this book, I have set out a proposed narrative of enrichment, reconnecting science and faith. This, I must emphasise, denies nothing about the empirical sciences, except any spurious claims to exclusivism or finality on their part. That may be in conflict with the *scientism* characteristic of the New Atheism, but it is certainly not in conflict with *science*, which has always been willing to recognise its limits, knowing that it raises questions that transcend its capacity to answer them – 'questions that science cannot answer and that no conceivable advance of science would empower it to answer' (Medawar).

So does engaging such questions mean abandoning science? No. It simply means acknowledging and respecting its limits and not forcing it to become something other than science. Christianity is able to enrich this vision of science – not by proposing itself as a competing science, but by being what it is and doing what it does best, which is raising and answering ultimate questions. Of course, it does much more than this – but it does this *distinctively* and it does it well. And it needs to be done.

The important point here is that science and faith can thus provide us with different, yet ultimately complementary, maps of human identity. As Mary Midgley suggests, Christian theology offers us a mental map which helps us to make sense of at least some aspects of the worlds within us and around us – and, I think I must emphasise, to make sense of the scientific enterprise in particular. That is the point made by William Inge (1860–1954), a former Lady Margaret Professor of Divinity at Cambridge University. God is not something that we prove by direct observation, as if God was a hitherto unnoticed moon orbiting the planet Mars. Rather, God is the ground of our existence and understanding in the first place.

> Rationalism tries to find a place for God in its picture of the world. But God . . . cannot be fitted into a diagram. He is rather the canvas on which the picture is painted, or the frame in which it is set.[25]

For Inge, the Christian faith offers a conceptual framework, a mental map, which both accommodates and encourages the scientific enterprise, as well as illuminates our understanding of the world and ourselves within it. We all need a canvas like that – something which can bear the weight of the world around us and our experiences within us, supporting and holding together a richly textured reality.

What about the question of *meaning*? Let's begin by reflecting on why this is so important to human beings, and then explore whether science can help us with this grand question of life.

Why meaning matters to us

There is now a firm consensus within the psychological research literature that having a sense of meaning to life matters to human well-being.[26] The ability to discern meaning within the complex pattern of events in our lives and in the world helps us to cope with ambiguity and bewilderment. The great Harvard psychologist William James made this point in an 1895 lecture entitled 'Is Life Worth Living?' James pointed out that a belief in the meaningfulness of life helped establish a resilience in the face of life's challenges. 'Believe that life is worth living, and your belief will help create the fact.'[27]

Many readers will be familiar with the work of Viktor Frankl (1905–97), an Austrian neurologist and psychiatrist who was interned in a series of Nazi concentration camps during the Second World War. His experiences in those camps led him to realise the importance of discerning meaning if people were to cope with traumatic and seemingly meaningless situations.[28] Frankl argued that survival in these situations depended on maintaining the will to live, which in turn depended on the discernment of meaning and purpose in even the most demoralising situations which were directly experienced as threats to survival and self-preservation. Those who coped best were those who had frameworks of meaning that enabled them to accommodate their experiences within their mental maps. In making this point, Frankl quoted the German philosopher Nietzsche: the person 'who has a why to live for can bear with almost any how'.

The role of theories of meaning – especially religious beliefs – in enabling people to cope with negative situations is thus well established, and its implications for dealing with those who face traumatic life events are being explored in pastoral care and nursing, to mention only two important fields.[29] There is a growing realisation of the importance of 'meaning-focused coping', in which people draw on their 'beliefs (e.g., religious, spiritual, or beliefs about justice), values (e.g., "mattering"), and existential goals (e.g., purpose in life or guiding principles) to motivate and sustain coping and well-being during a difficult time'.[30] Religious faith generates resilience – an ability to cope with situations that transcends a mere ability to understand.

In an influential study, the social psychologist Roy Baumeister summarised the findings of the research literature under four broad headings.[31] People feel a need to make sense of their lives and search for four main types of meaning: purpose, values, a sense of efficacy and a basis for self-worth. Although these four main needs for meaning could, in principle, be derived from a single source, empirical research suggests that people tend to draw meaning from multiple sources, including religion, work, family and personal relationships. These multiple sources of meaning in life protect individuals from the threat of meaninglessness, in that the erosion of one such source of meaning – for example, through a breakdown in family life – does not entail a *total* loss of meaning.

Empirical studies do not identify science as a significant source of meaning for most people – for example, in the quest for happiness and fulfilment.[32] Yet this does not mean that science cannot help illuminate the issues. Humans are meaning-seeking animals. Let's look at one recent discussion of the relevance of science for our understanding of the meaning of life.

A Failed Alternative: Scientism and Meaning

In his recent book *The Atheist's Guide to Reality* (2011), the atheist philosopher Alex Rosenberg sets out his understanding of what science can tell us about life's greatest questions. Rosenberg makes it clear that the only reality is that which can be disclosed by the application of the scientific method.

> Science provides all the significant truths about reality, and knowing such truths is what real understanding is all about . . . Being scientistic just means treating science as our exclusive guide to reality, to nature – both our own nature and everything else's.[33]

The Atheist's Guide to Reality demolishes all the great questions of philosophy and religion on the assumption that science is 'our exclusive guide to reality'. To save his readers having to follow his arguments in detail, Rosenberg provides a neat synopsis of life's big questions, along with what he considers to be scientifically reliable answers. A few examples:

What is the nature of reality? What physics says it is.
What is the purpose of the universe? There is none.
What is the meaning of life? Ditto.
What is the difference between right and wrong, good and bad? There is no moral difference between them.

Each of these points is developed in much greater detail later in the book. Rosenberg provides a thoroughly consistent exploration of an atheist worldview, based on the core assumption that reality is limited to and defined by what the natural sciences

– especially physics – are able to uncover. There is nothing *beyond* or *behind* the science. 'We have to be nihilists about the purpose of things in general, about the purpose of biological life in particular, and the purpose of life in general.'[34] Therefore, if science cannot disclose purpose in life, there is none to disclose.

Rosenberg tells us that this is a 'nice nihilism'. To me, it is just a reductive physicalism which claims that everything is just bosons and fermions. Adding the word 'nice' is purely cosmetic. It seems to me that Rosenberg needs to reflect on the words of the poet Muriel Rukeyser (1913–80): 'The universe is made of stories, not of atoms.'[35] Rukeyser is attuned to the subjective dimensions of life, the things that give human life meaning, where Rosenberg thinks only of coldly objective facts.

Yet in a puzzling move, Rosenberg declares that it is 'beyond reasonable doubt' that a 'core morality' exists – that is to say, a set of behavioural rules observed by all or nearly all societies across time. That is one of the main observations of C.S. Lewis's *The Abolition of Man*, and Lewis interprets this in a strongly theistic manner.[36] Rosenberg would doubtless object, but his concession opens the door to alternative visions of morality which are rather more persuasive and useful than those he himself appears to wish to adopt.

There is also a serious issue here, which Rosenberg fails to deal with adequately. Is this 'core morality' simply an historical 'given', which we have to accept whether we like it or not? Even the most pliable reader of Rosenberg's book might wonder whether these moral 'givens' might require review and revision, particularly in the light of rapid cultural change. Yet Rosenberg offers us no means by which science can offer an alternative moral vision, on the basis of which traditional ethical values might be corrected.

Rosenberg's philosophical rigour thus leads him to a moral nihilism, in that there are no 'correct' answers to moral questions. His critics would respond by arguing that this is not proper *science* at all; this is scientism, understood as the rather narrow and doctrinaire view that reality is limited to what the scientific method can disclose. It is also deeply problematic. How on earth could physics itself demonstrate that reality consists of only the kinds of things that physics recognises? Many will feel that the philosopher Roger Scruton puts his finger on a deep concern about the entire 'scientistic' enterprise:

> Scientism involves the use of scientific forms and categories in order to give the appearance of science to unscientific ways of thinking. It is a form of magic, a bid to reassemble the complex matter of human life, at the magician's command, in a shape over which he can exert control. It is an attempt to *subdue* what it does not understand.[37]

Rosenberg's views are framed in terms of a specific vision of reality, from which such issues as meaning and value are excluded for methodological reasons, in that the scientific method does not, and cannot, engage them. That is why Mary Midgley argues that we need multiple maps of reality – to enable us to avoid being improperly limited by the austerities of the scientific method. I agree entirely with Rosenberg when he says that science cannot tell us what is right. We are going to look at Sam Harris's flawed proposal that science *can* determine moral values in the next chapter. Harris's defiant and unpersuasive affirmation that science can tell us what is moral needs to be set against Rosenberg's robust and persuasive intellectual defence that it cannot. But that does not mean that we are unable to determine what is right and wrong. It just means that science cannot tell us the answers.

So what? It is like saying that reading a book on advanced nuclear physics cannot tell me how to get from Oxford to London. Knowing the structure of DNA does not – and cannot – tell me whether democracy is better than fascism. Evolutionary biology cannot tell me whether Mr Collins is the hero of *Pride and Prejudice*, the date of the battle of Waterloo, or the name of the second President of the United States of America. Now if science can help us answer these questions, and countless others like them, that is great. If not, we just look somewhere else for the answers. Life, most readers will conclude, is about rather more than bosons and fermions.

Science is a tool designed to answer certain questions and not others. We abuse science if we force it to answer the wrong questions. And we abuse ourselves if we pretend that, because this specific tool cannot answer moral or existential questions, there are no good answers to be found. Tools are designed for specific purposes, and if they are used for something else, we should not be surprised if they do not work. Why, many of us will wonder, can there not be things that can only be discovered by non-scientific means, if they can be discovered at all?

Meaning and Naturalism

Rosenberg's bold atheist manifesto has more to say, however. There is one more illusion that needs to be shattered by his rigorous scientistic thinking. Rosenberg argues that we believe many things that are actually wrong, as a result of our biological hardwiring. Our evolutionary past affects and distorts our ability to reason. 'There is strong evidence that natural selection produces lots of false but useful beliefs.'[38] Rosenberg's critics might, I think, be entitled to wonder whether the statement 'science provides all the significant truths about reality' is one of them. But Rosenberg cuts the ground from under his critics in a dramatic move – by undermining the credibility of 'thought' in the first place. 'Thinking about things', he tells us, is an 'overwhelmingly powerful illusion'.

> Ultimately, science and scientism are going to make us give up as illusory the very thing conscious experience screams out at us loudest and longest: the notion that when we think, our thoughts are about anything at all, inside or outside of our minds.[39]

This self-referentiality will leave most readers baffled. If we are naturally predisposed to have 'lots of false but useful beliefs', how then can we identify which of our beliefs are false, and correct them? After all, beliefs can only be true or false if they relate to *something*. Rosenberg sets out to liberate his readers from their illusions, but offers them no reliable criteria for identifying what is illusory and what is true. Rosenberg disallows us the tools we need to determine whether we are moving from illusion to truth, or simply from one illusion to another.

The best rebuttals of this approach do not come from religious writers, who often merely assume that it is so bizarre that it refutes itself, but from mainstream philosophers. Let me explore the approach set out by my colleague Timothy Williamson, presently Wykeham Professor of Logic at the University of Oxford.[40] Williamson points out that one obvious challenge to the kind of scientific imperialism developed by Rosenberg and others is that it has difficulty accounting for the success of mathematics, noted earlier (see pages 75–9). 'Naturalism privileges the scientific method over all others, and mathematics is one of the most spectacular success stories in the history of human knowledge.' Yet mathematics does not use experimental or empirical methods, but proves its results by pure reasoning. It does not fit into Rosenberg's severely impoverished account of how we investigate reality.

If we do not treat pure mathematics as a science, we are obliged to exclude mathematical proof from our understanding of the scientific method. After all, Williamson argues, mathematical proof is just as effective a route to knowledge as experimental or observational methods. Williamson concludes that any attempt 'to condense the scientific spirit into a philosophical theory' will fail, since 'no theory can replace that spirit'. Indeed, he concludes, 'naturalism as dogma is one more enemy of the scientific spirit'.

Perhaps more importantly, Williamson goes on to challenge the fundamental basis of Rosenberg's 'nice nihilism' with an argument that may well prove to be the final nail in its coffin.[41] Williamson invites us to consider 'the extreme naturalist claim that all truths are discoverable by hard science'. Why should we believe that this is right? What is its evidential basis? Williamson's response to this question needs to be read at least twice to grasp the point he is making. But once Williamson's point has been grasped, the plausibility of Rosenberg's position simply evaporates.

> If it is true that all truths are discoverable by hard science, then it is discoverable by hard science that all truths are discoverable by hard science. But it is not discoverable by hard science that all truths are discoverable by hard science. 'Are all truths discoverable by hard science?' is not a question of hard science. Therefore the extreme naturalist claim is not true.

When I was a science student at Oxford University back in the early 1970s, the main philosophical talking point among undergraduates was the 'logical positivism' of A.J. Ayer (1910–89) and his circle. Ayer – who was one of Williamson's predecessors as Wykeham Professor of Logic at Oxford from 1959 to 1978 – famously asserted that a statement could only be meaningful if it was *analytic* (for example, 'all vertebrates have backbones'), or *empirically verifiable* (for example, 'there are fish in the ocean'). This 'Verification Principle' thus held that all metaphysical statements and judgements of value were meaningless or subjective and therefore of no philosophical significance.

Those of us who were scientists tended to regard our fellow students in the humanities who held this position with slightly bemused contempt. Although they claimed to be 'scientific' in their approach, they often seemed to know remarkably little about scientific practice or theory development. Instead, they tended to focus exclusively on the question of what would make the language of philosophical discourse 'meaningful' – that is, empirically verifiable – without giving due attention to the problems that any scientist knew were associated with such a claim. We could see that this 'Verification Principle' led to the puzzling conclusion that scientific laws were meaningless statements, in that they could not be verified in the strict sense of the term.[42] Why? Because the corrigible nature of science leads to the conclusion that there are no statements we can hold as *absolutely* true on empirical grounds. Despite its supposedly empirical basis, the 'Verification Principle' actually excluded all scientific laws – and therefore most of the scientific enterprise – as meaningless.[43]

But we could also see something else. *By its own criteria of meaning, the 'Verification Principle' was meaningless.* It was itself a metaphysical assertion that could not be verified on the basis of its own criteria of judgement. And that is the same problem that emerges with the kind of overstated scientific imperialism that we find exemplified in Rosenberg – such as the absolutist, simplistic and unverifiable statement that 'science provides all the significant truths about reality'. Any suggestion that science is an 'exclusive guide to reality' cannot be justified by an appeal to science *without assuming that this conclusion is true*. It is a circular argument, comparable to the fatally flawed 'Verification Principle' in terms of its scope and foundations.

So where does this leave us? The simple truth is that none of this has much relevance for most practitioners of the natural sciences, who wisely avoid metaphysical speculation as a matter of principle and would probably regard Rosenberg's views as eccentric and totally unrepresentative of science. The kind of methodological naturalism which is intrinsic to the theory and practice of science concerns how reality is to be investigated and does not predetermine either the form or extent of that reality. This naturalism is a premise of the scientific method, not its conclusion. A working assumption can easily be petrified as a worldview. The problems start when we assume that science gives us *exclusive* access to the truth.

Rosenberg inflates his judgements, both verbally and evidentially. He declares that science tells us that there is 'no moral difference' between good and evil. That is just nonsense. I can only assume that he really means that science cannot tell us what is good or evil – a judgement with which I happily agree. Believing, with Rosenberg, that science tells us there is 'no moral difference' between good and evil runs counter to the most fundamental instincts and values of humanity, above all the belief in the importance of struggling against evil and injustice.

Science is a vitally important tool for investigating our world and living within it. But it illuminates only part of the picture, not the whole picture. To think otherwise is a delusion. And we need that whole picture if we are to live authentic and meaningful lives.

8

An Empirical Ethics? Science and Morality

Teenagers are expected to rebel against the banalities of conventional wisdom. I certainly did. As a rather doctrinaire teenage atheist, I regarded life as meaningless and my bold declaration of cosmic pointlessness as an act of intellectual bravery. As I saw things, I was bold enough to tell the bleak and austere truth, where others wallowed in the consoling delusion that life was somehow meaningful.

Now iconoclasm is great fun, but it is not especially productive. The downside of rebelling against an established position is that you are expected to provide constructive alternatives. This proved to be a little harder for me. One option certainly lay to hand. Some of the younger teachers at my school had been influenced by the radical thinkers of the late 1960s, who held that moral judgements merely expressed personal feelings or attitudes rather than expressing something that was intrinsically right or wrong. This might have been fashionable; it seemed intellectual nonsense to me. Surely there was a better way of pursuing the good life than either buying into a nonsensical self-serving individualism or following the dull moral conventions of the age?

It did not take me long to find my answer: *science* could tell us what is right and good. It solved my dilemma perfectly at that time. It seemed to be both culturally radical yet intellectually robust. Ethics was about making decisions that would advance or hinder human well-being. Since science was able to measure human well-being, it could tell us what is good for us and what is bad for us. Empirical facts determine what is right and what is wrong, not social convention or individual feelings. In effect, I was arguing that science was a kind of meta-language which was able to judge the validity of all other forms of human discourse and intellectual enterprise.

I shared my ideas with some of my friends in my last year at school, before going to Oxford University to study science in more detail. They were irritatingly obtuse, failing to grasp either the elegance or simplicity of what I proposed. One objected that what I believed to be scientifically verifiable 'moral values' were nothing more than empirical facts about how to achieve human well-being, which dubiously equated 'well-being' with 'morality'. Another was prepared to allow that science could *inform* moral questions, but not that it could *answer* them. I dismissed these unwelcome criticisms as deluded unscientific obscurantism, and thought no more about it. I need hardly add that mine turned out to be a hopelessly naïve view of ethics, and freely admit that it took me a few years to figure out why. But we are allowed to be simplistic when we are young.

Can Science Be the Foundation of Morality?

Richard Dawkins and I disagree on a number of matters. But there are some things on which we are firmly agreed. We both love science, and we both think it is intellectually stimulating and aesthetically enriching. And until recently, we both agreed that – to use Dawkins' own words – 'science has no methods for deciding what is ethical'.[1]

Dawkins was absolutely right to make this point back in 2003. Anyone who wants to defend the idea of a scientifically grounded morality has to deal with the lingering memory of earlier botched attempts to implement a 'scientific morality', especially the disastrous ethical experimentations of 'social Darwinism' in the first third of the twentieth century. Claiming to be 'scientific', this rather crude application of Darwinian principles to moral and political thought provided what is now widely seen as a spurious 'scientific' justification for repulsive social policies such as racism and eugenics.[2] However, the memory of such disastrous attempts to base social and political policies on allegedly 'scientific' values has now faded, allowing the emergence of fresh attempts to explore the question of whether moral values can be founded on science, especially neuroscience.[3]

Nevertheless, three serious concerns arising from the flawed 'social Darwinian' experiments of the past remain live issues today, and must be addressed. First, many of the supposedly 'scientific' values derived from evolutionary theory were little more than transpositions of what *happened* in nature to what *ought to happen* in human society. This all-too-easy transition from fact to value – this happens, and therefore this is right – lay behind some of the more objectionable social policies proposed by 'social Darwinism'. This is why we are right to be sceptical about any suggestion that value-laden policies and practices can be determined solely by empirical investigation.

Second, as we have seen, scientific theorisation – and any outcomes based upon it – is provisional. What one generation might regard as a 'scientific' response to a particular situation thus may be abandoned by a future generation with access to a better understanding of science or to a wider base of empirical knowledge. If we were to define moral values as 'doing things that enhance the quality of life', we would need to recognise that scientific understanding of what enhances the quality of life has shifted over the years, and will continue to shift.

And third, moral questions were treated as if they were scientific questions, capable of being answered simply by an appeal to empirical data. This can only be done in two ways, both of which are intellectually unacceptable. First, moral values are surreptitiously smuggled into what is essentially a scientific narrative – for example, by presupposing certain notions of what is good or moral and then showing how science helps us achieve those goals. Second, by identifying an empirically observable quality as either representing or determining morality, so that the empirical study of this quality can be equated with the scientific determination of moral values.

Yet in 2010, Dawkins changed his mind on this critically important point. After reading Sam Harris's *Moral Landscape*

(2010), he declared that he now realised he had 'unthinkingly bought into the hectoring myth that science can say nothing about morals'. I was surprised by this change of mind, particularly because my own reading of *The Moral Landscape* reinforced my conviction that science had no privileged insights in this field. Given this book's impact on Dawkins, and the importance of the questions it raised, we shall consider its fundamental themes and how it bears on the relation of science and the great human quest to live the good life.

Sam Harris on Science and Ethics

Sam Harris rose to fame in 2004 as one of the leading representatives of the 'New Atheism', arguing for a fundamental link between the irrationality of faith and its pursuit of violence – seen, for example, in the 9/11 terror attacks in New York City. His critique of religion was accompanied by some rather dubious moral views – such as a rather uncritical defence of the use of torture,[4] and his disturbing argument that 'some propositions are so dangerous that it may even be ethical to kill people for believing them'.[5] It made me wonder what Harris based his ethics on.

Happily, Harris has now provided an answer to that question. In 2010, he published *The Moral Landscape: How Science Can Determine Human Values*, in which he argued that science is able to provide a reliable objective basis for human ethics.[6] This book, based on Harris's 2009 PhD thesis in neuroscience at the University of California, offers a vigorous defence of 'moral realism' in the face of an endemic ethical pluralism and relativism. Where many in Western liberal culture endorse – though often fail to implement – an 'all moral views are equally valid' attitude, Harris offers a vigorous defence of the objectivity of moral values, which are held to be valid and binding, whether we like them or not.

Harris offers a good critique of some overstatements of evolutionary accounts of ethics, such as the sociobiologist E.O. Wilson's assertion that morality is 'merely an adaptation' to 'further our reproductive ends'.[7] Harris rightly observes that, while evolution did not design us 'to lead deeply fulfilling lives', human ethical reflection can hardly fail to take this goal into account. Few will dispute Harris's judgement that 'science should increasingly inform our values'.[8] For example, it is not difficult to see how the findings of experimental psychology concerning human cognitive biases can help us reason more effectively – a point noted by many moral philosophers as they reflect rather more rigorously than Harris on the nature of goodness.[9] Harris simply tends to assume his definition of morality for the purposes of exploration, rather than offer a rigorous defence of it.

Yet Harris's approach to ethics goes further than acknowledging and welcoming an *informing* scientific perspective on moral questions; it clearly demands that science should *determine* our values. Harris's advocation of a scientific morality has three main elements:

1. Morality concerns improving the 'well-being of conscious creatures'. It concerns 'the principles of behavior that allow people to flourish'.[10]
2. Facts about what promotes and harms the 'well-being of conscious creatures' are accessible to science.
3. Science is thus able to determine what is objectively 'moral', in that it can determine whether something increases, or decreases, the 'well-being of conscious creatures'.

The core assumption of Harris's approach is that our ethical thinking and moral actions should be motivated by the 'well-being of conscious creatures'. I am personally very sympathetic to this being recognised as one of several core values of responsible human reflection. But why should it be the *only* core value? And, much more importantly, just what is the *scientific* basis of this claim? It is clearly a *value judgement*, not an *empirical observation*. It is about what we ought to be doing, rather than what is observed.

This may be contrasted with Albert Einstein's observation that 'science can only ascertain what *is*, not what *should be*, and outside of its domain value judgements of all kinds remain necessary'.[11] That is why Harris has to smuggle in some decidedly unscientific presuppositions in order to 'allow' science to reach certain ethical conclusions that are simply not accessible through the scientific method alone. His scientific account of morality depends upon hidden non-empirical premises. Without intending to do so, Harris makes the case for needing to enrich a scientific narrative with supplementary perspectives – such as those drawn from the world of faith. That is what I think, and at least I am open about it.

It is interesting to note, as an aside, that Harris's position, if developed consistently, ought to lead him to regard religious faith as at least benign, and even as moral. Why? Because there is now a large body of serious empirical work on the impact of religious commitment on human well-being which shows a positive observed correlation between faith and well-being.[12] Harris's use of the enhancement of well-being as a criterion of morality clearly has unintended consequences. Yet this amusing outcome of his approach must not be allowed to obscure the fact that it is flawed and unworkable.

In the end, Harris merely asserts the untested and inherently untestable hypothesis that morality is to be deemed equivalent to maintaining or enhancing the 'well-being of conscious creatures'. Yet this core initial presupposition does not appear to be derived from any form of empirical investigation, however provisional. It is an unevidenced, metaphysical assumption, not a scientific conclusion. So what *scientific* reasons might be given for preferring Harris's definitions of moral terms over the rival versions offered by social contract theorists, virtue ethicists or any other of the many schools of moral theory currently active? I do not see any on offer.

Harris's emphasis on the 'maximisation of well-being' leads him to adopt the ethical position generally known as 'utilitarianism' (although Harris does not use this term to describe his position).[13] The difficulties with this position are well known. For example, it is easy to envisage morally complex situations in which it would not be clear what actions might maximise well-being, partly arising from disputes over what this 'well-being' is, and partly because it is unclear how to measure it. To give one very obvious example, of critical social importance, a 'maximal well-being' approach fails to help us work out how very scarce medical interventions such as organs and vaccines should be allocated.[14] Harris's approach does not help us work out whether we should treat all people equally, favour the worst off, maximise the total benefits of an intervention, or promote and reward its social usefulness. In practice, these issues are decided on non-scientific grounds, such as beliefs about social value, cultural utility or personal significance – none of which are 'scientific' notions.

Harris is aware of such difficulties in calculating optimal outcome, but argues that these should not be allowed to obscure the general principle of promoting well-being. It is a reasonable point. It is important not to fuss too much about details. Yet this makes it clear that Harris's approach suffers from a double deficiency, in that it is not merely theoretically indefensible, but it cannot be implemented in practice either. In the end, any viable ethics of this kind needs a metric of 'well-being', an algorithm of possibilities which can be evaluated in terms of the amount of 'well-being' that they entail.

If Harris's approach has any merit, it is not in adjudicating between the good and the better, but rather between good and evil – as, for example, when judging that certain harsh moral traditions are damaging to human beings. Yet even then, we are occasionally left wondering if things are quite as compelling as Harris believes. For example, Harris argues that there is a *scientific* rationale for declaring that the Taliban's treatment of women is objectively morally wrong. Why? Because an enforced wearing of a burqa is not conducive to the well-being of conscious creatures. That looks suspiciously like cultural prejudice being dressed up as a scientific fact.

In the end, Harris's defence of his ethical method turns out to be *philosophical*, not *scientific*. As the philosopher Whitley Kaufman points out, although Harris continually appeals to 'science', he is in fact defending a contentious and rather implausible moral philosophy.

> One of the oddities of this book is that the single concrete finding that Harris claims to have made in the book, that utilitarianism is the correct moral theory (the rest is mere promissory notes about a future science of ethics), is not in any reasonable sense a 'scientific' finding.[15]

Perhaps this ought not really to surprise us. One of Nietzsche's insights – ignored by the New Atheists – is that the problem atheism has with morality is not whether atheists can be moral in some general sense of the word, but rather what specific morality they should serve. The New Atheist appeal to science is ultimately an attempt to construct a morality based on something that is not transcendent or divine. Yet science simply cannot determine such moral issues. The history of the early twentieth century is littered with thoroughly illiberal, occasionally racist, attempts to construct a 'scientific' morality, none of which are now taken seriously.[16]

So where does this leave us? Harris's unrealistic and unpersuasive argument for the moral authority of science ignores the difficult history of this enterprise, and ultimately rests on unacknowledged core philosophical principles. He presupposes his own conclusions in an interesting but rather pointless act of intellectual circularity. This unsatisfactory essay in moral reflection is little more than an uncritical manifesto of a rather unperceptive form of scientism which seeks to extend the scope of science through a rhetorical trivialisation of the moral authority of its obvious cultural alternatives – philosophy and religion. And having created an artificial moral vacuum, Harris inflates science to occupy this space.

But there is no moral vacuum that needs to be filled in this way. Moral philosophy and theology have a long history of reflection on the classic themes of ethics and their application to everyday life. Science can, and should, *inform* our thinking about ethics. But, as Harris's failed experiment in scientific morality makes clear, it cannot function as the *basis* of ethics. In fact, despite all the hyped-up publicity surrounding his book, I do not think that Harris himself *really* believes that this is the case. Neither science nor scientists have any privileged insights into what is good, or how to achieve it. Harris needs to reconnect with the mainstream of moral reflection, not try to set himself above it.

Evolutionary Psychology and Ethics

In an earlier chapter, we explored Darwin's theory of evolution and reflected on some of its implications. One such implication which needs to be considered in more detail is whether a Darwinian metanarrative itself provides a basis for ethical reflection, either by showing that some of our most firmly established moral values are actually hangovers from our evolutionary past, or by offering its own set of such values.

The debate about the relation of evolution and ethics can be traced back to the nineteenth century. Herbert Spencer (1820–1903), perhaps best known for inventing the phrase 'the survival of the fittest' to describe Darwin's principle of natural selection, was an enthusiastic advocate of evolutionary ethics.[17] The critical reception he experienced was partly due to some questionable assumptions, particularly the rather dubious biological presupposition that evolution tended towards the greatest happiness. What came to be known as 'social Darwinism' generally held that the strong should be encouraged to become stronger – for example, through encouraging economic competition between individuals through *laissez-faire* capitalism, or through the manipulation of social structures.

It was perhaps inevitable that the popularisation of Darwin's theory would lead to the emergence of forms of social Darwinism, although it is important to note that this is not a *necessary* consequence of Darwin's theory of natural selection. Rather, it arises from regarding natural patterns underlying the phenomenon of evolution as being normative for human beings, arguing from observation of natural processes to the imposition of moral systems. Paradoxically, some of the themes evident in social Darwinism are actually Lamarckian, rather than Darwinian.

It is also important to note that other leading advocates of evolution in the late nineteenth century – such as Thomas Henry Huxley and Alfred Russel Wallace – were strongly opposed to the extension of evolution to the realm of morality, partly because they believed it *could* not be done, but perhaps mainly because they believed it *should* not be done.[18] Huxley's views on this were made explicitly clear in his Romanes Lecture at Oxford University in 1893, entitled 'Evolution and Ethics'. 'Let us understand once and for all,' Huxley declared, 'that the ethical progress of society depends, not on imitating the cosmic process, still less in running away from it, but in combatting it.'[19]

The most severe early critic of evolutionary ethics was the great philosopher G. E. Moore (1873–1958). Some see Moore as extending David Hume's earlier observation that it was logically impossible to move from a set of purely factual premises to a normative conclusion. In his *Principia Ethica* (1903), Moore set out his concerns about developing any ethical theory based on the observation of natural processes, such as evolution, inventing the term 'naturalistic fallacy' to refer to the error he believed to lie at the heart of Spencer's evolutionary ethics.

So what was that error? For Moore, the notion of 'goodness' was not capable of being determined or measured by any empirical means. Moore accused Spencer of committing the naturalistic fallacy, which consists in 'identifying the simple notion which we mean by "good" with some other notion'.[20] Spencer's equation of 'good' with 'happiness' was indefensible. Moore's critique of Spencer goes beyond the simple idea that what is found in nature is

good; it is based on the deeper idea that the 'good' cannot be correlated with empirical observations. While I personally find Moore's
'intuitionism' – the idea that we recognise the 'goodness' of an act
just as we recognise whether something is yellow – unpersuasive,
his criticism of Spencer remains important and is easily extended
to more recent speculation about science and ethics.

Evolutionary ethics faltered from about 1920 to 1975, largely
because its problems were seen to outweigh any slight benefits it
might bring. The situation changed, however, with the publication of Edward O. Wilson's book *Sociobiology* (1975), the final
sections of which argued that the evolutionary basis of ethics
should be recognised. 'Scientists and humanists should consider
together the possibility that the time has come for ethics to be
removed temporarily from the hands of the philosophers and
biologicized.'[21] The origins of human moral intuitions were to be
accounted for in terms of the evolutionary history of humanity.
The cumulative force of Wilson's argument created a new interest
in exploring the biological origins of our ethical beliefs.

Wilson's work did not actually propose an alternative ethic, but
probed some of the questions that he considered to require further
exploration. Are our moral instincts inherited from the past,
reflecting long-gone historical contexts? How exactly might we
determine which natural dispositions are 'good' and which are
'bad'? When viewed from a strictly scientific perspective, Wilson's
approach raised important questions, only some of which could
actually be answered scientifically.

It is, however, important to take such questions seriously. Is
the human capacity for normative guidance to be seen as a
biological adaptation, which may have conferred a selective
advantage in the past – though not necessarily in the present –
by enhancing social cohesion and co-operation within groups?
And if so, does this invalidate or confirm such norms of behaviour and feelings? The difficulties begin when anyone tries to
move from description to prescription.

At the descriptive level, it is relatively easy to appeal to evolutionary theory to offer an explanation of the origins of certain human capacities or patterns of thought and behaviour. Proving these explanations, of course, is rather more problematic, given the absence of secure hard evidence concerning our distant psychological past. Evolutionary psychology is often invoked to support a postmodern moral scepticism or relativism, or to undermine traditional moral realism.[22] Yet these claims cannot be validated, partly because of the serious difficulties in transitioning from description to prescription, and mainly because of the necessarily *provisional* and *tentative* nature of any scientific understanding of the evolutionary past.

The problem with approaches to morality based on evolutionary psychology lie not so much in the good questions that are being asked, as in the inadequate answers that are being given. Richard Alexander seems to me to sum up the issues rather well.

> Evolutionary analysis can tell us much about our history and existing systems of laws and norms, and also about how to achieve any goals deemed desirable; but it has essentially nothing to say about what goals are desirable, or the directions in which laws and norms should be modified in the future.[23]

My own reading of the recent literature in the field suggests that many are simply using 'evolutionary' arguments to lend 'scientific' support to their own moral precommitments, whether conservative, liberal or radical. They seem to use the prestige of science as a means of disguise and protection, allowing them to smuggle in their own unevidenced moral and metaphysical ideas as if these were the secure outcome of the scientific method. This 'scientific' analysis often rests on a gross oversimplification of the conception of ethics, usually equating 'good' with some measurable concept of well-being and failing to appreciate the difficulty in establishing any meaningful connection between actions that promote human survival and actions that are deemed to be moral. It is not difficult to see why so few people believe it offers a meaningful alternative or corrective to common sense, religious traditions or social conventions as an adequate base on which to build a viable system of ethics.

Yet ethics remain vitally important to personal and social existence. If science cannot provide us with moral guidance, we look for it somewhere else. The great dream of the Enlightenment was that reason might provide a universal and necessary foundation for ethics. So what about that vision? What remains of it today?

A Rational Ethic? The Limits of Reason

For some in contemporary culture, reason and science are the basis of clear and reliable thinking, displacing and deposing all rival sources of authority. It is a vision for which I have sympathy. After all, nobody wants to be irrational. Of course, it is not that simple. The core question that many of my more philosophical colleagues want to ask about an idea is whether it is *reasonable*. Yet this approach, often encountered within the New Atheism, merely locks us into some form of rationalism, which imprisons the scientific enterprise within a rationalist straitjacket, locked into the thought-world of the eighteenth century.

Let's look at this in more detail. Most scholars argue that the modern 'Age of Reason' began with Descartes' *Discourse on Method* (1637) and Spinoza's *Ethics* (1677), which held that philosophy was based on truths that were so luminous and arguments that were so compellingly persuasive that reason was able to attain certitude in matters of knowledge. Yet this view was generally abandoned as unworkable and unrealistic during the twentieth century. The New Atheism is really an Antiquated Rationalism which has failed to catch up with the philosophical revolution of the twentieth century, brought about by pivotal works such as Martin Heidegger's *Being and Time* (1927), Ludwig Wittgenstein's *Philosophical Investigations* (1953) and Hans-Georg Gadamer's *Truth and Method* (1960).

Enlightenment rationalism is now seen as something of a

period piece, a philosophy grounded in the assumptions of a long-dead and less critical period in human culture. Most philosophers would now follow Heidegger and the late Wittgenstein and argue that all human thinking – whether philosophical, theological or ethical – has to be regarded as 'fiduciary' (from the Latin term *fiducia*, 'trust'), in that its conclusions depend upon commitments whose truth has to be assumed and which cannot be demonstrated.[24] This is not to be seen as a problem (unless you are an old-fashioned rationalist, that is). It is just the way things are. We have to learn to live with this, and make the most of it.

And that is good news for both science and religion, both of which are now liberated from the old rationalist dogma that human reason can lay down what the universe is like. It does not, and it cannot. That is why the fundamental question a scientist is going to ask about a theory is not 'Is this reasonable?' but 'What are the reasons for thinking this is true?' We cannot lay down in advance what 'rationality' is characteristic of the universe. We have to find out either by letting the universe itself tell us, or by figuring out ways of uncovering it. Scientific rationality is thus best thought of as something that is discovered, rather than predetermined or predicted. And sometimes scientific rationality is in conflict with what we might call traditional rationality.

I first began to study quantum theory in detail at Oxford in 1971. I found myself being deeply challenged by its counterintuitive ideas, such as wave-particle duality. However, I soon came to see that what was counterintuitive for me was intuitive for those who were used to seeing the world through a quantum lens. My problem was that I was approaching quantum theory with a concept of rationality shaped by my experience of the everyday world of classical Newtonian physics. The quantum world was very different.

The same issues emerge within the Christian faith. To give one obvious example: the key question to ask about the doctrine of the Trinity is not 'Is this reasonable?' This question presupposes that the rationality of faith may be mapped onto a common-sense rationality, whereas the real task of any responsible Christian theology is to discover the internal logic of the Christian faith, not to lay down in advance what form this should take. Quantum mechanics and Christian theology alike are perfectly rational enterprises. The difficulty is that their logic seems counterintuitive, if they are judged by the socially constructed notion of 'common sense', which is based on an amalgam of cultural expectations and experiences. The doctrine of the Trinity makes perfect sense within the logic of the Christian faith, but not within the austere and inadequate notion of rationality associated with the Enlightenment.[25]

The Enlightenment took the view that reason was capable of disclosing a universally valid ethic. It was a wonderful vision, and one that I gladly absorbed when I was a highly idealistic teenager. Although I now regard the idea of a universal rational morality as a fiction – a 'dead time's exploded dream' (Matthew Arnold) – it clearly could be a very *useful* fiction. If everyone could sign up to it as an act of faith, it might sort out a few of the world's problems. So what is wrong with it?

The main concern is that this understanding of human reason fails to appreciate the extent to which our patterns of reasoning are shaped by our culture. Sure, $2 + 2 = 4$ wherever you are. Mathematics and logic are clearly in a class of their own, transcending the boundaries of history and culture. And so is the scientific method, which has universal validity, despite its limits. Yet moral thinking belongs to none of these classes. We now realise that it is dependent on values and judgements embedded within the social context of the thinker. As the philosopher Stephen Toulmin pointed out, the exercise of rational judgement is itself an activity carried out in a particular context and essentially dependent on it. The attraction of pure mathematics to rationalist writers lay partly in the fact that it was seen to be the only intellectual activity whose problems and solutions are 'above time'.[26] But mathematics is one thing; reasoning is another. Karl Marx's great insight, originally framed in terms of ideas being the outcomes of socio-economical reality, is that reason is embedded in, and shaped by, a cultural context.[27]

The philosopher Alasdair MacIntyre, one of the more perceptive critics of the attempt by the 'Age of Reason' to forge a universal morality, argues that it tried to confront the world in an empirical, presuppositionless way, which looked good in theory, but failed in practice. In both his *After Virtue* (1981) and *Whose Justice? Which Rationality?* (1988), MacIntyre argued that the thinkers of the Enlightenment set out to replace what they took to be discredited traditional and superstitious forms of morality by a kind of secular morality of such impeccable rational credentials that it would secure the assent of any rational person.[28] Yet these attempts to formulate moral principles to which no adequately reflective rational person could refuse allegiance failed. Why? Because it became clear that the Enlightenment actually developed a variety of methodologies and conclusions, each claiming to have a compelling rational justification and refusing to concede that its rivals could claim to be 'rational'.

> Both the thinkers of the Enlightenment and their successors proved unable to agree as to precisely what those principles were which would be found undeniable by all rational persons ... Nor has subsequent history diminished the extent of such disagreement. Consequently, the legacy of the Enlightenment has been the provision of an ideal of rational justification which it has proved impossible to attain.[29]

MacIntyre argues that the Enlightenment rejected the Aristotelian idea of a 'virtuous life' which had shaped Western thought for nearly two millennia, including its central theme of a *telos* – the idea that human beings exist for a purpose and that to 'be good' is about acting in a way that enables us to fulfil that purpose. Instead, human beings were conceived as moral agents who possessed no true purpose or goal other than those they created for themselves. This theme is taken up in Michael Sandel's perceptive criticism of liberal theories of justice, which often ignore the fact that ethical debates are unacknowledged conflicts about understandings of human nature and destiny. Sandel – Professor of Government at Harvard University – emphasises that justice is 'inescapably judgmental', resting on unprovable visions of the true goals of humanity.[30] Despite all our best intentions to make the law neutral, we cannot define or defend principles of justice without making assumptions about the meaning of the good life.

MacIntyre's work did much to challenge the very idea of a 'rational' ethic on the basis of the contested nature of rationality itself, which he had little difficulty in demonstrating from the tangled history of rationalist attempts to construct ethical norms. Yet he also did much to reinstate traditional ideas of ethics as 'virtue', which have had considerable impact on contemporary moral philosophy and theology.[31] The idea of a rationalist ethic lingers on, though it is now largely confined to popular writers within the New Atheist movement – such as the trite, godless banalities set out at the end of Richard Dawkins' *The God Delusion*.

As we have seen, the natural sciences fail to provide us with a compelling basis for envisaging and living a good life. But in the end, this is not important. To criticise science for failing to deliver moral principles is like blaming a microscope for not making good coffee. Tools are designed for purposes. If we want to investigate the structure and behaviour of the material world, we turn to science; for ethics, we turn to moral philosophy or theology. We cannot afford to be stifled and imprisoned by forms of intellectual tunnel vision which result from declaring that only one method of investigating and representing reality is permissible.

Since these things cannot be proved, we have to make judgements about what is right and what is true. Yet these are not arbitrary or irrational judgements, as if rational thought is suspended in order to reach them. As we have argued throughout this work, when one narrative proves inadequate for a given purpose, we are perfectly entitled to draw on additional narratives to help us in our quest for justice in society and personal integrity in our own lives. If we are to engage these deep questions, we need a larger narrative, another map of meaning, to enrich and expand our vision.

You may not agree with the specific vision of interconnected narratives that I articulate in this book, but you will end up developing one of your own, whether this is explicitly justified or implicitly assumed. Human beings seem to be meant to develop and work within a greater narrative, however partial and provisional, if we are to provide coherent and credible answers to the great debates about meaning and value now taking place in our culture. That is what we need – and that is certainly what can be developed.

In the final chapter of this book, we shall explore how such a greater narrative can be developed and inhabited.

9

Science and Faith: Making Sense of the World – Making Sense of Life

In 1930, the British novelist Evelyn Waugh (1903–66) discovered Christianity, and the new landscape of intellectual and imaginative possibilities that this opened up for him. Writing later to a friend, he spoke of 'the delicious process of exploring it limitlessly'.[1] This book describes something of my own journey of exploration of the landscape of life, which led me first to an abiding love of science, then to the discovery of the intellectual capaciousness of Christianity, and finally into a deeper and richer personal vision of reality that resulted from weaving their threads together. I have tried to explain some of the insights and concerns I experienced and encountered along the way.

In bringing this work to a close, I am conscious that I may have failed to convey the sense of excitement that I felt, and continue to feel, as I explore the landscape of the world in this way. The journey of discovery set out in this work has been made by countless others before me, and I have not hesitated to look through their eyes as I have reflected on the deeper questions that arise as I travel. In the course of this book, I have tried to reflect on concerns that some readers may wish to raise, and engage with others who might wish to commend different ways of seeing things.

This book is not about *defending* either science or Christianity; I am happy to leave those tasks to others. What I can do, and perhaps can do better than most, is to explore how they might intertwine and interconnect, offering us a rich palette of colours as we try to depict our beautiful yet complex world and live meaningfully within it. This work is thus more a celebration of intellectual and existential possibilities than a treatise on the foundations of human knowledge.

Perhaps the most significant discovery I made while journeying in this way was the limits placed on us as human beings. I mentioned earlier (see page 45) my own hopelessly optimistic views about human nature and capacities as a young man, which led me to ridicule Bertrand Russell's declaration that philosophy taught us how to live 'without certainty'.[2] As a teenager, I was angry that Russell made things needlessly complicated. Now I realise that things *are* complicated, and that simplistic answers to life's great questions are for children and fools. I have come to terms with the dilemma we all face as human beings, so power-fully affirmed by postmodern philosophy – namely, that we cannot prove the things we believe on the basis of good reasons, but believe that we are justified in believing them all the same.

Some might see this as a counsel of despair. It is not. It is just an honest recognition of the complexity of our world and our limited ability to grasp its inner workings and deepest meanings. I often share Charles Darwin's 'horrid doubt' about 'whether the convictions of man's mind, which has been developed from the mind of the lower animals, are of any value or at all trustworthy'.[3] Richard Dawkins makes a similar point when he observes that our minds have developed to help us survive in a world in which 'the objects that mattered to our survival were neither very large nor very small; a world where things either stood still or moved slowly'.[4] So how can we expect ourselves to deal adequately and reliably with vastly more complex matters, such as the meaning of life?

Yet we do – or, at least, we do our best to cope with questions that matter to us but ultimately lie tantalisingly beyond the best tools of enquiry at our disposal. The danger – and it is a real danger – is that we just reduce our vast and complex world to the intellectually manageable, and treat this impoverished and trun-cated mental representation of reality as if it *is* reality. We should hardly be surprised when a serious and committed attempt to think about our world or God causes us mental discomfort, in that our minds are being asked to cope with something that lies considerably beyond what they are best adapted to doing – ensuring our survival.

In one of his short stories, the Argentinian writer Jorge Luis Borges (1889–1986) tells of a moment when a degree of clarity is unexpectedly brought to a decidedly unpromising conversation. It seemed as if a 'more complex interlocutor' had joined the dialogue and moved it on.[5] That is one of the basic themes of this work – the need for a richer, deeper narrative than that offered by science alone – or, indeed, by *anything* on its own. Reality is too complex to be comprehended by any form of intellectual tunnel vision. We need multiple windows on our complex world if we are to appreciate it to the full and act rightly and meaningfully within it. Now there is nothing wrong with seeing only part of the truth, so long as we realise that this is an incomplete vision. The problems begin if we think that reality is limited to what one tradition of investigation can disclose, and refuse to listen to any voices other than our own.

Reality is complicated. Sure, some people try to reduce it to the intellectually manageable and ridicule those who protest against this simplistic reductionism. Yet our universe is just too rich to be exhaustively, or even representatively, described by one tradition of investigation, one angle of approach or one level of description. There are so many facets of existence that need to be explored, so many levels of reality to be engaged. We need a dialogue of humanity's greatest and most significant voices, not a monologue from people who think they know everything already and are too heavily invested in defending their own disciplines to listen to anyone else. We need to interweave ideas, approaches and narratives. Let's see how this might work out in practice.

Interweaving stories about reality

Human beings cannot stop thinking and talking about God, science and faith. We are naturally drawn to religious questions and intuitions. That is why the rationalist sectarians who feel threatened by the persistence of the divine try to have it excluded from the public domain as 'irrational'. But we are meant to ask these questions just as much as we are meant to eat and drink to survive, or to be attracted to other humans to reproduce. That is what our identity and well-being as human beings requires. These conversations must be allowed to happen! To ask these questions and seek for answers is an integral part of being human.

The idea that an interest in questions of faith is something imposed on human beings by religious institutions or authorities is a social construction of the 'Age of Reason', anxious to portray itself as an intellectual liberator and distract our attention from its notoriously impoverished notion of 'rationality'. But science has moved on, and we now know that religion comes naturally to us – sometimes in the form of a fascination with the 'transcendent', sometimes through a sense of presence or agency, sometimes through a sense of something ultimate beyond the realm of reason and experience, and sometimes through an awareness of our place within a deeper order of things. That is why we cannot stop talking about ultimate questions – such as God and the meaning of life. We seem to be *meant* to ask such questions.

Science and faith are not the only voices in today's culture that need to be taken seriously. They are, however, widely regarded as two of the most important – if not *the* most important – movements in our world. This book represents a plea for dialogue, opening the door to an enriched vision of reality. There are some within both the religious and scientific communities who would resist this move, fearing intellectual contamination or loss of focus, or who persist in believing that science and faith are locked in some kind of eternal warfare. We have moved beyond these outdated isolationist ideologies, which are now known to rest on highly questionable foundations. There are clearly boundary issues that need to be negotiated in this most rewarding and creative conversation. But that is true of any relationship worth having in the first place. A 'significant other' often sparks off lines of thought, moments of insight and challenges to settled ideas that may be initially threatening, but so often lead to new and richer ways of seeing things.

C.S. Lewis once argued that the task of a creative writer was to point away from herself to what she had discovered, in the hope of encouraging others to make that same discovery.[6] In this book, I have set out something of my own personal journey from a sense of rapturous amazement at nature to discovering initially the intellectual delight of the natural sciences, then the elevating and enriching experience of religious faith, and finally the exploration of the richer vision of reality that resulted from allowing science and faith to inform and illuminate each other. My own journey is not normative. It does not define the way in which this engagement must take place. It simply illustrates the possibilities opened up by this principled and respectful interweaving of narratives,[7] which allows the reconnection of the otherwise fragmented aspects of our worlds of meaning.

My task in this book is not to provide a defence of either science or Christianity, but to explore what happens when they are allowed to speak to each other, quietly and respectfully, disregarding the predictable outrage of those tiresome and small-minded guardians of a spurious cultural purity who feel threatened by this discussion and want to close it down before it even gets under way. This book can be seen as both an argument for the interweaving of a scientific and a Christian narrative and an exploration of the issues and possibilities that emerge *when this is done*, mapping out the intellectual landscape that is opened up when things are seen in this way. And let me emphasise again that there is no question of turning science into religion, or religion into science. Science is science; religion is religion. All that I am proposing is that they talk to each other, seriously and respectfully, and reflect on the more richly textured way of seeing things which results from this.

Now of course there are many important questions which need to be discussed in any such conversation about interweaving narratives, some of which I have hinted at in this book. But I have painted this picture with broad strokes, hoping to appeal to my readers' imagination as well as to their reason, leaving the finer brushwork to heavily annotated and probably rather dull monographs. And in one sense I have said nothing new, in that such a narrative of enrichment was the common currency of earlier ages.[8] Yet this older narrative has been displaced by a narrative of conflict, which assumed cultural dominance for reasons of historical contingency and has sustained that cultural dominance largely through ignorance of the work of a new generation of historians. It is time to move on – or perhaps to look back, and reappropriate and expand what can now be seen to be a wiser and more reflective approach that weaves together science and faith into a deeply satisfying way of seeing our world and grasping our possibilities within it.

Now some readers will rightly want to raise concerns at this point. Let me try and anticipate three of them. The first is more likely to be raised by scientists, the second by religious believers, and the third by both. They are all fair concerns, and need more engagement.

An Invented Universe? Making Things Up – Or Seeing Things More Clearly?

I remember well the first time I saw the moons of the planet Jupiter. Having read some books about astronomy, I built myself a little telescope. On a cold, crisp winter's evening long ago, I turned it to look at the Milky Way and was overwhelmed by the number of stars I could now see. Then I found the planet Jupiter, and looked at it. For the first time, I saw its moons. Now, both those moons and the stars were there before I looked at them through my telescope. Yet the telescope enabled me to see them by extending the reach of my natural vision.

But sometimes optics distort our vision. During my time as a research student in Oxford University's Department of Biochemistry, I used advanced optical techniques to study temperature-induced changes in biological samples. One set of results from my micro-scope was especially impressive. If right, they would have changed our understanding of how one particular cell worked. I was natu-rally suspicious at my unexpected good fortune, and got a technician to check out the optics. They were faulty. What I was seeing was an 'artefact', an illusion created by badly aligned lenses, not some-thing that was really there.

That is the concern some will rightly have about the idea of having multiple windows on reality – especially if one of them is religious. Although Richard Dawkins' jaunty little soundbite about God being a 'delusion' is both trite and simplistic, some readers will share a concern about the rationality of faith. Might that window turn out to be like my telescope, which allowed an enhancement of vision so that I saw the real world more clearly? Or might it be like my faulty microscope, which created an illusion so that I saw an invented universe, with no counterpart in reality?

Now let me be clear: I cannot prove that the approach I am commending is right. But what I can do is invite my readers to step into this way of seeing things and imagine how things look from this perspective. Does it seem to make sense? Does it allow new insights, or bring new depths to older ones? I hope that some of the ideas I have explored in the course of this book may be helpful here.

But religious readers will also want to raise a point of concern. Let's look at this.

A Rational Religion: Where Is the Mystery?

In this book, I have emphasised how Christianity makes sense of things, offering a map of the landscape of reality. I gladly endorse C.S. Lewis's words, 'I believe in Christianity as I believe that the Sun has risen, not only because I see it, but because by it, I see everything else.'[9] Why? Because I have found them to be true to my own experience of reflection and engagement. But some readers may feel that my approach represents a dilution, perhaps even a distortion, of the Christian faith. Is Christianity *really* just about making sense of things? What about the other major themes of faith? Have I not overlooked them, or even airbrushed them out of things?

I know what these readers mean, and it is a fair point. There is far more to the Christian faith than I have allowed. I have said little, if anything, about the relational aspects of faith – such as the powerful notion that God is with us even in life's darkest moments. It is a theme beautifully expressed in Psalm 23: 'The LORD is my shepherd.' This sums up the essence of their faith for many Christians. Life is a journey, and God is our constant and faithful companion along its way. And what about beauty and joy, more easily known through worship than through reading works of theology? Or prayer? Or the care of the socially marginalised and disadvantaged, such an important theme in the ministry of Jesus of Nazareth? Or the many other themes of the Christian faith that go beyond its thinking about creation or human nature?

And what about the imaginative side of faith? Not, I stress, *imaginary* – that is just something that is made up. The word 'imaginative' invites us to appreciate how an image or a story captures our imagination and gives new meaning to our lives by allowing us to see things afresh. It protests against what the French poet Paul Claudel (1868–1955) termed the 'starved imagination' of rationalism.[10] For many religious believers, what lies at the heart of the Christian faith is what C.S. Lewis termed a 'baptised imagination'. And it is hard to translate this into the abstract ideas of theology, which often fail to excite our minds or elicit a sense of wonder. Theology is the conversion into words of something that totally resists any such reduction in the first place. That is one of the reasons why Lewis argued that the Christian *story* took precedence over Christian *doctrines*.[11] For Lewis, the Christian metanarrative captured the human imagination and acted as a vehicle for the theological ideas expressed in the creeds.

Some readers will feel that I have presented a rationalised faith, shorn of its sense of wonder, joy and hope. I can understand this concern. Yet I need to make two points about the approach I have adopted. First, given cultural concerns about the 'irrationality' of faith found in the writings of Richard Dawkins and others, it is clearly important to reassure readers that faith makes sense – in terms of both its grounds and its outcomes. And second, my own discovery of the intellectual capaciousness of faith was an important milestone in my journey of understanding and exploration. It was an unexpected and important moment of insight for me, particularly as I had absorbed the ideas of the more simplistic forms of atheism I encountered as a teenager, above all its rhetoric about the irrationality of both religious faith and religious believers alike.

Of course there is more – much more – to Christianity than this intellectual capaciousness. Others have written far more eloquently than I could about the fields of Christianity and spirituality, art and music. Many theologians emphasise that human reason is ultimately incapable of grasping massive realities – such as God. That is why theology talks about 'mystery', meaning 'something that human reason cannot grasp in its totality'.[12]

Yet, despite its religious limits, the approach I have taken works well in exploring the relation of faith and science. It is not the full picture, I willingly concede. But it is an integral aspect of the 'big picture' which is especially important for the purposes of this book.

An Improper Synthesis? Why I Am Not Merging Science and Religion

A third concern, which might well be raised by readers with either scientific or religious backgrounds, is that my approach ultimately amounts to the merging of science and religion, blurring their distinctive boundaries and improperly converting one into the other. I concede that this has happened in the past,[13] but it is not what I am proposing. I gladly acknowledge, respect and value the distinctive identities and concerns of science and religion, and I make no attempt to fuse them.

A colleague of mine died some years ago. He was a distinguished scholar and I joined many others at his memorial service as a small way of paying my respect to his memory. During the service itself, and at the reception afterwards, I heard stories about my colleague. What he was like as a scholar. As a husband. As a father. As a friend. As someone who loved walking. Each of these stories illuminated one of his aspects, but none defined him as a person. He was each of these, and yet more than any of them. We need these multiple perspectives to do justice to the complexity and richness of our universe.

My approach is best described in terms of the 'interweaving of narratives'. We saw earlier how human beings construct their identities using multiple narratives.[14] That is how human beings function as social animals. We weave together religious, political, social and cultural narratives as we try to make sense of our world. They are the colours of our palette, which enable us to avoid a simplistic and inadequate black-and-white view of the world. It is natural for us to weave the threads of these narratives together, just as it is natural for us to try and sort out how they interact – which takes priority at which points, and how we resolve tensions or seeming contradictions between them. Mary Midgley's idea of 'multiple maps' or 'multiple windows' through which we view reality expresses a similar theme. No one story, no one angle of gaze or tradition of investigation is adequate to deal with human existence in all its richness and complexity.

This interweaving of narratives is essential as we deal with the 'ultimate questions' that persistently refuse to go away. To answer these properly, we need to bring together multiple approaches and recognise the existence of multiple levels of meaning – such as purpose in life, values, a sense of individual efficacy and a basis for self-worth.[15] What I am proposing is not some crude homogenisation of narratives. It is like an artist's palette: each colour needs to be valued in its own right and used appropriately to render the rich texture and vibrancy of our world.

It is an approach with potentially rich scientific, religious and cultural elements, which connects up with many discussions and concerns today – such as the problem of 'Two Cultures', set out by C.P. Snow in a lecture at Cambridge University on 7 May 1959.[16] Whatever Snow actually intended to say in that lecture, it has been seized upon as marking the dichotomisation of the modern mind, positing the mutual ignorance and hostility that exists between the natural sciences and the humanities, and pleading for the cultural and intellectual enrichment that could result from greater interaction. This book is a small contribution to Snow's plea for interdisciplinary dialogue, aiming to explore some of the intellectual possibilities that might result.

So how might science enrich faith? Or faith enrich science? There are many ways in which the natural sciences can enrich a narrative of faith. For example, consider the words of Psalm 19:1: 'The heavens are telling the glory of God.' Science expands our vision of those heavens, enabling us to grasp more of their vastness and thus deepening our sense of wonder as we reflect on our universe. It helps us to appreciate the immensity of the heavens, adding rich layers of interpretation to our sense of amazement at the night sky.

Or think of the theme of forgiveness, of central importance to the Christian faith, which is given theological articulation in doctrines of the atonement. Science expands our grasp of this notion by helping us understand the empirical difference that forgiveness makes to individuals and communities, thus enabling the development of more effective pastoral strategies.[17]

Yet I suspect that few readers of this book will need to be persuaded of how science might bring added depth to faith. They will more likely want to ask hard questions about ways in which a narrative of faith might enrich a scientific way of thinking. Let's turn to think about this.

How Religion Enriches a Scientific Narrative

In my own experience, there are three main ways in which Christianity enriches a scientific narrative. First, it provides us with a reassurance of the *coherence of reality* – that however fragmented our world of experience may seem, there is a half-glimpsed 'bigger picture' which holds things together, its threads connecting together in a web of meaning what might otherwise seem incoherent and pointless. This theme resonates throughout the poetic and religious writings of the Middle Ages. As might be expected, it is a major issue in perhaps that greatest of medieval literary classics, Dante's *Divine Comedy*. As the poem draws to its close, Dante catches a glimpse of the unity of the cosmos in which its aspects and levels are seen to converge into a single whole.[18]

Yet the modern period has seen doubts about the coherence of reality, many arising from the 'new philosophy' of the Scientific Revolution. Do new scientific ideas destroy any idea of a meaningful reality? The English poet John Donne (1572–1631) spoke movingly of this concern in the early seventeenth century, as scientific discoveries seemed to some to erode any sense of connectedness and continuity within the world. ''Tis all in pieces, all cohaerence gone,' he wrote of this unsettling new world.[19] How could it be held together?

So have we lost sight of the idea of some deeper unity of reality?[20] Where once there was a sense of intellectual and moral coherence to reality, there now seems to be what the great German poet and novelist Hermann Hesse (1877–1962) once described as a mere aggregation of 'intellectual fashions' and the 'transitory values of the day'.[21] Other intellectual developments have also posed a threat to the notion of a coherent reality, including Nancy Cartwright's idea of a 'dappled world'.[22] Where C.S. Lewis argued that 'we are not reading rationality into an irrational universe, but responding to a rationality with which the universe has always been saturated',[23] Cartwright holds that we are imposing an order or rationality when there may be none – or, indeed, there may be a variety of orderings, requiring multiple accounts of the natural world and its structures. For Lewis, we are responding to the universe as it actually is; for Cartwright, we run the risk of inventing our own universe and disregarding the one around us.

Christianity provides a web of meaning, a deep belief in the fundamental interconnectedness of things, which holds Donne's 'pieces' together. Christians find this theme eloquently expressed in the New Testament, which speaks of all things 'holding together' in Christ (Colossians 1:17).[24] There is a hidden web of meaning and connectedness behind the ephemeral and incoherent world that we experience. This was the insight which constantly eluded the novelist Virginia Woolf (1882–1941), who occasionally experienced short, stabbing instances of insight which seemed to her to reveal 'some real thing behind appearances'.[25] These transitory and rare 'moments of being' (as she called them) convinced her that there were hidden webs of meaning and connectedness behind the world she knew. Yet she could never enter this hidden world; it always seemed to retreat from her as she approached its door, as if she were grasping at smoke.

Second, as we noted earlier, Christianity provides *answers to the scientifically unanswerable* – to what Karl Popper termed 'ultimate questions', such as the meaning of life and our place in a greater scheme of things. These are to be seen as supplementations of the rigorous and consistent application of the scientific method, protecting us against the existential vacuum that results from seeing science alone as the foundation of meaning and value.

Religious faith thus provides a framework of meaning which not only helps us grasp the contours of reality more firmly, but inspires us to want to pursue the good and the beautiful. Like many before me, I found that this enabled me to 'reconcile the intellectual demands and pleasures of scientific thought with the sense of purpose and fulfilment that a rich spiritual life can provide'.[26] Of course, such religious frameworks of meaning cannot be rationally or empirically verified. Yet this is a disadvantage that they share with *any* metanarrative that goes beyond the empirical evidence and reflects on deeper questions of meaning and value.

The author Salman Rushdie is severely – and rightly – critical of 'any ideology that claims to have a complete, totalized explanation of the world'.[27] Both science and religion can easily become ideologies – above all, when they assert that they alone have a monopoly on truth. That is the error of both religious fundamentalism and scientific imperialism. But it is an *avoidable* error. I have argued for multiple maps and levels of reality and multiple narratives about life, not simply because reality itself is so complex that it *demands* this form of representation, but also to challenge any pretensions of ultimacy on the part of either science or religion.

And third, religion is able to enrich a scientific narrative by preventing it from collapsing into a technocratic 'dull catalogue of common things' (John Keats). The sociologist Max Weber used the term 'disenchantment' to refer to an excessively intellectual and rationalising way of looking at nature which limited it to what could be measured and quantified.[28] A religious perspective does not in any way deny the scientific utility of such a rationalising approach. It simply insists that there is more that needs to be said if a full and satisfying account of reality is to be provided, and offers a supplementation of a scientific narrative by which this might be achieved.

To bring this work to a close, I shall reflect on some remarks by two outstanding scientists, Albert Einstein and Carl Sagan. These help us to consider how the narrative of faith might enrich and deepen a scientific way of looking at things.

The 'Problem of the Now': Subjectivity and Science

I first began to read about Einstein's theory of relativity in my early teens. I found Einstein's account of the complex world of x, y, z and t fascinating, not least the deep conceptual questions that it raised about the nature of space and time. It did not bother me at the time, but I could not help noticing that this was a remarkably impersonal and abstract account of space and time, framed in terms of 'world lines'. Where, I wondered, did I fit into this map of space and time?

This thought came back to me when reading Einstein's correspondence as background research for this book. I was particularly struck by one of his later letters, written a few months before his death. It was a letter of condolence, written to the family of Michele Besso, a lifelong friend of Einstein who died in March 1955. In the letter, Einstein expressed his sadness at his friend's death and reflected on his reaction to the news.

> Now he has departed from this strange world a little ahead of me. That means nothing. For believing physicists like us know that the distinction between past, present and future has only the meaning of a persistent illusion.[29]

If you know your theory of relativity, you can see exactly what Einstein meant. At one level, he is right. But for most of us, his comment will be existentially unsatisfying. That Besso had died before Einstein means *nothing*? For most people the *subjective* distinction between past, present and future is real and matters profoundly. Physics says one thing, psychology something very different. Yes, human life is incredibly brief when seen against the backdrop of cosmic time. But it is the only life we have. We only occupy a tiny slice of the four dimensions of space-time, and we want to live good and meaningful lives.

While we can certainly organise our experiences of time using the abstract framework of 'space-time', this framework is not in itself capable of delivering the existential payload that is of such personal significance to most of us. Human beings are both objects and subjects. Each of us has our own 'Now', which we distinguish from earlier events which we remember, and from future events which we anticipate or imagine.[30] That is why narratives are so important: they allow us to make sense of our place in the flow of time.[31] Our construction of the present is often framed in terms of recalling the past and anticipating the future. As Einstein's analysis makes clear, all too often science treats us as objects rather than as subjects, so that its descriptions of our situation are not descriptions of what we actually feel. That is why we need a greater narrative which can weave together fact and meaning. That is why we seek for a richer vision of reality which engages both the cognitive and existential dimensions of life.

Einstein himself was acutely aware of this problem, as can be seen from a conversation with the philosopher Rudolf Carnap (1891–1970). Carnap spent some time at the Institute for Advanced Studies at Princeton, where he had the opportunity to talk with Einstein about philosophical issues arising from his research. As Carnap later recalled in his personal memoirs:

> The problem of 'Now' worried Einstein seriously. He explained that the experience of the 'Now' means something special for men, something different from the past and the future, but that this important difference does not and cannot occur within physics.[32]

Carnap described Einstein as painfully resigned to the inability of science to grasp this experience, the existential importance of which could hardly be denied.

> Einstein thought that these scientific descriptions cannot possibly satisfy our human needs; that there is something essential about the 'Now' which is just outside of the realm of science.

The problem here arises from the exclusion of the perceiving subject from physical science – a development which the Austrian physicist Erwin Schrödinger traced back to ancient Greek natural philosophy.[33] Yet the 'I' perspective lies at the root and heart of the human condition. It cannot be excluded from any existentially meaningful account of reality. It has to be brought back in – and that requires the expansion, enrichment or correction of narratives that are deficient in this critically important respect.

The point is clear. According to Carnap, Einstein believed that 'scientific descriptions cannot possibly satisfy our human needs'. There is no suggestion on Einstein's part that the existential shortcomings of these scientific descriptions were an indication of their falsity, which is clearly not the case. Einstein was simply aware that we, as thinking and reflecting human beings, need more than these scientific descriptions.[34] Our needs as human beings – which should and must be incorporated into any humane philosophy – require that these should be supplemented from beyond the realm of science. Though representing a different level of engagement, such approaches are capable of supplementing this scientific account, allowing a richer engagement with the issue than would otherwise be the case.

It is not difficult to see how this issue fits into a greater narrative, with a long history in philosophy and theology, concerning the intensely problematic 'object-subject relation'. Schrödinger himself identified this relation as lying at the heart of quantum mechanics in a letter to the physicist Arnold Sommerfeld (1868–1951) in 1931.[35] The Austrian philosopher Ferdinand Ebner (1882–1931) and the German Jewish philosopher and mystic Martin Buber (1878–1965) both wrote significant works on this theme in the 1920s,[36] picking up on a concern that excessive objectivism was inadequate to do justice to the existential and relational needs of human beings – precisely the point that Einstein was apparently concerned about.

The same themes were developed in more explicitly religious ways in the fifth century by Augustine of Hippo, now widely regarded as one of the earliest writers to explore the issue of autobiographical memory.[37] Augustine's analysis of the nature of time emphasises both the awareness of the subjective time in which the individual thinker exists and the awareness of the individual existing in subjective time. The research of Karl Szpunar at Harvard University has highlighted the importance of the notion of 'subjective time' for human identity,[38] as well as creating space for a religious or metaphysical enrichment of the notion along the lines found in Augustine's classic text *The Confessions*.

Without in any way losing sight of the insights about space and time embedded in Einstein's theory of relativity, Augustine offers a framework which articulates and preserves the subjective importance of the present moment, providing a framework for affirming the significance of memories of the past and hopes for the future. This richer narrative allows multiple insights to be integrated in a manner that respects disciplinary boundaries, while at the same time ensuring that the 'big picture' – and not just part of it – is fully grasped and appreciated.[39]

Now this is a complex and perhaps demanding example. Yet it helps us to see how a scientific narrative can be (and, in Einstein's view, *needed* to be) enriched without being distorted. David Mermin remarks that it is time to consider 'what other foundational puzzles can be resolved by restoring the balance between subject and object in physical science'. He is right. And the greater narratives that might help us with this task are already there, just waiting to be used.

The Night Sky: On Seeing the Heavens

Einstein's anguished recognition that scientific descriptions cannot satisfy human existential needs led him to conclude that something else of essential importance lay 'just outside of the realm of science'. Many know that experience, within and beyond the natural sciences. C.S. Lewis had a haunting awareness of something lying beyond the horizon of experience, like a distant flower whose fragrance was wafted towards him by a passing breeze. The author Salman Rushdie spoke of these moments of intuitions of transcendence as the 'flight of the human spirit outside the confines of its material, physical existence'.[40] Isaac

Newton expressed much the same idea when he spoke of science as standing on the shoreline of a greater truth, too often preoccupied with the accumulation of observations and missing their ultimate significance:

> I seem to have been only like a small boy playing on the seashore, diverting myself in now and then finding a smoother pebble or a prettier shell than the ordinary, whilst the great ocean of truth lay all undiscovered before me.[41]

I know that feeling. I remember looking at the night sky in the winters of the late 1960s, and seeing the 'Belt of Orion' – three bright stars in the constellation of Orion. I was an atheist back in those days, with no interest in God. Like many, I felt a deep sense of awe at the wonder of nature, which was intensified by the beauty of the night sky. I had a sense of standing on the threshold of something that my reason told me was imaginary, yet some deeper intuition told me was profoundly significant. That intuition never entirely went away, remaining as a soft voice within me, whispering words of doubt about my slick and simple atheism.

I have to admit that at that time I found the sight of the night sky unsettling, calling into question the existential adequacy of my settled rationalist assumptions. I knew enough about astronomy to know that light took hundreds of years to travel to earth from those stars. To look at those stars in the Belt of Orion was, in effect, to travel back in time. I was seeing them as they were, not as they are. By the time the light now leaving those stars reached earth, I would be dead. Those stars thus became symbols of my own mortality, chilling silent reminders of the brevity of human life. The universe might be very beautiful. But it also seemed totally pointless.

My atheist 'mental map' of that time led me to believe that the universe was cold and indifferent to me. There seemed to be a 'chilling impersonality' in the laws of nature.[42] I was of no consequence. As the atheist chemist Peter Atkins later put it, the universe was a machine 'driven by motiveless, purposeless decay'.[43] Although I was, in one sense, a product of nature, it did not care about me. At that stage in my life, I saw the night sky as a talisman of a heartless cosmic indifference, similar to that which I had found in the classic Persian poem *The Rubáiyát of Omar Khayyám*:

> And that inverted Bowl they call the Sky,
> Whereunder crawling coop'd we live and die,
> Lift not your hands to *It* for help – for It
> As impotently moves as you or I.[44]

That sense of cosmic pointlessness haunts many today, particularly within the scientific community. Ursula Goodenough, a biologist at the University of Washington, recalls being 'overwhelmed with terror' at the thought of the immensity of the universe and the fact that it would one day come to an end. No longer could she appreciate the beauty of the stars; they came to represent or symbolise deeper and unsettling truths that she found unbearable.

> The night sky was ruined. I would never be able to look at it again. I wept into my pillow, the long slow tears of adolescent despair . . . A bleak emptiness overtook me whenever I thought about what was really going on out in the cosmos or deep in the atom. So I did my best not to think about such things.[45]

I know exactly how Goodenough felt, although in my own phase as an atheist I was willing to stare into the abyss of despair. If that was the way things were, I thought, I had better get used to it. I would have to face up to reality and ignore any seductive thoughts of meaning or hope of 'metaphysical comfort' (Nietzsche).

In my first term studying science at Oxford University, I finally realised that this was simply a way of looking at things, not a factual account of things. I was imposing meaninglessness onto the cosmos. It was what you saw when you looked at the world with one (unacknowledged) set of theoretical spectacles. So what would happen if you put on a different set of spectacles? What if the world was to be seen through a God lens? Through a theistic schema? I came to discover that the night sky looked rather different when seen from the standpoint of faith.

The narrative of faith affirmed my sense of awe in the presence of a vast universe, while adding a layer of interpretation that enabled me to see myself in a new manner. I might be very small, overwhelmed by the majesty of the cosmos. *But I mattered to God*. As I write those words, they seem trite, even simplistic. Yet that thought changes everything. As Salman Rushdie points out, 'Religion helps us understand why life so often makes us feel small, by telling us what we are *smaller than*; and, contrariwise, because we also have a sense of being special.'[46] The narrative of faith gives us a framework which allows us to hold together the ideas of cosmic vastness and personal significance in a coherent whole.

One of the world's most famous photographs was taken in 1990 from the Voyager space probe during its mission to study the outer solar system. Twelve years after its launch, it reached the planet Saturn and sent back images of this great planet. The astronomer Carl Sagan suggested the probe's cameras should send back an image of earth, seen from a distance of about 6 billion kilometres. After much discussion, NASA agreed. Back came the famous image of a 'pale blue dot', set against the darkness of space – a 'lonely speck in the great enveloping cosmic dark'.[47] As Sagan rightly pointed out, this 'distant image of our tiny world' set everything in perspective. How small, how insignificant we are, compared with the vastness of space!

To this day, I keep on looking at that image from Voyager – that minuscule 'pale blue dot' which is our cosmic home. And I find my thoughts straying to one of the psalms, which seems to anticipate the thoughts and emotions I experience when looking at that 'lonely speck in the great enveloping cosmic dark'.

> When I look at your heavens, the work of your fingers,
> the moon and the stars that you have established;
> what are human beings that you are mindful of them,
> mortals that you care for them? (Psalm 8:3–4)

The psalm exults that human beings are part of God's creation and are named and loved by the God from whom all things come. Our lives are touched by transcendence. If this narrative of faith is right (and I cannot prove that it is), then there is a bigger picture – a *vast* picture. But each of us is part of it, and each of us can make a difference.

Conclusion

This book is an interim report from the frontiers of science and faith, a promissory note which can never aspire to be 'finished' or 'perfect', partly because the fields are moving and partly because there is too much for one person to take in and assimilate. Like science, any enriched narrative must be provisional; like religion, it can be illuminating and inspiring. I am still on my voyage of discovery, which has led me to see the world and myself in a new way, through new eyes, and to reflect on the great questions of life through interacting with other minds and imaginations greater than my own. Marcel Proust (1871–1922) captures the challenge and promise of such an intellectual journey beautifully in one of his novels:

> The only true voyage of discovery, the only fountain of youth, would be not to travel to new landscapes, but to possess other eyes, to behold the universe through the eyes of another, of a hundred others.[48]

This book maps my own journey of discovery and intellectual realignment, which led me to develop and embrace an enriched narrative of reality, weaving together the narratives of science and the Christian faith. I am not seeking to impose this on anyone; I do, however, want to share what I have found and explain why I find it so intellectually resilient and existentially satisfying. This method of weaving narratives together is not limited to science and Christianity; other strands can easily be added.

I have tried (and probably failed) to convey the sense of delight and intellectual fulfilment that I find in exploring the vibrant vision of reality that results when science and faith are allowed to critique and enrich each other. The borderlands of science and faith are contested and poorly marked. Yet where some see borders as things to be defended and policed, I see them as porous, calling out to be explored and transgressed creatively and productively. As human beings, we are free to choose our own stories of meaning and have the right to rebel against the constricting and limiting narratives which our culture tries to impose upon us. The old narrative of the conflict of science and religion is now seen as historically under-determined and ideologically driven. Its spell has been broken. It is time to move on and embrace a better approach, such as the narrative of enrichment proposed in this volume.

This narrative of enrichment of science and faith respects both dialogue partners, while recognising that interweaving their themes allows us a deeper grasp on the things that really matter in life. This is not about inventing a make-believe universe, but about discerning the deeper levels of meaning and beauty that are already present within our universe yet which are too easily missed if we limit ourselves to one tradition of enquiry or one map of reality.

We all need a greater narrative to make sense of the world and our lives, naturally weaving together multiple narratives, levels and maps to give us the greatest traction on reality. Reality is just too complex to be engaged and inhabited using only one tradition of investigation. Despite its shortcomings, this book tries to act as Borges' 'more complex interlocutor', aiming to move our cultural conversation on in more satisfying directions.

We need the best picture of reality that we can devise if we are to inhabit it meaningfully and authentically.[49] Why should we rest content with a monochrome picture of reality, when an enriched vision allows us to use a full palette of colours and appreciate it more fully? This richer vision provides a 'big picture' of things which possesses existential traction and not merely cognitive functionality. It is a way of seeing things which enables us not simply to *exist*, but to *live*.

For Further Reading

The following works are recommended as excellent resources to follow through the themes explored in the book's nine chapters.

General Reading

Brooke, John Hedley, *Science and Religion: Some Historical Perspectives*. Cambridge: Cambridge University Press, 2014.

Dixon, Thomas, *Science and Religion: A Very Short Introduction*. Oxford: Oxford University Press, 2008.

Ferngren, Gary B., *Science and Religion: A Historical Introduction*. Baltimore, MD: Johns Hopkins University Press, 2002.

McGrath, Alister E., *Science and Religion: An Introduction*. 2nd ed. Oxford: Blackwell, 2011.

Ruse, Michael, *Science and Spirituality: Making Room for Faith in the Age of Science*. Cambridge: Cambridge University Press, 2014.

Sacks, Jonathan, *The Great Partnership: God, Science and the Search for Meaning*. London: Hodder & Stoughton, 2011.

Stump, J.B. and Alan G. Padgett (eds), *The Blackwell Companion to Science and Christianity*. Oxford: Wiley-Blackwell, 2012.

Chapter 1

Coulson, C.A., *Science and Christian Belief*. London: Oxford University Press, 1955.

Harrison, Peter, *The Territories of Science and Religion*. Chicago: University of Chicago Press, 2015.

Medawar, Peter, *The Limits of Science*. Oxford: Oxford University Press, 1987.

Numbers, Ronald L. (ed.), *Galileo Goes to Jail and Other Myths about Science and Religion*. Cambridge, MA: Harvard University Press, 2009.

Chapter 2

Dear, Peter R., *The Intelligibility of Nature: How Science Makes Sense of the World*. Chicago: University of Chicago Press, 2008.

Hannam, James, *God's Philosophers: How the Medieval World Laid the Foundations of Modern Science*. London: Icon, 2010.

Midgley, Mary, *Evolution as a Religion: Strange Hopes and Stranger Fears*. 2nd ed. London: Routledge, 2002.

Ward, Keith, *More than Matter: Is Matter All We Really Are?* Oxford: Lion Hudson, 2010.

Chapter 3

Gauch, Hugh G., *Scientific Method in Practice*. New York: Cambridge University Press, 2003.

Kuhn, Thomas S., *The Copernican Revolution*. New York: Random House, 1959.

McGrath, Alister E., *Surprised by Meaning: Science, Faith, and How We Make Sense of Things*. Louisville, KY: Westminster John Knox Press, 2011.

Numbers, Ronald L. (ed.), *Galileo Goes to Jail and Other Myths about Science and Religion*. Cambridge, MA: Harvard University Press, 2009.

Chapter 4

Gingerich, Owen, *God's Universe*. Cambridge, MA: Harvard University Press, 2006.

Kragh, Helge, *Conceptions of Cosmos: From Myths to the Accelerating Universe: A History of Cosmology*. Oxford: Oxford University Press, 2007.

McGrath, Alister E., *A Fine-Tuned Universe: The Quest for God in Science and Theology*. Louisville, KY: Westminster John Knox Press, 2009.

McLeish, Tom, *Faith and Wisdom in Science*. Oxford: Oxford University Press, 2014.

Polkinghorne, John, *Science and Creation: The Search for Understanding*. London: SPCK, 1988.

Chapter 5

Alexander, Denis, *Creation or Evolution: Do We Have to Choose?* 2nd ed. Oxford: Monarch Books, 2014.

Brooke, John Hedley, *Science and Religion: Some Historical Perspectives*. Cambridge: Cambridge University Press, 2014.

Collins, Francis S., *The Language of God: A Scientist Presents Evidence for Belief*. New York: Free Press, 2006.

McGrath, Alister E., *Dawkins' God: From the Selfish Gene to the God Delusion*. 2nd ed. Oxford: Wiley-Blackwell, 2015.

Chapter 6

Brown, Warren S., Nancey C. Murphy and H. Newton Malony (eds), *Whatever Happened to the Soul? Scientific and Theological Portraits of Human Nature*. Minneapolis: Fortress Press, 1998.

Feingold, Lawrence, *The Natural Desire to See God According to St Thomas and His Interpreters*. Rome: Apollinare Studi, 2001.

Smith, Christian, *Moral, Believing Animals: Human Personhood and Culture*. Oxford: Oxford University Press, 2009.

Wiley, Tatha, *Original Sin: Origins, Developments, Contemporary Meaning*. New York: Paulist Press, 2002.

Chapter 7

Baumeister, Roy F., *Meanings of Life*. New York: Guilford Press, 1991.

Frankl, Viktor E., *Man's Search for Meaning*. New York: Simon and Schuster, 1963.

Hicks, Joshua A. and Clay Routledge (eds), *The Experience of Meaning in Life: Classical Perspectives, Emerging Themes, and Controversies*. New York: Springer, 2013.

Seligman, Martin, *Flourish: A Visionary New Understanding of Happiness and Well-Being*. New York: Simon & Schuster, 2011.

Chapter 8

MacIntyre, Alasdair, *After Virtue: A Study in Moral Theory*. 3rd ed. Notre Dame, IN: University of Notre Dame Press, 2007.

Murdoch, Iris, *The Sovereignty of Good*. London: Macmillan, 1970.

Sandel, Michael, *Justice: What's the Right Thing To Do?* London: Penguin Books, 2010.

Taylor, Charles, *A Secular Age*. Cambridge, MA: Belknap Press, 2007.

Chapter 9

Harrison, Peter, *The Territories of Science and Religion*. Chicago: University of Chicago Press, 2015.

Sagan, Carl, *Pale Blue Dot: A Vision of the Human Future in Space*. London: Headline, 1995.

Smith, Christian, *Moral, Believing Animals: Human Personhood and Culture*. Oxford: Oxford University Press, 2009.

Steane, Andrew, *Faithful to Science: The Role of Science in Religion*. Oxford: Oxford University Press, 2014.

Notes

Chapter 1

1. Albert Einstein, 'Religion and Science', in *Ideas and Opinions*, New York: Crown Publishers, 1954, pp. 6–40; quote at p. 38.
2. Johann Peter Eckermann, *Gespräche mit Goethe in den letzten Jahren seines Lebens*, 3 vols, Leipzig: F.A. Brockhaus, 1836, vol. 2, p. 50.
3. Aristotle, *Metaphysics*, 982b. See also Plato, *Theaetetus*, 154b–155c. For useful reflections on this theme, see Jerome Miller, *In the Throe of Wonder*, Albany: State University of New York Press, 1992, pp. 11–52.
4. Thomas Aquinas, *Summa Theologiae* IaIIae q. 32, a. 8. For discussion, see Reinhard Hütter, *Dust Bound for Heaven: Explorations in the Theology of Thomas Aquinas*, Grand Rapids, MI: Eerdmans, 2012, pp. 244–6.
5. Peter Medawar, *The Limits of Science*, Oxford: Oxford University Press, 1987, p. 66.
6. José Ortega y Gasset, 'El origen deportivo del estado', *Citius, Altius, Fortius* 9, no. 1–4, 1967, pp. 259–76; quote at p. 259.
7. John Dewey, *The Quest for Certainty*, New York: Capricorn Books, 1960, p. 255.
8. On wisdom, see William G. Compton and Edward Hoffman, *Positive Psychology: The Science of Happiness*, 2nd ed., Belmont, CA: Wadsworth, 2013, pp. 199–228.
9. C.S. Lewis, *Essay Collection*, London: HarperCollins, 2002, p. 21. For further reflection, see Alister E. McGrath, 'The Privileging of Vision: Lewis's Metaphors of Light, Sun, and Sight', in *The Intellectual World of C.S. Lewis*, Oxford: Wiley-Blackwell, 2013, pp. 83–104.
10. Letter to L.T. Duff, 10 May 1943, in *The Letters of Dorothy L. Sayers: Volume II, 1937 to 1943*, ed. Barbara Reynolds, New York: St Martin's Press, 1996, p. 401.
11. Letter to William Temple, Archbishop of Canterbury, 7 September 1943, in ibid., p. 429.
12. Salman Rushdie, *Is Nothing Sacred?*, The Herbert Read Memorial Lecture 1990, Cambridge: Granta, 1990, p. 8.

13. Albert Einstein, letter to Heinrich Zangger, 10 March 1914, in Martin J. Klein, A.J. Kox and Robert Schulmann (eds), *The Collected Papers of Albert Einstein, Volume 5: The Swiss Years: Correspondence, 1902–1914*, Princeton, NJ: Princeton University Press, 1993, p. 381.

14. Eugene Wigner, 'The Unreasonable Effectiveness of Mathematics', *Communications on Pure and Applied Mathematics* 13, 1960, pp. 1–14.

15. For these phrases, see C.A. Coulson, *Science and Christian Belief*, London: Oxford University Press, 1955, pp. 19–20.

16. ibid., pp. 97–102.

17. I later found a similar line of argument in Sir Peter Medawar's famous 1968 Romanes Lecture at Oxford. Peter Medawar, 'Science and Literature', *Encounter*, January 1969, pp. 15–23.

18. Richard Dawkins, 'A Survival Machine', in *The Third Culture*, ed. John Brockman, New York: Simon & Schuster, 1996, pp. 75–95.

19. Thomas Aquinas, *Disputed Questions about the Power of God*, q.6, a.2.

20. Richard Dawkins, *Unweaving the Rainbow: Science, Delusion and the Appetite for Wonder*, London: Penguin Books, 1998, p. xiii.

21. For this important theme, see Kalevi Kull and Claus Emmeche (eds), *Towards a Semiotic Biology: Life Is the Action of Signs*, London: Imperial College Press, 2011. On its philosophical and theological aspects, see Luigi Giussani, *Il Senso Religioso*, 2nd ed., Milan: Jaca Books, 1977, pp. 29–40; C. Stephen Evans, *Natural Signs and Knowledge of God*, Oxford: Oxford University Press, 2010, pp. 26–46.

22. Augustine of Hippo, *Sermons* 68, 6.

23. For example, see Dacher Keltner and Jonathan Haidt, 'Approaching Awe, a Moral, Spiritual and Aesthetic Emotion', *Cognition and Emotion* 17, 2003, pp. 297–314.

24. Mary Midgley, *Evolution as a Religion: Strange Hopes and Stranger Fears*, 2nd ed., London: Routledge, 2002, pp. 17–18.

25. Dawkins, *Unweaving the Rainbow*, p. xii.

26. See Alister E. McGrath, *Dawkins' God: From the Selfish Gene to the God Delusion*, 2nd ed, Oxford: Wiley-Blackwell, 2015.

27. Christopher Hitchens, *Letters to a Young Contrarian*, New York: Basic Books, 2001, p. 55.

28. Greg M. Epstein, 'Less Anti-theism, More Humanism', *Washington Post*, 1 October 2007.

29. Plato, *Republic*, 560e–561a.

Notes

30. See especially Ronald L. Numbers (ed.), *Galileo Goes to Jail and Other Myths about Science and Religion*, Cambridge, MA: Harvard University Press, 2009. For the specific social origins of the 'conflict' model in the late nineteenth century, see Frank Miller Turner, 'The Victorian Conflict between Science and Religion: A Professional Dimension', *Isis* 69, 1978, pp. 356–76. For a good survey of the main historical issues involved, see J.B. Stump and Alan G. Padgett (eds), *The Blackwell Companion to Science and Christianity*, Malden, MA: Wiley-Blackwell, 2012, pp. 3–60.

31. See the excellent general survey in Thomas Dixon, *Science and Religion: A Very Short Introduction*, Oxford: Oxford University Press, 2008, pp. 1–17.

32. ibid., p. 3.

33. Charles Taylor, *A Secular Age*, Cambridge, MA: Belknap Press, 2007. For an excellent series of essays exploring these themes, see Michael Warner, Jonathan Van Antwerpen and Craig J. Calhoun (eds), *Varieties of Secularism in a Secular Age*, Cambridge, MA: Harvard University Press, 2010.

34. http://www.krishnaconsciousnessmovement.com/moonlanding.html. Accessed 21 October 2014. The reference is to *Shrimad Bhagavatam* 5.22.8. This view should not be seen as representative of the complex interaction of science and religion within Hinduism. For important assessments, see David L. Gosling, *Science and the Indian Tradition: When Einstein Met Tagore*, London: Routledge, 2007; C. Mackenzie Brown, *Hindu Perspectives on Evolution: Darwin, Dharma and Design*, London: Routledge, 2012; Jonathan B. Edelmann, *Hindu Theology and Biology: The Bhagavata Purana and Contemporary Theory*, Oxford: Oxford University Press, 2012.

35. Barbara Herrnstein Smith, *Natural Reflections: Human Cognition at the Nexus of Science and Religion*, New Haven, CT: Yale University Press, 2009, pp. 121–49.

36. Eugenie C. Scott, 'Darwin Prosecuted: Review of Johnson's *Darwin on Trial*', *Creation/Evolution Journal* 13, no. 2, 1993, pp. 36–47; quote at p. 43 (emphasis in original). The *Creation/Evolution Journal* became a part of *Reports of the National Center for Science Education* in 1997.

37. Alvin Plantinga, *Where the Conflict Really Lies: Science, Religion, and Naturalism*, New York: Oxford University Press, 2011, pp. 168–74.

38. Stephen Jay Gould, 'Nonoverlapping Magisteria', *Natural History* 106, March 1997, pp. 16–22.

39. See especially Peter Harrison, *The Territories of Science and Religion*, Chicago: University of Chicago Press, 2015. Harrison rightly notes that our concepts of science and religion are recent, having emerged only in the last three centuries, and that it is those categories themselves (rather than their underlying ideas) that now shape our thinking about science, faith and God.

Chapter 2

1. C.S. Lewis, *Christian Reflections*, Grand Rapids: Eerdmans, 1967, p. 65.
2. Peter R. Dear, *The Intelligibility of Nature: How Science Makes Sense of the World*, Chicago: University of Chicago Press, 2008, p. 173.
3. Crystal L. Park, 'Religion as a Meaning-Making Framework in Coping with Life Stress', *Journal of Social Issues* 61, no. 4, 2005, pp. 707–29.
4. Karl R. Popper, 'Natural Selection and the Emergence of Mind', *Dialectica* 32, 1978, pp. 339–55; quote at p. 342.
5. Thomas H. Huxley, *Darwiniana*, London: Macmillan, 1893, p. 252.
6. Stephen Jay Gould, 'Impeaching a Self-Appointed Judge', *Scientific American* 267, no. 1, 1992, pp. 118–21.
7. See especially Mary Midgley, *Evolution as a Religion: Strange Hopes and Stranger Fears*, 2nd ed., London: Routledge, 2002.
8. Mary Midgley, *The Solitary Self: Darwin and the Selfish Gene*, Durham: Acumen, 2010.
9. For example, Mary Midgley, *The Myths We Live By*, London: Routledge, 2004.
10. David E. Rumelhart, 'Schemata: The Building Blocks of Cognition', in *Theoretical Issues in Reading Comprehension: Perspectives from Cognitive Psychology*, ed. R.J. Spiro, B.C. Bruce and W.F. Brewer, Hillsdale, NJ: Erlbaum, 1980, pp. 33–58.
11. Charles Taylor, *A Secular Age*, Cambridge, MA: Belknap Press, 2007.
12. Michel Foucault, *Madness and Civilization: A History of Insanity in the Age of Reason*, London: Routledge, 1995.
13. Richard Dawkins, *The Selfish Gene*, 2nd ed., Oxford: Oxford University Press, 1989, p. 330 (this passage was added in the second edition).
14. Freeman Dyson, 'The Scientist as Rebel', in *Nature's Imagination: The Frontiers of Scientific Vision*, ed. John Cornwell, Oxford: Oxford University Press, 1995, pp. 1–11.

15. George M. Marsden, *A Short Life of Jonathan Edwards*, Grand Rapids, MI: Eerdmans, 2008, p. 131.

16. For reflections on Shaw's disturbing misjudgement, see Sally Peters, 'Commentary: Bernard Shaw's Dilemma: Marked by Mortality', *International Journal of Epidemiology* 32, no. 6, 2003, pp. 918–19.

17. Maurice A. Finocchiaro, *Defending Copernicus and Galileo: Critical Reasoning in the Two Affairs*, New York: Springer, 2010. See also Stephen Mason, 'Galileo's Scientific Discoveries, Cosmological Confrontations, and the Aftermath', *History of Science* 40, 2002, pp. 377–406.

18. John Paul II, 'Faith Can Never Conflict with Reason', *L'Osservatore Romano* 49, November 1992, p. 2.

19. 'A Pox on Cell-Stem Research', *New York Times*, 1 August 2006.

20. For a systematic demolition of 25 such myths – including this one – see Ronald L. Numbers (ed.), *Galileo Goes to Jail and Other Myths about Science and Religion*, Cambridge, MA: Harvard University Press, 2009.

21. James R. Moore, *The Post-Darwinian Controversies: A Study of the Protestant Struggle to Come to Terms with Darwin in Great Britain and America, 1870–1900*, Cambridge: Cambridge University Press, 1979, pp. 99–100.

22. For an early work advocating this position, see David C. Lindberg and Ronald L. Numbers, *God and Nature: Historical Essays on the Encounter between Christianity and Science*, Berkeley, CA: University of California Press, 1986. The best recent study is David C. Lindberg and Peter Harrison, 'Early Christianity', in *Science and Religion around the World: Historical Perspectives*, ed. John Hedley Brooke and Ronald L. Numbers, Oxford: Oxford University Press, 2011, pp. 67–91.

23. For the history of this absurd idea, see Jeffrey Burton Russell, *Inventing the Flat Earth: Columbus and Modern Historians*, New York: Praeger, 1991; Christine Garwood, *Flat Earth: The History of an Infamous Idea*, London: Macmillan, 2007.

24. Paul Davies, *The Mind of God: Science and the Search for Ultimate Meaning*, London: Penguin, 1992, p. 77.

25. For an excellent case study, see Peter Harrison, 'Sentiments of Devotion and Experimental Philosophy in Seventeenth-Century England', *Journal of Medieval and Early Modern Studies* 44, no. 1, 2014, pp. 113–33.

26. This point is developed in the important study of Peter Harrison, *The Fall of Man and the Foundations of Science*, Cambridge: Cambridge University Press, 2007.

27. For one of the best empirical studies of how scientists now view the 'conflict' narrative, see Elaine Howard Ecklund, *Science vs. Religion: What Scientists Really Think*, Oxford: Oxford University Press, 2010, p. 5.

28. F.J. Tipler, C.J.S. Clarke and G.F.R. Ellis, 'Singularities and Horizons – A Review Article', in *General Relativity and Gravitation: One Hundred Years after the Birth of Albert Einstein*, ed. A. Held, New York: Plenum Press, 1980, pp. 97–206, quote at p. 110.

29. This point was clearly understood by the end of the 1980s: see, for example, Frank Miller Turner, 'The Victorian Conflict between Science and Religion: A Professional Dimension', *Isis* 69, 1978, pp. 356–76; Colin A. Russell, 'The Conflict Metaphor and Its Social Origins', *Science and Christian Faith* 1, 1989, pp. 3–26.

30. Jack Morrell and Arnold Thackray, *Gentlemen of Science: Early Years of the British Association for the Advancement of Science*, Oxford: Oxford University Press, 1981, p. 395.

31. Matthew Stanley, *Huxley's Church and Maxwell's Demon: From Theistic Science to Naturalistic Science*, Chicago: University of Chicago Press, 2015, pp. 242–63.

32. http://scienceblogs.com/pharyngula/2007/06/14/high-priest-epstein-in-newswee/

33. Mary Midgley, *Are You an Illusion?* Durham: Acumen, 2014, p. 5.

34. Peter Medawar, *The Limits of Science*, Oxford: Oxford University Press, 1987, p. 66.

35. Roy Baumeister, *Meanings of Life*, New York: Guilford Press, 1991, pp. 29–57.

36. Ludwig Wittgenstein, *Philosophical Investigations*, 3rd ed., Oxford: Blackwell, 1968, p. 48.

37. Midgley, *The Myths We Live By*, pp. 26–8.

38. Mary Midgley, unpublished essay 'Dover Beach', cited in Nelson Rivera, *The Earth is Our Home: Mary Midgley's Critique and Reconstruction of Evolution and its Meanings*, Exeter: Imprint Academic, 2010, p. 179 n. 21.

39. Mary Midgley, *Wisdom, Information, and Wonder: What Is Knowledge For?* London: Routledge, 1995, p. 199.

40. Roy Bhaskar, *The Possibility of Naturalism: A Philosophical Critique*

of the Contemporary Human Sciences, 3rd ed., London: Routledge, 1998.

41. See, for example, Leslie Stevenson and David L. Haberman (eds), *Twelve Theories of Human Nature*, New York: Oxford University Press, 2012.

42. F.H.T. Rhodes, 'Christianity in a Mechanistic Universe', in *Christianity in a Mechanistic Universe and Other Essays*, ed. D.M. MacKay, London: InterVarsity Press, 1965, pp. 11–50, quotes at p. 42.

43. Christian Smith, *Moral, Believing Animals: Human Personhood and Culture*, Oxford: Oxford University Press, 2009, p. 64.

44. Elinor Ochs and Lisa Capps, 'Narrating the Self', *Annual Review of Anthropology* 25, 1996, pp. 19–43.

45. Hendrik L. Bosman, 'Origin and Identity: Rereading Exodus as a Polemical Narrative Then (Palestine) and Now (Africa)', *Scriptura* 90, 2005, pp. 869–77.

46. For an interdisciplinary survey, see Lewis P. Hinchman and Sandra K. Hinchman (eds), *Memory, Identity, Community: The Idea of Narrative in the Human Science*, Albany, NY: State University of New York Press, 1997.

47. See especially C.S. Lewis, 'Is Theology Poetry?', in *Essay Collection*, London: HarperCollins, 2002, pp. 1–21. For Lewis's use of the literary category of 'myth' as a metanarrative, see Alister E. McGrath, 'A Gleam of Divine Truth: The Concept of Myth in Lewis's Thought', in *The Intellectual World of C.S. Lewis*, Oxford: Wiley-Blackwell, 2013, pp. 55–82.

48. Smith, *Moral, Believing Animals*, pp. 63–94.

49. See the important study of Cristine Legare, E. Margaret Evans, Karl S. Rosengren and Paul L. Harris, 'The Coexistence of Natural and Supernatural Explanations across Cultures and Development', *Child Development* 83, no. 3, 2012, pp. 779–93.

50. A good example is the Renaissance metaphor of the 'Two Books' of science and religion: see Giuseppe Tanzella-Nitti, 'The Two Books Prior to the Scientific Revolution', *Annales Theologici* 18, 2004, pp. 51–83.

Chapter 3

1. 'To teach how to live without certainty, and yet without being para-lyzed by hesitation, is perhaps the chief thing that philosophy, in our

age, can still do for those who study it.' Bertrand Russell, *A History of Western Philosophy*, London: George Allen & Unwin Ltd, 1946, p. xiv.

2. Richard Dawkins, *The Selfish Gene*, 2nd ed., Oxford: Oxford University Press, 1989, p. 330.

3. For a good discussion of the 'Lysenko affair' of the 1940s, see Nikolai L. Krementsov, *Stalinist Science*, Princeton, NJ: Princeton Univesity Press, 1997, pp. 54–83.

4. For an excellent study of this point and its implications for medicine, see Mark H. Waymack, 'Yearning for Certainty and the Critique of Medicine as "Science"', *Theoretical Medicine and Bioethics* 30, no. 3, 2009, pp. 215–29.

5. Henry Miller, *Big Sur and the Oranges of Hieronymus Bosch*, New York: New Directions, 1957, p. 25.

6. Carl Sagan, 'Why We Need To Understand Science', *Skeptical Inquirer* 14, no. 3, Spring 1990.

7. Charles Gore, *The Incarnation of the Son of God*, London: John Murray, 1922, pp. 105–6.

8. For the science, see Helge Kragh, *Conceptions of Cosmos: From Myths to the Accelerating Universe: A History of Cosmology*, Oxford: Oxford University Press, 2007, pp. 46–65.

9. See the classic study of Thomas S. Kuhn, *The Copernican Revolution*, New York: Random House, 1959.

10. For a very accessible account, see Allan Chapman, *Stargazers: Copernicus, Galileo, the Telescope and the Church*, Oxford: Lion, 2014.

11. For a collection of essays from leading thinkers exploring the options, see Bernard Carr (ed.), *Universe or Multiverse?* Cambridge: Cambridge University Press, 2007.

12. Abigail J. Lustig, 'Darwin's Difficulties', in *The Cambridge Companion to the 'Origin of Species'*, ed. Michael Ruse and Robert J. Richards, Cambridge: Cambridge University Press, 2009, pp. 109–28.

13. Pietro Corsi, 'Before Darwin: Transformist Concepts in European Natural History', *Journal of the History of Biology* 38, 2005, pp. 67–83.

14. Charles Darwin, *Origin of Species*, London: John Murray, 1859, p. 171.

15. Hugh G. Gauch, *Scientific Method in Practice*, New York: Cambridge University Press, 2003, p. 152.

Notes

16. Richard Dawkins, *A Devil's Chaplain*, London: Weidenfield & Nicholson, 2003, p. 81.

17. William T. Scott and Martin X. Moleski, *Michael Polanyi: Scientist and Philosopher*, Oxford: Oxford University Press, 2005.

18. Leon M. Lederman, *The God Particle: If the Universe Is the Answer, What Is the Question?* Boston: Houghton Mifflin, 1993. For more recent developments, see Leon M. Lederman and Christopher T. Hill, *Beyond the God Particle*, Amherst, NY: Prometheus Books, 2013.

19. Sami Paavola, 'Peircean Abduction: Instinct, or Inference?' *Semiotica* 153, 2005, pp. 131–54.

20. The text of the speech is reproduced in August Kekulé, 'Benzolfest Rede', *Berichte der deutschen chemischen Gesellschaft zu Berlin* 23, 1890, pp. 1302–11.

21. See the collection of important essays in Mark J. Boda and Gordon T. Smith (eds), *Repentance in Christian Theology*, Collegeville, MN: Liturgical Press, 2006.

22. Kathleen Norris, *Dakota: A Spiritual Geography*, New York: Houghton Mifflin, 2001, p. 197.

23. N.R. Hanson, *Patterns of Discovery: An Inquiry into the Conceptual Foundations of Science*, Cambridge: Cambridge University Press, 1961.

24. G.K. Chesterton, 'The Return of the Angels', *Daily News*, 14 March 1903.

25. W.V.O Quine, 'Two Dogmas of Empiricism', in *From a Logical Point of View*, 2nd ed., Cambridge, MA: Harvard University Press, 1951, pp. 20–46, quote at p. 42.

26. C.S. Lewis, *Surprised by Joy*, London: HarperCollins, 2002, p. 201. See further Alister E. McGrath, 'An Enhanced Vision of Rationality: C.S. Lewis on the Reasonableness of Christian Faith', *Theology* 116, no. 6, 2013, pp. 410–17.

27. Lewis, *Surprised by Joy*, p. 197.

28. This statement is found in the manuscript known as 'Early Prose Joy', held at the Wade Center, Wheaton College, Illinois.

29. For some of the issues, see Scott A. Kleiner, 'Explanatory Coherence and Empirical Adequacy: The Problem of Abduction, and the Justification of Evolutionary Models', *Biology and Philosophy* 18, 2003, pp. 513–27; David H. Glass, 'Coherence Measures and Inference to the Best Explanation', *Synthese* 157, 2007, pp. 275–96; Stathis

Psillos, 'The Fine Structure of Inference to the Best Explanation', *Philosophy and Phenomenological Research* 74, 2007, pp. 441–8.

30. C. S. Lewis, 'Is Theology Poetry?', in *C. S. Lewis: Essay Collection*, London: Collins, 2000, p. 21.

31. For an excellent (and relatively non-technical) overview of this theory, see Neil Lambert, 'M-Theory and Maximally Supersymmetric Gauge Theories', *Annual Review of Nuclear and Particle Science* 62, 2012, pp. 285–313.

32. Peter Woit, *Not Even Wrong: The Failure of String Theory and the Search for Unity in Physical Law*, London: Jonathan Cape, 2006, p. 167.

33. C.S. Lewis, 'The Poison of Subjectivism', in *Essay Collection*, p. 250.

34. William James, *The Will to Believe*, New York: Dover Publications, 1956, p. 51.

35. Terry Eagleton, *Reason, Faith, and Revolution: Reflections on the God Debate*, New Haven, CT: Yale University Press, 2009, p. 7.

36. Simone Weil, *First and Last Notebooks*, London: Oxford University Press, 1970, p. 147.

37. Peter B. Medawar and Jean Medawar, *The Life Science: Current Ideas of Biology*, London: Wildwood House, 1977, p. 171.

Chapter 4

1. Richard Dawkins, *River out of Eden: A Darwinian View of Life*, London: Phoenix, 1995, p. 133.

2. Henry A. Wolfson, 'Patristic Arguments against the Eternity of the World', *Harvard Theological Review* 59, 1966, pp. 351–67; Richard Sorabji, *Time, Creation and the Continuum*, Ithaca, NY: Cornell University Press, 1983.

3. Simo Knuuttila, 'Time and Creation in Augustine', in *The Cambridge Companion to Augustine*, ed. Eleonore Stump and Norman Kretzmann, Cambridge: Cambridge University Press, 2001, pp. 103–15.

4. Steven Snyder, 'Albert the Great: Creation and the Eternity of the World', in *Philosophy and the God of Abraham*, ed. R. James Long, Toronto, ON: Pontifical Institute of Biblical Studies, 1991, pp. 191–202.

5. Svante Arrhenius, *Worlds in the Making: The Evolution of the Universe*, New York: Harper, 1908, p. xiv.

6. See Edward R. Harrison, *Cosmology: The Science of the Universe*, 2nd ed., Cambridge: Cambridge University Press, 2000; Helge Kragh,

Conceptions of Cosmos: From Myths to the Accelerating Universe: A History of Cosmology, Oxford: Oxford University Press, 2007.

7. For an excellent study, see Robert W. Smith, *The Expanding Universe: Astronomy's 'Great Debate', 1900–1931*, Cambridge: Cambridge University Press, 2010.

8. The story is told in Jeremy Bernstein, *Three Degrees above Zero: Bell Laboratories in the Information Age*, New York: Scribner's, 1984.

9. Douglas Scott, 'The Standard Cosmological Model', *Canadian Journal of Physics* 84, 2006, pp. 419–35.

10. On which see R.B. Partridge, *3K: The Cosmic Microwave Background Radiation*, Cambridge: Cambridge University Press, 1995.

11. See, for example, John H. Walton, *Genesis 1 as Ancient Cosmology*, Winona Lake, IN: Eisenbrauns, 2011; William Brown, *The Seven Pillars of Creation*, New York: Oxford University Press, 2010; Stephen Barton and David Wilkinson (eds), *Reading Genesis After Darwin*, Oxford: Oxford University Press, 2009.

12. Rémi Brague, *The Wisdom of the World: The Human Experience of the Universe in Western Thought*, Chicago, IL: University of Chicago Press, 2003, pp. 17–25.

13. Roger Scruton, *The Face of God*, London: Bloomsbury, 2014, p. 8.

14. John Polkinghorne, *Science and Creation: The Search for Understanding*, London: SPCK, 1988, p. 20.

15. Eugene Wigner, 'The Unreasonable Effectiveness of Mathematics', *Communications on Pure and Applied Mathematics* 13, 1960, pp. 1–14.

16. For examples and discussion, see Mario Livio, *Is God a Mathematician?* New York: Simon & Schuster, 2009.

17. Polkinghorne, *Science and Creation*, pp. 20–1.

18. See, for example, Max Tegmark, *Our Mathematical Universe: My Quest for the Ultimate Nature of Reality*, New York: Alfred A. Knopf, 2013.

19. Albert Einstein, 'Physics and Reality' (1936), in *Ideas and Opinions*, New York: Bonanza, 1954, p. 292.

20. Roger Penrose, *The Road to Reality: A Complete Guide to the Laws of the Universe*, London: Jonathan Cape, 2004.

21. See Daniel C. Dennett, *Darwin's Dangerous Idea: Evolution and the Meaning of Life*, New York: Simon & Schuster, 1995; Daniel C. Dennett, *Breaking the Spell: Religion as a Natural Phenomenon*, New York: Viking Penguin, 2006. For a cultural and scientific deconstruction of Dennett's very American view of religion, see Donovan Schaefer, 'Blessed, Precious

Mistakes: Deconstruction, Evolution, and the American New Atheism,',
International Journal for Philosophy of Religion 76, 2014, pp. 75–94.

22. Arthur Balfour, *The Foundations of Belief*, New York: Longmans, 1895, p. 117.
23. Alvin Plantinga, *Where the Conflict Really Lies: Science, Religion, and Naturalism*, New York: Oxford University Press, 2011.
24. See especially Philip Kitcher, 'Explanatory Unification', *Philosophy of Science* 48, no. 4, 1981, pp. 507–31; Rebecca Schweder, 'A Defense of a Unificationist Theory of Explanation', *Foundations of Science* 10, 2005, pp. 421–35.
25. Mark Balaguer, *Platonism and Anti-Platonism in Mathematics*, New York: Oxford University Press, 1998.
26. Peter Lipton, *Inference to the Best Explanation*, 2nd ed., London: Routledge, 2004.
27. Martin J. Rees, *Just Six Numbers: The Deep Forces that Shape the Universe*, London: Phoenix, 2000; Paul Davies, *The Goldilocks Enigma: Why Is the Universe Just Right for Life?* London: Allen Lane, 2006, pp. 147–71.
28. Freeman J. Dyson, *Disturbing the Universe*, New York: Harper & Row, 1979, p. 250.
29. Fred Hoyle, 'The Universe: Past and Present Reflections', *Engineering and Science* 45, no. 2, 1981, pp. 8–12, quote at p. 12.
30. Stephen Hawking and Leonard Mlodinow, *The Grand Design*, London: Bantam Books, 2010.
31. ibid., p. 5.
32. ibid., p. 180.
33. For a critical analysis, see John C. Lennox, *God and Stephen Hawking: Whose Design Is It Anyway?* Oxford: Lion, 2010.
34. Hawking and Mlodinow, *The Grand Design*, p. 172.
35. Lawrence M. Krauss, *A Universe from Nothing: Why There Is Something Rather Than Nothing*, New York: Free Press, 2012.
36. For discussion, see Alister E. McGrath, *Dawkins' God: From 'The Selfish Gene' to 'The God Delusion'*, 2nd ed., Oxford: Wiley-Blackwell, 2015.
37. 'On the Origin of Everything', *New York Times*, 23 March 2012; http://www.nytimes.com/2012/03/25/books/review/a-universe-from-nothing-by-lawrence-m-krauss.html. Accessed 24 October 2014.
38. C.S. Lewis, 'The Poison of Subjectivism', in *Essay Collection*, London: HarperCollins, 2002, p. 664.

Notes

Chapter 5

1. Edward J. Larson, *Evolution: The Remarkable History of a Scientific Theory*, New York: Modern Library, 2004, pp. 134–5.
2. Martin J.S. Rudwick, *Worlds before Adam: A Reconstruction of Geohistory in the Age of Reform*, Chicago: University of Chicago Press, 2008.
3. Ralph O'Connor, *The Earth on Show: Fossils and the Poetics of Popular Science, 1802–1856*, Chicago: University of Chicago Press, 2007.
4. Deborah Cadbury, *The Dinosaur Hunters: A Story of Scientific Rivalry and the Discovery of the Prehistoric World*, London: Fourth Estate, 2000.
5. James A. Secord, 'Monsters at the Crystal Palace', in *Models: The Third Dimension of Science*, ed. Soraya de Chadarevian and Nick Hopwood, Stanford, CA: Stanford University Press, 2004, pp. 236–69.
6. James A. Secord, *Victorian Sensation: The Extraordinary Publication, Reception, and Secret Authorship of Vestiges of the Natural History of Creation*, Chicago: University of Chicago Press, 2000.
7. Adrian Desmond, *The Politics of Evolution: Morphology, Medicine, and Reform in Radical London*, Chicago: University of Chicago Press, 1989; Pietro Corsi, *Evolution before Darwin*, Oxford: Oxford University Press, 2010.
8. See Shirley A. Rowe, 'Biology, Atheism, and Politics in Eighteenth-Century France', in *Biology and Ideology: From Descartes to Dawkins*, ed. Denis R. Alexander and Ronald Numbers, Chicago: University of Chicago Press, 2010, pp. 36–60.
9. Alister E. McGrath, *Darwinism and the Divine: Evolutionary Thought and Natural Theology*, Oxford: Wiley-Blackwell, 2011, pp. 85–142.
10. There are many excellent studies, such as the material presented in Jonathan Hodge and Gregory Radick (eds), *The Cambridge Companion to Darwin*, Cambridge: Cambridge University Press, 2003.
11. Ulrich Kutschera, 'A Comparative Analysis of the Darwin–Wallace Papers and the Development of the Concept of Natural Selection', *Theory in Biosciences* 122, no. 4, 2003, pp. 343–59.
12. The text of this larger work can be found in Robert C. Stauffer (ed.), *Charles Darwin's Natural Selection, Being the Second Part of his Big Species Book Written from 1856 to 1858*, Cambridge: Cambridge University Press, 1975.
13. I here follow the excellent summary found in Ernst Mayr, *The Growth*

   of Biological Thought, Cambridge, MA: Belknap Press, 1982, pp. 479–80.

14. Spencer used the phrase in his *Principles of Biology* (1864); Darwin incorporated it into the fifth edition of the *Origin*: 'This preservation of favourable variations, and the destruction of injurious variations, I call Natural Selection, or the Survival of the Fittest.' Charles Darwin, *Origin of Species*, 5th ed., London: John Murray, 1869, pp. 91–2.

15. On which see Michael Bulmer, 'Did Jenkin's Swamping Argument Invalidate Darwin's Theory of Natural Selection?' *The British Journal for the History of Science* 37, 2004, pp. 281–97.

16. The best study is John Hedley Brooke, 'Darwin and Victorian Christianity', in *The Cambridge Companion to Darwin*, ed. Jonathan Hodge and Gregory Radick, Cambridge: Cambridge University Press, 2003, pp. 192–213. The excellent online Darwin Project has a section which brings together the most important historical evidence in an historically objective and trustworthy way: http://www.darwinproject. ac.uk/

17. Frank Burch Brown, *The Evolution of Darwin's Religious Views*, Macon, GA: Mercer University Press, 1986.

18. Randal Keynes, *Annie's Box: Charles Darwin, His Daughter and Human Evolution*, London: Fourth Estate, 2001. Darwin lost three of his children at an early age.

19. Letter to John Fordyce, 7 May 1879, *The Life and Letters of Charles Darwin*, ed. F. Darwin, 3 vols, London: John Murray, 1887, vol. 1, p. 304.

20. See the important analysis in John Hedley Brooke, '"Laws Impressed on Matter by the Creator"? The *Origins* and the Question of Religion', in *The Cambridge Companion to The 'Origin of Species'*, ed. Michael Ruse and Robert J. Richards, Cambridge: Cambridge University Press, 2009, pp. 256–74.

21. Stauffer (ed.), *Charles Darwin's Natural Selection*, p. 224.

22. Charles Kingsley to Charles Darwin, 18 November 1859, *Life and Letters of Charles Darwin*, vol. 2, p. 287. Thomas H. Huxley had a long and important exchange of letters with Kingsley over issues of science and religion: Paul White, *Thomas Huxley: Making the 'Man of Science'*, Cambridge: Cambridge University Press, 2003, pp. 114–21.

23. Charles Kingsley, 'The Natural Theology of the Future', in *Westminster Sermons*, London: Macmillan, 1874, pp. v–xxxiii, quote at p. xxv.

24. John R. Lucas, 'Wilberforce and Huxley: A Legendary Encounter',

Notes

Historical Journal 22, 1979, pp. 313–30; J. Vernon Jensen, 'Return to the Wilberforce-Huxley Debate', *British Journal for the History of Science* 21, no. 2, 1988, pp. 161–79; John Hedley Brooke, 'The Wilberforce-Huxley Debate: Why Did It Happen?', *Science and Christian Belief*, 13, 2001, pp. 127–41; Frank A.J.L. James, 'An "Open Clash between Science and the Church"? Wilberforce, Huxley and Hooker on Darwin at the British Association, Oxford, 1860', in *Science and Beliefs: From Natural Philosophy to Natural Science*, ed. David M. Knight and Matthew D. Eddy, Aldershot: Ashgate, 2005, pp. 171–93.

25. This comment is taken from Wilberforce's review of *The Origin of Species*, published in *The Quarterly Review* 108, July 1860, pp. 225–64.

26. Jensen, 'Return to the Wilberforce-Huxley Debate', p. 176.

27. Charles Darwin to Joseph Hooker, 20(?) July 1860, *Life and Letters of Charles Darwin*, vol. 2, p. 234.

28. Matthew Stanley, *Huxley's Church and Maxwell's Demon: From Theistic Science to Naturalistic Science*, Chicago: University of Chicago Press, 2015.

29. Frederick Temple, *The Present Relations of Science and Religion: A Sermon*, Oxford: Parker, 1860, p. 15.

30. On Temple's significance in shaping Victorian attitudes towards evolution, see Peter Hinchliff, *Frederick Temple, Archbishop of Canterbury*, Oxford: Oxford University Press, 1998, pp. 166–93.

31. Frederick Temple, *The Relations between Religion and Science*, London: Macmillan, 1885, p. 115.

32. Charles Darwin, *The Descent of Man*, 2 vols, London: John Murray, 1871, vol. 1, p. 168.

33. David J. Galton and Clare J. Galton, 'Francis Galton and Eugenics Today', *Journal of Medical Ethics* 24, 1998, pp. 99–105.

34. Elazar Barkan, *The Retreat of Scientific Racism: Changing Concepts of Race in Britain and the United States between the World Wars*, Cambridge: Cambridge University Press, 1992, p. 242.

35. Marie Carmichael Stopes, *Radiant Motherhood: A Book for Those Who Are Creating the Future*, London: Putnam's Sons, 1920, p. 223.

36. ibid., p. 225.

37. ibid., p. 220.

38. See Gillian Beer, *Darwin's Plots: Evolutionary Narrative in Darwin, George Eliot and Nineteenth-Century Fiction*, Cambridge: Cambridge

University Press, 2000; Gowan Dawson, *Darwin, Literature and Victorian Respectability*, Cambridge: Cambridge University Press, 2007.

39. Darwin, *The Descent of Man*, vol. 2, p. 404.

40. ibid., p. 405.

41. David N. Livingstone and Mark A. Noll, 'B.B. Warfield (1851–1921): A Biblical Inerrantist as Evolutionist', *Isis* 91, 2000, pp. 283–304.

42. See the two important studies by William E. Carroll: 'Creation, Evolution, and Thomas Aquinas', *Revue des Questions Scientifiques* 171, 2000, pp. 319–47; 'At the Mercy of Chance? Evolution and the Catholic Tradition', *Revue des Questions Scientifiques* 177, 2006, pp. 179–204.

43. For reflections on these themes from a Jewish perspective, see Jonathan Sacks, *The Great Partnership: God, Science and the Search for Meaning*, London: Hodder & Stoughton, 2011, pp. 209–32.

44. James Barr, 'Why the World Was Created in 4004 BC: Archbishop Ussher and Biblical Chronology', *Bulletin of the John Rylands University* 67, 1984–5, pp. 575–608.

45. William R. Brice, 'Bishop Ussher, John Lightfoot and the Age of Creation', *Journal of Geological Education* 30, 1982, pp. 18–24.

46. For example, see Stephen Barton and David Wilkinson (eds), *Reading Genesis After Darwin*, Oxford: Oxford University Press, 2009; William Brown, *The Seven Pillars of Creation*, New York: Oxford University Press, 2010.

47. Keith A. Francis, 'Nineteenth-Century British Sermons on Evolution and *The Origin of Species*', in *A New History of the Sermon: The Nineteenth Century*, ed. Robert Ellison, Leiden: Brill, 2010, pp. 269–308.

48. See the authoritative work of Ronald L. Numbers, *The Creationists: The Evolution of Scientific Creationism*, New York: Knopf, 1992.

49. For details, see Ernan McMullin, *Evolution and Creation*, Notre Dame, IN: University of Notre Dame Press, 1985, pp. 1–58; Alister E. McGrath, *Darwinism and the Divine*, Oxford: Wiley-Blackwell, 2011, pp. 222–30.

50. Two of the best are Denis Alexander, *Creation or Evolution: Do We Have To Choose?* 2nd ed., Oxford: Monarch Books, 2014; Francis S. Collins, *The Language of God: A Scientist Presents Evidence for Belief*, New York: Free Press, 2006. See also Michael Ruse, *Can a Darwinian Be a Christian? The Relationship between Science and Religion*, Cambridge: Cambridge University Press, 2001.

Notes

Chapter 6

1. 'Soul has Weight, Physician Thinks', *New York Times*, 11 March 1907.
2. Andreas Hüttemann and Alan C. Love, 'Aspects of Reductive Explanation in Biological Science: Intrinsicality, Fundamentality, and Temporality', *British Journal of Philosophy of Science* 62, no. 3, 2011, pp. 519–49.
3. Francis Crick, *The Astonishing Hypothesis: The Scientific Search for the Soul*, London: Simon & Schuster, 1994, pp. 3, 11.
4. For the issues, see William R. Stoeger and Nancey C. Murphy (eds), *Evolution and Emergence: Systems, Organisms, Persons*, Oxford: Oxford University Press, 2007.
5. Desmond Morris, *The Naked Ape: A Zoologist's Study of the Human Animal*, London: Jonathan Cape, 1967.
6. See, for example, Jonathan Marks, 'The Biological Myth of Human Evolution', *Contemporary Social Science* 7, no. 2, 2012, pp. 139–65. Marks stresses that 'culture' is to be understood here as 'a symbolic, linguistic, historical environment', rather than simply as 'learned behaviour'.
7. For a discussion of Dawkins' views, see Alister E. McGrath, *Dawkins' God: From The Selfish Gene to The God Delusion*, 2nd ed., Oxford: Wiley-Blackwell, 2015.
8. Richard Dawkins, *The Selfish Gene*, 2nd ed., Oxford: Oxford University Press, 1989, p. 21.
9. For a brief overview, see Uwe Sauer, Matthias Heinemann and Nicola Zamboni, 'Genetics: Getting Closer to the Whole Picture', *Science* 316, no. 5824, 2007, pp. 550–1. For Noble's recent views, see Denis Noble, 'A Theory of Biological Relativity: No Privileged Level of Causation', *Interface Focus* 2, no. 1, 2011, pp. 55–64.
10. Denis Noble, *The Music of Life: Biology Beyond the Genome*, Oxford: Oxford University Press, 2006, pp. 11–15, quote at p. 13.
11. Noble would now argue that the cumulative weight of observation would count against Dawkins: Denis Noble, 'Neo-Darwinism, the Modern Synthesis and Selfish Genes: Are They of Use in Physiology?' *Journal of Physiology* 589, no. 5, 2011, pp. 1007–15.
12. C.S. Lewis, *The Voyage of the Dawn Treader*, London: HarperCollins, 2009, p. 215.
13. For an excellent introduction to this idea, see Robert B. Laughlin,

A Different Universe: Reinventing Physics from the Bottom Down, New York: Basic Books, 2005.

14. Plato, *Cratylus*, 400c. For the background, see John P. Wright and Paul Potter (eds), *Psyche and Soma: Physicians and Metaphysicians on the Mind-Body Problem from Antiquity to Enlightenment*, Oxford: Clarendon Press, 2000.

15. C.F. Fowler, *Descartes on the Human Soul*, Boston: Kluwer Academic Publishers, 1999, pp. 67–160. Descartes later framed this in terms of a 'mind-body' dualism.

16. H. Wheeler Robinson, *Inspiration and Revelation in the Old Testament*, Oxford: Clarendon Press, 1946, p. 70.

17. James D.G. Dunn, *The Theology of Paul the Apostle*, Grand Rapids, MI: Eerdmans, 1998, pp. 51–78.

18. See Warren S. Brown, Nancey C. Murphy and H. Newton Malony (eds), *Whatever Happened to the Soul? Scientific and Theological Portraits of Human Nature*, Minneapolis: Fortress Press, 1998.

19. For example, see Charles C. Conti, *Metaphysical Personalism: An Analysis of Austin Farrer's Metaphysics of Theism*, Oxford: Clarendon Press, 1995.

20. Augustine of Hippo, *Confessions*, I.1.i.

21. The best study is Lawrence Feingold, *The Natural Desire to See God According to St Thomas and His Interpreters*, Rome: Apollinare Studi, 2001.

22. Alister E. McGrath, 'Arrows of Joy: Lewis's Argument from Desire', in *The Intellectual World of C.S. Lewis*, Oxford: Wiley-Blackwell, 2013, pp. 105–28.

23. Paul Bloom, 'Religion Is Natural', *Developmental Science* 10, no. 1, 2007, pp. 147–51.

24. Brent Nongbri, *Before Religion: A History of a Modern Concept*, New Haven, CT: Yale University Press, 2013, pp. 15–24.

25. See, for example, Peter Harrison, '*Religion*' and the Religions in the English Enlightenment*, Cambridge: Cambridge University Press, 1990.

26. For various approaches, see Pascal Boyer, *Religion Explained: The Evolutionary Origins of Religious Thought*, New York: Basic Books, 2001; Scott Atran, *In Gods We Trust: The Evolutionary Landscape of Religion*, Oxford: Oxford University Press, 2002; Justin L. Barrett, *Why Would Anyone Believe in God?* Lanham, MD: AltaMira Press, 2004.

27. Robert N. McCauley, *Why Religion Is Natural and Science Is Not*, New York: Oxford University Press, 2011, pp. 83–143.

28. ibid., pp. 254–68.
29. Ara Norenzayan, Will M. Gervais and Kali H. Trzesniewski, 'Mentalizing Deficits Constrain Belief in a Personal God', *PLoS One* 7, no. 5, 2012, e36880, doi:10.1371/.
30. It is instructive to compare Lewis with Jesse Bering, *The Belief Instinct: The Psychology of Souls, Destiny, and the Meaning of Life*, New York: W.W. Norton, 2012.
31. Justin L. Barrett, *Born Believers: The Science of Children's Religious Belief*, New York: Free Press, 2012.
32. See the sociological analysis in Christian Smith, *Moral, Believing Animals: Human Personhood and Culture*, Oxford: Oxford University Press, 2009.
33. For example, see Boyer, *Religion Explained*, pp. 4–33; Atran, *In Gods We Trust*, pp. 12–13.
34. As argued by Candace S. Alcorta and Richard Sosis, 'Ritual, Emotion, and Sacred Symbols: The Evolution of Religion as an Adaptive Complex', *Human Nature* 16, 2005, pp. 323–59.
35. Peter J. Richerson and Lesley Newson, 'Is Religion Adaptive? Yes, No, Neutral. But Mostly We Don't Know', in *The Believing Primate: Scientific, Philosophical and Theological Reflections on the Origin of Religion*, ed. Jeffrey Schloss and Michael Murray, Oxford: Oxford University Press, 2009, pp. 100–17.
36. David Sloan Wilson, 'Beyond Demonic Memes: Why Richard Dawkins is Wrong About Religion', e*Skeptic*, Wednesday 4 July 2007. Published online at http://www.skeptic.com/eskeptic/07-07-04/. Accessed 10 December 2014.
37. For one of the outcomes of this research, see Alister E. McGrath, *The Intellectual Origins of the European Reformation*, 2nd ed., Oxford: Blackwell, 2003.
38. See Ronald G. Witt, *In the Footsteps of the Ancients: The Origins of Humanism from Lovato to Bruni*, Leiden: Brill, 2000; Charles G. Nauert, *Humanism and Renaissance Civilization*, Variorum Collected Studies Series, Burlington, VT: Ashgate, 2012.
39. Erika Rummel, *Erasmus' Annotations on the New Testament: From Philologist to Theologian*, Toronto: University of Toronto Press, 1986.
40. See, for example, Paul Kurtz, *What is Secular Humanism?* Amherst, NY: Prometheus Books, 2006.
41. For an excellent account, see Mason Olds, *American Religious Humanism*, Minneapolis, MN: University Press of America, 1996.

42. Mary Midgley, 'The Paradox of Humanism', in *James M. Gustafson's Theocentric Ethics: Interpretations and Assessments*, ed. Harlan R. Beckley and Charles M. Swezey, Macon, GA: Mercer University Press, 1988, pp. 187–99, quote at p. 193.

43. Terry Eagleton, *Reason, Faith, and Revolution: Reflections on the God Debate*, New Haven, CT: Yale University Press, 2009, p. 28.

44. George Steiner, *Language and Silence: Essays 1958–1966*, London: Faber, 1967, p. 15.

45. Mark Roseman, *The Villa, the Lake, the Meeting: Wannsee and the Final Solution*, London: Penguin Books, 2003.

46. Note especially his *Answer to Job* (1952), widely regarded as one of the finest recent explorations of evil. For further discussion, see Paul Bishop, *Jung's 'Answer to Job': A Commentary*, New York: Brunner-Routledge, 2002.

47. See further Marie Vejrup Nielsen, *Sin and Selfish Genes: Christian and Biological Narratives*, Leuven: Peeters, 2010.

48. Dawkins, *The Selfish Gene*, 2nd ed., pp. 9–10, 200–1.

49. For a good account, see Tatha Wiley, *Original Sin: Origins, Developments, Contemporary Meaning*, New York: Paulist Press, 2002.

50. Aleksandr I. Solzhenitsyn, *A World Split Apart: Commencement Address Delivered at Harvard University*, New York: Harper and Row, 1978, p. 55.

51. For this theme in the New Testament, see Romans 7:18–19. 'I can will what is right, but I cannot do it. For I do not do the good I want, but the evil I do not want is what I do.'

52. See the blog 'Retraction Watch' for detailed reports. For a well-known older example, see Frank Spencer, *Piltdown: A Scientific Forgery*, Oxford: Oxford University Press, 1990.

53. Louis F. Fieser, 'The Synthesis of Vitamin K', *Science* 91, 1940, pp. 31–6.

54. Robert M. Neer, *Napalm: An American Biography*, Cambridge, MA: Belknap Press, 2013.

55. William Temple, *Nature, Man and God*, London: Macmillan, 1934, p. 22.

56. Michael Shermer, *How We Believe: Science, Skepticism, and the Search for God*, New York: Freeman, 2000, p. 71.

57. Bernard Williams, *Ethics and the Limits of Philosophy*, London: Collins, 1985, pp. 159–60.

Notes

58. Bernard Williams, *Morality: An Introduction to Ethics*, Cambridge: Cambridge University Press, 1993, p. 80.

59. Christopher Hitchens, *God Is Not Great: How Religion Poisons Everything*, New York: Twelve, 2007, p. 8.

60. ibid., p. 5.

61. John Gray, 'What Scares the New Atheists?', *Guardian*, 3 March 2015.

62. For the origins and influence of this story, see Jon Turney, *Frankenstein's Footsteps: Science, Genetics and Popular Culture*, New Haven, CT: Yale University Press, 1998, pp. 13–42.

63. See Sven Wagner, *The Scientist as God: A Typological Study of a Literary Motif, 1818 to the Present*, Heidelberg: Universitätsverlag Winter, 2012.

64. For this and other understandings of the movement, see William Grassie and Gregory R. Hansell (eds), *H±: Transhumanism and Its Critics*, Philadelphia, PA: Metanexus Institute, 2011.

65. See, for example, Eugene V. Koonin and Yuri I. Wolf, 'Is Evolution Darwinian or/and Lamarckian?' *Biology Direct*, 11 November 2009, 4:42. doi: 10.1186/1745-6150-4-42.

66. On which see Nick Bostrom, *Superintelligence: Paths, Dangers, Strategies*, Oxford: Oxford University Press, 2014.

67. See the overview in Nick Bostrom, 'Existential Risk as Global Priority', *Global Policy* 4, no. 1, 2013, pp. 15–31.

68. Ingmar Persson and Julian Savulescu, *Unfit for the Future: The Need for Moral Enhancement*, Oxford: Oxford University Press, 2012.

Chapter 7

1. Albert Einstein, *Out of My Later Years*, New York: Littlefield, Adams, & Co., 1967, p. 29 (emphasis in original).

2. Bertrand Russell, *Religion and Science*, London: Oxford University Press, 1935, p. 243.

3. José Ortega y Gasset, 'El origen deportivo del estado', *Citius, Altius, Fortius* 9, no. 1–4, 1967, pp. 259–76, quote at p. 259.

4. ibid., p. 260.

5. For a sympathetic account of the background to, and ongoing debate concerning, this statement, see Tim Madigan, *W.K. Clifford and 'The Ethics of Belief'*, Newcastle: Cambridge Scholars, 2008.

6. See the analysis in James T. Cushing, *Quantum Mechanics: Historical Contingency and the Copenhagen Hegemony*, Chicago: University of Chicago Press, 1994.

7. See Thomas Bonk, *Underdetermination: An Essay on Evidence and the Limits of Natural Knowledge*, Dordrecht: Springer, 2008.

8. For recent discussions, see Robert Audi, 'Belief, Faith, and Acceptance', *International Journal for Philosophy of Religion* 63, 2008, pp. 87–102.

9. On which see Abigail J. Lustig, 'Darwin's Difficulties', in *The Cambridge Companion to the 'Origin of Species'*, ed. Michael Ruse and Robert J. Richards, Cambridge: Cambridge University Press, 2009, pp. 109–28.

10. Richard Dawkins, *The Selfish Gene*, 2nd ed., Oxford: Oxford University Press, 1989, p. 1.

11. Richard Dawkins, *River out of Eden: A Darwinian View of Life*, London: Phoenix, 1995, p. 133.

12. Alister E. McGrath, *Dawkins' God: From The Selfish Gene to The God Delusion*, 2nd ed., Oxford: Wiley-Blackwell, 2015, pp. 120–35.

13. 'Richard Dawkins: "Immoral" Not to Abort if Foetus Has Down's Syndrome', *Guardian*, 21 August 2014, http://www.theguardian.com/science/2014/aug/21/richard-dawkins-immoral-not-to-abort-a-downs-syndrome-foetus

14. See, for example, Robert J. Richards, *The Meaning of Evolution: The Morphological Construction and Ideological Reconstruction of Darwin's Theory*, Chicago: University of Chicago Press, 1992.

15. George Steiner, *Nostalgia for the Absolute*, Toronto: Anansi, 2004, p. 4.

16. Richard Dawkins, *A Devil's Chaplain: Selected Writings*, London: Weidenfield & Nicholson, 2003, p. 81.

17. Stephen Jay Gould, 'Foreword', in Peter Medawar, *The Strange Case of the Spotted Mice*, Oxford: Oxford University Press, 1996, p. v.

18. For an assessment, see Neil Calver, 'Sir Peter Medawar: Science, Creativity and the Popularization of Karl Popper', *Notes and Records of the Royal Society* 67, 2013, pp. 301–14.

19. Peter Medawar, 'Critical Notice', *Mind* 70, no. 277, 1961, pp. 99–106.

20. Peter Medwar, *Advice to a Young Scientist*, New York: Harper & Row, 1979, p. 101.

21. Peter Medawar, *The Limits of Science*, Oxford: Oxford University Press, 1985, p. 66. For Medawar's dependence on Popper, see Calver, 'Sir Peter Medawar', pp. 301–14.

22. Medawar, *The Limits of Science*, p. 66.

23. Ludwig Wittgenstein, *Notebooks 1914–1916*, Chicago: University of Chicago Press, 1979, 74e (entry for 7 August 1916).

24. Terry Eagleton, 'Lunging, Flailing, Mispunching: A Review of Richard

Dawkins' *The God Delusion*', *London Review of Books*, 19 October 2006.

25. William Ralph Inge, *Faith and Its Psychology*, New York: Charles Scribner's Sons, 1910, p. 197.

26. For example, Phillip R. Shaver and Mario Mikulincer (eds), *Meaning, Mortality, and Choice: The Social Psychology of Existential Concerns*, Washington DC: American Psychological Association, 2012; Joshua A. Hicks and Clay Routledge (eds), *The Experience of Meaning in Life: Classical Perspectives, Emerging Themes, and Controversies*, New York: Springer, 2013.

27. William James, *The Will to Believe and Other Essays in Popular Philosophy*, New York: Longmans, Green, and Co., 1897, p. 62.

28. Viktor E. Frankl, *Man's Search for Meaning*, New York: Simon and Schuster, 1963. For a biography, see Anna Redsand, *Viktor Frankl: A Life Worth Living*, New York: Clarion Books, 2006.

29. For example, see B.G. Skaggs and C.R. Barron, 'Searching for Meaning in Negative Events: Concept Analysis', *Journal of Advanced Nursing* 53, no. 5, 2006, pp. 559–70.

30. Susan Folkman, 'The Case for Positive Emotions in the Stress Process', *Anxiety, Stress, & Coping* 21, no. 1, 2008, pp. 3–14.

31. Roy F. Baumeister, *Meanings of Life*, New York: Guilford Press, 1991; Michael J. MacKenzie and Roy F. Baumeister, 'Meaning in Life: Nature, Needs, and Myth', in *Meaning in Positive and Existential Psychology*, ed. Alexander Batthyany and Pninit Russo-Netze, New York: Springer, 2014, pp. 25–38.

32. Martin Seligman, *Flourish: A Visionary New Understanding of Happiness and Well-Being*, New York: Simon & Schuster, 2011. See also Richard M. Ryan and Edward L. Deci, 'On Happiness and Human Potentials: A Review of Research on Hedonic and Eudaimonic Well-Being', *Annual Review of Psychology* 52, 2001, pp. 141–66.

33. Alexander Rosenberg, *The Atheist's Guide to Reality: Enjoying Life without Illusions*, New York: W.W. Norton, 2011, pp. 7–8.

34. ibid., p. 92.

35. Muriel Rukeyser, *The Speed of Darkness*, 1968.

36. See the important analysis in Michael D. Aeschliman, *The Restitution of Man: C.S. Lewis and the Case against Scientism*, Grand Rapids, MI: Eerdmans, 1998.

37. Roger Scruton, 'Scientism in the Arts and Humanities', *The New Atlantis*, no. 40, Fall 2013, pp. 33–46.

38. Rosenberg, *Atheist's Guide to Reality*, pp. 110–11.
39. ibid., pp. 162–3.
40. Timothy Williamson, 'What Is Naturalism?', *New York Times*, 4 September 2011. For his own approach, see Timothy Williamson, *The Philosophy of Philosophy*, Oxford: Blackwell, 2007.
41. Timothy Williamson, 'On Ducking Challenges to Naturalism', *New York Times*, 28 September 2011.
42. The point at issue was first made by David Hume: no finite number of observations, however large, can allow a logically defensible and unrestrictedly general conclusion to be drawn, in that future observations might disconfirm it.
43. See Bryan Magee, *Confessions of a Philosopher: A Journey through Western Philosophy*, London: Phoenix, 1998, pp. 42–68.

Chapter 8

1. Richard Dawkins, *A Devil's Chaplain*, London: Weidenfeld & Nicholson, 2003, p. 34.
2. Rutledge M. Dennis, 'Social Darwinism, Scientific Racism, and the Metaphysics of Race', *Journal of Negro Education* 64, no. 3, 1995, pp. 243–52; Edwin Black, *War against the Weak: Eugenics and America's Campaign to Create a Master Race*, Westport, CT: Dialogue Press, 2012.
3. A good example is Laurence R. Tancredi, *Hardwired Behavior: What Neuroscience Reveals About Morality*, New York: Cambridge University Press, 2005.
4. Harris continues to defend this view: http://www.huffingtonpost.com/sam-harris/in-defense-of-torture_b_8993.html
5. Sam Harris, *The End of Faith: Religion, Terror, and the Future of Reason*, New York: W.W. Norton & Co., 2004, pp. 52–3.
6. Sam Harris, *The Moral Landscape: How Science Can Determine Human Values*, New York: Free Press, 2010.
7. ibid., pp. 48–9.
8. ibid., p. 21.
9. For example, see John Cottingham's recognition of the importance of Sigmund Freud's understanding of human behaviour as in large part governed by the operation of unconscious forces which are opaque to reason. See Nafsika Athanassoulis and Samantha Vice (eds), *The Moral Life: Essays in Honour of John Cottingham*, London: Palgrave, 2008.
10. Harris, *The Moral Landscape*, p. 19.

Notes

11. Albert Einstein, *Out of My Later Years*, New York: Littlefield, Adams, & Co., 1967, p. 29 (emphasis in original).

12. The classic study, now supplemented by many others, is Harold G. Koenig and Harvey J. Cohen, *The Link between Religion and Health: Psychoneuroimmunology and the Faith Factor*, Oxford: Oxford University Press, 2002.

13. See Whitley R.P. Kaufman, 'Can Science Determine Moral Values? A Reply to Sam Harris', *Neuroethics* 5, no. 1, 2012, pp. 55–65.

14. For an analysis of the moral intractability of this genuine ethical issue, see Govind Persad, Alan Wertheimer and Ezekiel J. Emanuel, 'Principles for Allocation of Scarce Medical Interventions', *The Lancet* 373, no. 9661, 2009, pp. 423–31.

15. Kaufman, 'Can Science Determine Moral Values?', p. 59.

16. For example, see Elazar Barkan, *The Retreat of Scientific Racism: Changing Concepts of Race in Britain and the United States between the World Wars*, Cambridge: Cambridge University Press, 1992.

17. Paul Lawrence Farber, *The Temptations of Evolutionary Ethics*, Berkeley, CA: University of California Press, 1994, pp. 38–57. For a sympathetic account of Spencer's ideas, see Michael W. Taylor, *The Philosophy of Herbert Spencer*, London: Continuum, 2007.

18. See the excellent analysis in Fritz Allhoff, 'Evolutionary Ethics from Darwin to Moore', *History and Philosophy of the Life Sciences* 25, no. 1, 2003, pp. 51–79.

19. T.H. Huxley, *Evolution and Ethics and Other Essays*, London: Macmillan, 1894, p. 83.

20. G.E. Moore, *Principia Ethica*, Cambridge: Cambridge University Press, 1903, p. 58.

21. E.O. Wilson, *Sociobiology: The New Synthesis*, Cambridge, MA: Harvard University Press, 2000, p. 562.

22. For example, Sharon Street, 'A Darwinian Dilemma for Realist Theories of Value', *Philosophical Studies* 127, 2006, pp. 109–66.

23. Richard D. Alexander, *Darwinism and Human Affairs*, Seattle: University of Washington Press, 1979, p. 220.

24. Lee Braver, *Groundless Grounds: A Study of Wittgenstein and Heidegger*, Cambridge, MA: MIT Press, 2012.

25. See Paul Chang-Ha Lim, *Mystery Unveiled: The Crisis of the Trinity in Early Modern England*, New York: Oxford University Press, 2012.

26. Stephen Toulmin, *The Uses of Argument*, Cambridge: Cambridge University Press, 2003, p. 118.

27. Philip Smith, *Cultural Theory: An Introduction*, Oxford: Blackwell, 2001, pp. 6–9.
28. Terry Pinkard, 'MacIntyre's Critique of Modernity', in *Alasdair MacIntyre*, ed. Mark C. Murphy, Cambridge: Cambridge University Press, 2003, pp. 176–200.
29. Alasdair MacIntyre, *Whose Justice? Which Rationality?* London: Duckworth, 1988, p. 6. See also Alasdair MacIntyre, *After Virtue: A Study in Moral Theory*, 3rd ed., Notre Dame, IL: University of Notre Dame Press, 2007.
30. Michael Sandel, *Justice: What's the Right Thing to Do?* London: Penguin Books, 2010, pp. 10, 207, 261.
31. See Daniel C. Russell (ed.), *The Cambridge Companion to Virtue Ethics*, Cambridge: Cambridge University Press, 2013.

Chapter 9

1. Letter to Edward Sackville-West, cited in Michael de-la-Noy, *Eddy: The Life of Edward Sackville-West*, London: Bodley Head, 1988, p. 237.
2. Bertrand Russell, *A History of Western Philosophy*, London: George Allen & Unwin Ltd, 1946, p. xiv.
3. Letter to William Graham, 3 July 1881, in *The Life and Letters of Charles Darwin*, ed. F. Darwin, 3 vols, London: John Murray, 1887, vol. 1, p. 315.
4. Richard Dawkins, *The God Delusion*, London: Bantam, 2006, pp. 363–4.
5. Jorge Luis Borges, 'El acercamiento a Almotásim', in *Nueva antología personal*, Buenos Aires: Siglo XXI Editores Argentina, 2004, pp. 60–75, quote at p. 72.
6. C.S. Lewis, *The Personal Heresy: A Controversy*, London: Oxford University Press, 1939. p. 11.
7. See Peter Harrison, *The Territories of Science and Religion*, Chicago: University of Chicago Press, 2015.
8. A good example is the Renaissance metaphor of the 'Two Books' of science and religion: see Giuseppe Tanzella-Nitti, 'The Two Books Prior to the Scientific Revolution', *Annales Theologici* 18, 2004, pp. 51–83.
9. C.S. Lewis, *Essay Collection*, London: HarperCollins, 2002, p. 21.
10. Paul Claudel, 'Introduction à un poème sur Dante', in *Positions et propositions*, Paris: Gallimard, 1928, pp. 161–86.

Notes

11. For detailed discussion, see Alister E. McGrath, 'A Gleam of Divine Truth: The Concept of Myth in Lewis's Thought', in *The Intellectual World of C.S. Lewis*, Oxford: Wiley-Blackwell, 2013, pp. 55–82.

12. See the fine exposition in Andrew Louth, *Discerning the Mystery: An Essay on the Nature of Theology*, Oxford: Clarendon Press, 1983.

13. For example, in Anglican 'modernist' circles in the period between the two world wars: see W. Mark Richardson, 'Evolutionary-Emergent Worldview and Anglican Theological Revision: Case Studies from the 1920s', *Anglican Theological Review* 92, no. 2, 2010, pp. 321–45.

14. Christian Smith, *Moral, Believing Animals: Human Personhood and Culture*, Oxford: Oxford University Press, 2009, pp. 63–94.

15. As argued by Roy F. Baumeister, *Meanings of Life*, New York: Guilford Press, 1991.

16. C.P. Snow, *The Two Cultures*, Cambridge: Cambridge University Press, 1959.

17. See Everett L. Worthington Jr, et al., 'A Psychoeducational Intervention to Promote Forgiveness in Christians in the Philippines', *Journal of Mental Health Counselling* 32, no. 1, 2010, pp. 75–93.

18. Dante, *Paradiso* XXXIII, 85–90.

19. John Donne, 'The First Anniversarie: An Anatomy of the World', line 213; in W. Milgate (ed.), *The Epithalamions, Anniversaries, and Epicedes*, Oxford: Clarendon Press, 1978, p. 28.

20. See, for example, the reflections in C.S. Lewis, *The Discarded Image: An Introduction to Medieval and Renaissance Literature*, Cambridge: Cambridge University Press, 1964.

21. Hermann Hesse, 'Die Sehnsucht unser Zeit nach einer Weltanschauung', *Uhu* 2, 1926, pp. 3–14.

22. Nancy Cartwright, *The Dappled World: A Study of the Boundaries of Science*, Cambridge: Cambridge University Press, 1999.

23. C.S. Lewis, *Christian Reflections*, Grand Rapids: Eerdmans, 1967, p. 65.

24. For an exploration of this theme, see Giuseppe Tanzella-Nitti, 'La dimensione cristologica dell'intelligibilità del reale', in *L'intelligibilità del reale: Natura, uomo, macchina*, ed. Sergio Rondinara, Rome: Città Nuova, 1999, pp. 213–25.

25. Virginia Woolf, 'Sketch of the Past', in *Moments of Being*, ed. Jeanne Schulkind, 2nd ed., New York: Harcourt Brace & Company, 1985, p. 72.

26. John C. Avise, *The Genetic Gods: Evolution and Belief in Human Affairs*, Cambridge, MA: Harvard University Press, 1998, p. vii.

27. Salman Rushdie, *Is Nothing Sacred?*, The Herbert Read Memorial Lecture 1990, Cambridge: Granta, 1990, p. 9.

28. For the process, see Wolfgang Schluchter, *Die Entstehungsgeschichte des modernen Rationalismus*, Frankfurt am Main: Suhrkamp, 1998.

29. Letter of 21 March 1955, in *Albert Einstein–Michele Besso Correspondence, 1903–55*, ed. Pierre Speziali, Paris: Hermann, 1972, pp. 537–8. 'Nun ist er mir auch mit dem Abschied von dieser sonderbaren Welt ein wenig vorausgegangen. Dies bedeutet nichts. Für uns gläubige Physiker hat die Scheidung zwischen Vergangenheit, Gegenwart und Zukunft nur die Bedeutung einer wenn auch hartnäckigen Illusion.'

30. See the excellent analysis of the problem in N. David Mermin, 'Physics: QBism puts the Scientist back into Science', *Nature* 507, 2014, pp. 421–3. For a fuller account of 'Quantum Bayesianism', usually abbreviated as 'QBism', see Christopher A. Fuchs, N. David Mermin and Rüdiger Schack, 'An Introduction to QBism with an Application to the Locality of Quantum Mechanics', *American Journal of Physics* 82, no. 749, 2014, doi: 10.1119/1.4874855.

31. See the classic study of Paul Ricouer, 'Narrative Time', *Critical Inquiry* 7, no. 1, 1980, pp. 169–90.

32. P.A. Schilpp (ed.), *The Philosophy of Rudolf Carnap*, La Salle, IL: Open Court Publishing, 1963, pp. 37–8.

33. Erwin Schrödinger, *'Nature and the Greeks' and 'Science and Humanism'*, Cambridge: Cambridge University Press, 2014.

34. This point is developed in an excellent essay by Roger Scruton, 'Scientism in the Arts and Humanities', *The New Atlantis*, no. 40, Fall 2013, pp. 33–46.

35. Karl von Meyenn (ed.), *Eine Entdeckung von ganz außerordentlicher Tragweite: Schrödingers Briefwechsel zur Wellenmechanik und zum Katzenparadoxon*, Berlin: Springer, 2011, p. 490.

36. Samuel Hugo Bergman, *Dialogical Philosophy from Kierkegaard to Buber*, Albany, NY: State University of New York Press, 1991.

37. Liliann Manning, Daniel Cassel and Jean-Christophe Cassel, 'St Augustine's Reflections on Memory and Time and the Current Concept of Subjective Time in Mental Time Travel', *Behavioral Sciences* 3, no. 2, 2013, pp. 232–43.

38. See, for example, Karl K. Szpunar, 'On Subjective Time', *Cortex* 47, 2011, pp. 409–11; idem, 'Evidence for an Implicit Influence of Memory on Future Thinking', *Memory & Cognition* 38, 2010, pp. 531–40.

39. For reflections on how scientists negotiate these boundaries, see Elaine Howard Ecklund, Jerry Z. Park and Katherine L. Sorrell, 'Scientists Negotiate Boundaries between Religion and Science', *Journal for the Scientific Study of Religion* 50, no. 3, 2011, pp. 552–69.

40. Rushdie, *Is Nothing Sacred?*, p. 7.

41. David Brewster, *Life of Sir Isaac Newton*, new ed., rev. W.T. Lynn, London: Tegg, 1875, p. 303.

42. Steven Weinberg, *Dreams of a Final Theory: The Search for the Fundamental Laws of Nature*, London: Hutchinson Radius, 1993, p. 196.

43. Peter W. Atkins, *Creation Revisited*, Harmondsworth: Penguin, 1994, p. 21.

44. *The Rubáiyát of Omar Khayyám*, trans. Edward Fitzgerald, 1879, p. lxxii.

45. Ursula Goodenough, *The Sacred Depths of Nature*, New York: Oxford University Press, 1998, p. 10.

46. Rushdie, *Is Nothing Sacred?*, p. 8.

47. Carl Sagan, *Pale Blue Dot: A Vision of the Human Future in Space*, London: Headline, 1995, p. vi.

48. Marcel Proust, *La prisonnière*, Paris: Gallimard, 1925, p. 69. 'Le seul véritable voyage, le seul bain de Jouvence, ce ne serait pas d'aller vers de nouveaux paysages, mais d'avoir d'autres yeux, de voir l'univers avec les yeux d'un autre, de cent autres.'

49. Smith, *Moral, Believing Animals*, p. 64.

Index

Index

Index

Index

Index

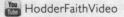